Educated by Initiative

Educated by Initiative

The Effects of Direct Democracy on
Citizens and Political Organizations in
the American States

Daniel A. Smith and Caroline J. Tolbert

THE UNIVERSITY OF MICHIGAN PRESS   Ann Arbor

Published in the United States of America by
The University of Michigan Press
Manufactured in the United States of America
⊗ Printed on acid-free paper

2007   2006   2005   2004   4   3   2   1

A CIP catalog record for this book is available from the British Library.

Library of Congress Cataloging-in-Publication Data

Smith, Daniel A., 1966–
    Educated by initiative : the effects of direct democracy on
citizens and political organizations in the American states / Daniel
A. Smith and Caroline J. Tolbert.
        p.   cm.
    Includes bibliographical references and index.
    ISBN 0-472-09870-5 (cloth : alk. paper) — ISBN 0-472-06870-9
(pbk. : alk. paper)
    1. Political participation—United States—States.
2. Referendum—United States—States.   3. Direct democracy—United
States—States.   4. Progressivism (United States politics)
I. Tolbert, Caroline J.   II. Title.

JK1764.S547   2004
328.273—dc22   2004006181

To Eliot and Safi
—DAS

To Jacqueline, Eveline, and Edward
—CJT

Contents

Illustrations

Figures

Boxes

Preface

This book is about democracy. Like many other valued skills—reading, arithmetic, swimming, riding a bicycle—democracy must be practiced lest we forget how to be democratic citizens. Citizens in a democracy are expected not only to vote in elections and participate in civic affairs but also to be knowledgeable about public issues, to be interested in the making of public policy by elected officials, and to be confident that democratic governance works. In his best-selling book *Bowling Alone*, Robert Putnam warns that civic engagement in the United States is at an all-time low. Among the many measures of civic engagement he compiles, Putnam points to declining meeting attendance, political awareness and engagement, voter turnout, and trust in government, with the young having the lowest levels of political participation.[1] For those concerned about the apparent decline of social capital and what Putnam calls the "strange disappearance of civic America," these trends are disturbing. Yet they are not new. One hundred years ago, Progressive Era reformers were equally concerned about the failing health of American democracy. Progressives contended that democracy must be regularly practiced to be sustainable.

Toward achieving this goal, Progressive Era educators and reformers pressed for the American states to adopt the tripartite mechanisms of direct democracy: the initiative, the referendum, and the recall. All three of these plebiscitary devices authorize citizens to participate directly in the making of public policy by encouraging them to gather a prescribed number of valid signatures to force a popular vote on a policy question on Election Day. With the initiative (which we refer to alternatively as "citizen lawmaking," "direct legislation," and, more generically, "ballot measures"), petitioners collect a specified number of signatures to place either a statutory measure or a constitutional amendment on the ballot for fellow voters to adopt or reject. The initiative may be either immediately binding (a direct initiative) or first considered by the state legislature (an indirect initiative) before going into effect.[2] With the referendum (more accurately called the "popular referendum" to distinguish it from a measure the state legislature places on the ballot for a popular vote), citizens gather signatures to place a disputed law (or a section of a law) on the ballot for voters to consider. Unfortunately, the popular press often refers to initiatives as referendums, muddling the two distinct mechanisms. Finally, while rarely used (notwithstanding conservatives' successful 2003 effort to recall California's Democratic governor, Gray Davis), the recall permits citizens to collect signatures to force a vote on the retention of an elected official. Citizens in numerous states voted to add one or more of these populist mechanisms to state constitutions during the early 1900s. Progressive educators and reformers contended that initiatives in particular would directly involve citizens in the policymaking process and would help members of the public become better-informed democratic citizens.

Drawing on the recent experiences in the American states that permit citizen lawmaking, we examine empirically whether the Progressive reformers who celebrated the use of direct democracy were correct about the beneficial value of the initiative process in educating the citizenry. Direct democracy and the initiative process in particular are red-hot-button topics among those who follow state politics as well as American politics more generally. The initiative process as practiced in roughly half the American states has lately received prominent scholarly and journalistic attention. Contemporary proponents of the initiative laud it as an unadulterated form of "government of, by and for the people." The initiative, as oft-cited David Schmidt notes in his historical overview of the process, enables "the public itself to decide what constitutes the public interest." Prior to the 2000 elections, the *Wall Street Journal* opined that "the initiative process is overwhelmingly popular" because "voters want a final trump card over entrenched incumbents, who often feel free to ignore voters." *Boston Globe* columnist Jeff Jacoby concurred: "Initiatives are the last resort of desperate citizens, a way to check the power of remote or arrogant lawmakers."[3]

Conversely, critics of the process lambaste the initiative as a "grassroots charade," with ballot measures increasingly the handiwork of special interests. In his scathing study of initiative politics in California, Peter Schrag, the former editor of the *Sacramento Bee,* decries how the initiative has been ironically co-opted by "'the interests'—the insurance industry, the tobacco companies, the trial lawyers, public employee unions." Journalist Lydia Chavez contends that rather than giving power to the people, the process encourages "anyone with a million dollars to pay for the signatures necessary to put an initiative on the ballot." In *Democracy Derailed,* Washington, DC, pundit David Broder argues that the initiative "threatens to challenge or even subvert the American system of government." "Identifying the democratic delusions that shroud the initiative process in a sacrosanct veil," political scientist Richard Ellis insists, "is one small but necessary step in the larger project of restoring our collective faith in deliberative and representative government."[4]

It is an overstatement to claim that the initiative has replaced representative governance in the 24 states that permit citizens to author and adopt new state laws and amend the state constitutions. Nevertheless, direct legislation has left an indelible mark on the more than 135 million Americans living in the states where the process exists. During the twentieth century, voters approved more than 800 of the more than 2,000 initiatives that citizens placed on statewide ballots.[5] Controversial propositions—ranging from tax reform to gay rights to educational reform to affirmative action to abortion restrictions to environmental and animal protection to legalization of marijuana—have shaped the policy contours of these states, providing "innovative" solutions that reflect "the diversity of groups that use the process."[6] This is especially the case concerning many governance issues that are politically intractable in state legislatures, such as legislative term limits, tax and expenditure limitations, tax increases, party primaries, campaign finance restrictions, and public financing of campaigns. Of the 19 states with term limitations for state legislators, for example, 18 of the laws were enacted by voters via initiative elections. Because of the initiative's apparent effectiveness, governors and other public officials increasingly call for the extension of the initiative to municipal, county, state, and even national jurisdictions.[7]

The Dual Purpose of the Initiative

While other scholars have studied the substantive impact that ballot measures have on public policy, the role of interest groups and money, the passage or defeat of initiatives, and voter response to the initiative process, our book diverges from these lines of inquiry, taking an alternative tack. We systematically assess how ballot initiatives shape the broader democratic landscape in the American states by examining how the process itself affects citizens and political organizations. As social scientists, we are interested in how institutions structure politics—specifically, how the mechanism of the initiative affects the attitudes and behaviors of individuals as well as the interests and tactics of political organizations. In contrast to our inquiry, most of the research conducted on direct democracy in the American states examines policy outcomes of ballot measures. While the policies adopted by voters unquestionably have had a major impact on the public policies of the two dozen states that permit citizen lawmaking, we argue that individuals and organizations are also influenced by the plebiscitary process itself. Our orientation, then, is on the educative by-products of the initiative process.

Since the initiative, popular referendum, and recall were first adopted in the American states during the early twentieth century, practitioners and scholars have noted both the instrumental and educative purposes of direct democracy. Today, the instrumental goal of the initiative is often highlighted in scholarly and journalistic studies. The instrumental purpose of the initiative is clearly stipulated in the constitutions of the states permitting the process. The plebiscitary mechanism is first and foremost intended to provide citizens with an institutional check on the system of representative governance. From this perspective, the initiative can empower citizens to initiate and approve substantive laws and constitutional amendments, circumventing the state legislature in the process. For example, article V of the Colorado state constitution reads,

> The legislative power of the state shall be vested in the general assembly consisting of a senate and house of representatives, both to be elected by the people, but the people reserve to themselves the power to propose laws and amendments to the constitution and to enact or reject the same at the polls independent of the general assembly and also reserve power at their own option to approve or reject at the polls any act or item, section, or part of any act of the general assembly.[8]

As such, citizens of Colorado as well as those residing in 23 other states have the authority to make or alter public policy independent of their elected legislative bodies.

The underlying premise of the instrumental function of the initiative, which devolves to citizens the authority to make public policy, is that it can help prevent state legislatures from becoming unrepresentative. In an unusually evenhanded assessment of the mechanism during the Progressive Era, Harvard political scientist William Munro observed, "The first argument in favor of direct legislation rests, accordingly, upon the allegation that existing legislative methods and results are unsatisfactory to the majority of the electorate; that representatives do not properly represent."[9] Interested citizens or groups functioning outside the traditional legislative process may introduce substantive issues either ignored or thwarted by elected representatives. Although scholars continue to debate whether the primary function of the initiative—that it directly or indirectly allows the popular will to check the power of state governments by enabling citizens to enact public policy—is effective, the instrumental purpose of the initiative tells only half the story.[10]

A second rationale for the adoption and use of the initiative is a procedural by-product of its instrumental function. In addition to any substantive changes in public policy it may exact, the initiative process is itself educational. Writing in 1912, Munro noted,

> Emphasis is laid, for example, upon the educative value of direct legislation. By means of the initiative, a spirit of legislative enterprise is promoted among the voters; men are encouraged to formulate political ideas of their own and to press these upon public attention with the assurance that they shall have a fair hearing. If the welfare often suffers from public apathy; if the mass of the voters manifest little interest in the contents of the statute-book, this is due in large measure, it is claimed, to the feeling of electoral helplessness which in some states amounts to a popular conviction.[11]

Thus Progressive reformers during the most formative period of initiative adoption and usage saw citizen lawmaking as a pedagogical process. Progressives thought that having plebiscites on policy issues would encourage citizens to become more politically engaged, thereby mitigating the declining state of civic affairs and public discourse.

At the apex of the Progressive Era, advocates of the process routinely touted the educative values of the initiative. In 1912, for example, University of Wisconsin–Madison professor Paul Reinsch stated with confident equanimity that direct legislation "will assist the people, the body of the electorate, in the development of its political consciousness," because "it will make the body of the electorate more familiar with legislative programs and more interested."[12] Irrespective of any substantive policy changes that might result from the mechanism, numerous Progressives thought that the initiative would stimulate an array of positive educative externalities. Questions placed on the ballot would increase political participation by bolstering turnout on Election Day. Progressives argued that ballot measures would also encourage civic engagement, help edify the electorate, and even increase citizens' trust in government. Furthermore, reformers believed that the process's educative effects would mitigate the power of interest groups and party machines.

Leaving to others any evaluation of the substantive outcomes that result from successful ballot initiatives, this book takes a critical look at the pedagogy that accompanies citizen lawmaking. Despite the Progressive Era recognition of the secondary, procedural effects of the process, scholars have not thoroughly examined the initiative's educative effects and their repercussions for democracy in the American states. Our objective, then, is to critically examine the educative externalities of the initiative process.

Educating Citizens and Political Organizations

We investigate the possible educative effects of ballot initiatives on both citizens and political organizations. With respect to citizens' attitudes and behaviors, we are interested in whether individuals living in initiative states are more civically involved than those living in noninitiative states. Are citizens more knowledgeable about politics and civically engaged when they are presented with the opportunity to place measures on the ballot and vote on them? Are citizens living in states with initiatives on the ballot more likely to turn out to vote when they may participate as Election Day lawmakers? Does the act of citizen lawmaking provide citizens with a greater sense of political efficacy—namely, confidence in government—because they directly participate in the policymaking process? With respect to political organizations, we are interested in whether the initiative process significantly affects interest groups' and political parties' activities and strategies. Do states allowing the initiative have more robust and diverse interest group systems, or are special interests (and their members) merely afforded another venue in which to influence public policy? Does having an active initiative process encourage people to give money to interest groups, thereby strengthening citizen groups? Conversely, has the ostensibly nonpartisan initiative weakened political parties, as Progressives had hoped, or have parties devised creative ways to use the process to further partisan goals? Throughout the book, we examine these secondary effects of the initiative process, at each turn endeavoring to provide a balanced appraisal of citizen lawmaking's impact on the broader democratic process.

Of course, individuals and political organizations that become directly involved with promoting or opposing ballot propositions generally do not do so to realize some indirect educative effects that might be derived from the process. Rather, they desire to change public policies. Nevertheless, inspired by theories of new institutionalism, which examines how political processes help to shape individual and organizational preferences and motivations, as well as the spate of recent historical and quantitative inquiries into the workings of direct democracy, we argue that the pedagogic externalities of the initiative process may be just as—if not more—important than any substantive changes brought about by successful initiatives.[13] After all, more than half of all initiatives placed on statewide ballots fail, and many of the measures that voters approve are subsequently overturned by the courts, fail to be implemented, or are reversed in whole or in part by state legislatures.[14]

Notwithstanding the ultimate fate of ballot measures, we argue that the institutional rules permitting citizen lawmaking affect individuals' behavior and attitudes and political organizations' tactics, which, in turn, shape the broader political context. While public policies resulting from direct democracy come and go, the secondary effects of the initiative may have a more enduring impact on a democratic body politic as well as on the institutions of representative government. By highlighting the procedural process, we reassess whether the initiative threatens to undermine republican government, as Beltway journalist Broder and other skeptics contend, or, conversely, whether the educative aspects of citizen lawmaking paradoxically strengthen and complement our system of representative democracy.

Chapter Outline and Audience

To evaluate the educative facets of the initiative process, we begin by recasting the normative debate in the United States concerning the merits and pitfalls of citizen lawmaking. In chapter 1, we assess the normative arguments and empirical claims made by Progressive Era proponents and opponents of the process. An appreciation of the historical context surrounding the adoption of the initiative is essential to demonstrating how citizen lawmaking's current educative effects may be both compatible and incompatible with the visions of direct democracy's early proponents. In all too many ways, the current dialogue about the initiative mirrors the palaver heard a century ago, yet recent studies have all but neglected the historical context in which this dialogue has transpired. Our historical rendering offers the reader a ledger sheet of sorts on which the current discussion of the initiative process can be held to account.

Using the Progressive Era as a benchmark, we assess the educative impact of the initiative by drawing from the experiences of the two dozen American states that currently permit citizen lawmaking. We employ a variety of different research designs and draw on an array of data sets to analyze how initiatives affect citizens' attitudes and behavior and condition political organizations. The results of the data analysis form the basis of this book, but we hope that what we present is much more than an aggregation of data. We seek to push the boundaries of the policy debate regarding direct democracy and to make the information accessible to a wide audience. With respect to citizens' behavior and attitudes, we examine the education of citizens in terms of voter participation (chapter 2), civic engagement (chapter 3), and confidence in government (chapter 4). Regarding political organizations, we examine how both interest groups (chapter 5) and political parties (chapter 6) have educated themselves in response to the institutionalization of citizen lawmaking.

We conclude the book by critically appraising the significance of how citizens and political organizations have become "educated by initiative." We consider the larger implications of how these pedagogical effects of citizen lawmaking might impact the democratic process and representative government. In light of the empirical evidence, we reflect on whether the initiative process today operates in accordance with Progressive reformers' intentions. Does the process—which critics argue can tyrannize minorities by dividing citizens along racial, ethnic, religious, and geographic lines as well as activate the interest group and party systems that purportedly dilute citizen power—undermine the central tenets of republican government? Or, conversely, does the process, which may increase and enliven political and civic participation, political knowledge, and trust in government, strengthen and complement representative democracy? As proponents gather momentum in the drive to extend the initiative to other states and possibly to establish a national initiative and referendum, we contend that previous studies portraying initiatives as pillaging representative government or as providing a panacea for political apathy are not only too extreme but also too limited in their scope. We argue instead that the initiative process has a range of educative effects.

Our research is presented in a way that requires no knowledge of statistical methods, even though the study is conducted according to academic standards and at times uses sophisticated quantitative analyses. In addition to students of direct democracy, we hope to reach policymakers, practitioners, both advocates and critics of citizen lawmaking, and thoughtful individuals who are touched by this issue. We have written the text in such a manner that a formal training in statistics and research methods is not a necessary requirement to digest our findings. Throughout the text, we use "What Matters" boxes to highlight statistically significant results and to keep track of what might be an otherwise dizzying array of data. We often provide details of "what matters" without relying on numerical indicators or with probabilities presented as simple percentages. Behind these comparisons, however, are multivariate regression analyses that statistically control for the effect of multiple influences. We offer the full regression tables in the appendix for those who are interested in examining our statistical findings in more detail. We discuss our methods to some extent within the text, but we carefully explain our approach in clear language and leave more detailed and technical discussions in the endnotes.

In short, we hope this book will inject new life into the debate regarding the possibilities and limitations of direct democracy by moving beyond the current scholarly and general preoccupation with the policy outcomes of ballot measures. In the two dozen states that permit citizen lawmaking, the educative effects—and not just the substantive outcomes of ballot measures—will continue to shape the contours of representative governance and democratic participation for years to come.

Both of us began conducting research on ballot initiatives and direct democracy in the early 1990s. This book evolved from our individual as well as collaborative research on the topic over more than a decade. The book testifies to the compatibility of our different strengths as social scientists. At the University of Michigan Press, Jim Reische and Jeremy Shine encouraged us to develop the manuscript. Their suggestions, along with those of the rest of the staff, especially Ellen Goldlust-Gingrich, have made this a better book.

Individually and jointly, we have numerous people to thank. We have worked and collaborated with several talented students at Kent State University, the University of Denver, and the University of Florida. Graduate students John Grummel, Carolyn Hribar, and Ramona McNeal of Kent State University provided valuable statistical analysis. Ramona McNeal and John Grummel are coauthors of journal articles in which the results presented in chapter 2 were first published. We also thank the political science department at Kent State, which provided funding for academic year and summer graduate research assistants who contributed to this project. At the University of Denver, former undergraduate students Jennifer Berg, Nate Golich, Robert Herrington, and Joey Lubinski were much more than research assistants: they were all valued coauthors. A Small Research Grant awarded by the American Political Science Association made possible some of the archival research on the initiative process and scholarly dialogue during the Progressive Era, and Virginia Gray and David Lowery kindly made available to us their state interest group data.

We have benefited greatly from the generosity of numerous scholars and practitioners who have educated the two of us about the dynamics and wonders of direct democracy. In addition to the extensive critical comments provided by the anonymous reviewers who scrutinized the entire manuscript, we would be remiss if we did not acknowledge our rich conversations about direct democracy with John Allswang, Paula Baker, Mark Bender, Fred Boehmke, Shaun Bowler, Rich Braunstein, David Broder, Andy Busch, Bruce Cain, Anne Campbell, Jack Citrin, Susan Clarke, Tom Cronin, Richard Ellis, Stan Elofson, Ken Fernandez, Beth Garrett, Zoltan Hajnal, Tom Holbrook, Craig Holman, Ted Lascher, Dan Lowenstein, Skip Lupia, John Matsusaka, Dave McCuan, Ken Miller, Chris Mooney, Galen Nelson, Dennis Pohill, Beth Rosenson, Peter Schrag, David Sears, Gary Segura, John Shockley, Ron Smith, Dane Waters, Kristina Wilfore, and Joe Zimmerman. Special thanks are extended to Larry Dodd, Todd Donovan, Elisabeth Gerber, Rodney Hero, and Dave Magleby, talented scholars and good friends who have served as mentors to us both.

Finally, we are deeply indebted to our families. Our spouses, Brenda Chalfin and David Dowling, are educators in their own right who regularly ply us with critical feedback. Our children never do. We dedicate the book to them. We hope that they will live in a country where the Progressive Era spirit of participatory democracy is rekindled and children (and adults) become educated about the importance of being active participants rather than passive bystanders not only in politics but also in life.

1 | The Progressive Era Vision
Instrumental and Educative Justifications of Direct Democracy

"I tell you," Woodrow Wilson stressed to a reporter in May 1911, "the people of this state and this country are determined at last to take over the control of their own politics."[1] Well before his successful run for the presidency the following year, the New Jersey governor had begun broadening his appeal to a national audience, selectively employing a more populist rhetoric. An avowed progressive liberal, Wilson was a relatively late convert to the direct democracy crusade, which included the devices of initiative, referendum, and recall. A little more than a decade earlier, in 1898, the formally trained political scientist and president of Princeton University had harshly criticized direct legislation as it was practiced in Switzerland. "Where it has been employed," Wilson penned, "it has not promised either progress or enlightenment, leading rather to doubtful experiments and to reactionary displays of prejudice than to really useful legislation."[2] Notwithstanding the "native impulses" that he had acquired as an "academic Mugwump," Wilson had convinced himself by the time of his bid for the presidency of the virtues of a "populistic conception of democracy."[3] Pragmatism as well as presidential aspirations clearly informed his change of heart.[4] As governor, he faced the ever-increasing reality that representative government, despite its theoretical brilliance, was becoming an abject failure in practice. For Wilson, the initiative offered a practical remedy that could free citizens from living in "a fool's paradise." Rationalizing his newfound support for the initiative, the Democratic governor inveighed, "We are simply trying to square the facts of our government with the theory with which we have been deceiving ourselves."[5]

During his presidential campaign, Wilson waxed poetic about direct democracy serving as a curative to representative government, envisioning how populist mechanisms could "cut down the jungle in which corruption lurks." He mused publicly about how the initiative—the mechanism whereby people collect a specified number of valid signatures to place either a statute or a constitutional amendment on the ballot for the electorate to adopt or reject—might help to "drag things into the light, break down private understandings and force them to be public understandings." Drawing on the nascent experiences of the handful of states that had adopted plebiscitary mechanisms during the previous decade, Wilson argued in 1911 that citizens could use the initiative in particular to apply tacit pressure on capricious state legislatures, forcing them to abide by the will of the people. By way of analogy, Wilson understood the practice of citizen lawmaking as the "gun behind the door—for use only in case of emergency, but a mighty good persuader, nevertheless."[6]

Wilson's pragmatic defense of the initiative underscores its instrumental uses. If a state legislature was unable or unwilling to pass popular legislation, citizens could directly propose and adopt laws to correct any legislative "sins of omission."[7] Even indirectly, the mere threat of an initiative could pressure recalcitrant legislators to act. For recent converts such as Wilson, direct legislation was not a radical solution. Unlike the zealous supporters who envisioned citizen lawmaking replacing representative government, Wilson foresaw the device being used sparingly. "Once this direct access of the people to the execution of their own purposes is accomplished," he maintained, "the initiative and referendum will not be the ordinary means of legislation."[8] Rather, the initiative would serve as a stopgap mechanism, a benign tool that would "restore" rather than "destroy" representative government. For the erstwhile professor, the expedience of direct legislation could bring "our representatives back to the consciousness that what they are bound in duty and in mere policy to do is represent the sovereign people whom they profess to serve."[9] As a prod, then, the initiative had the potential to directly or indirectly bring forth substantive policy changes in the American states.

Though the instrumental defense of the initiative advanced by Wilson and other early-twentieth-century reformers continues to be expressed today, it was not the sole Progressive Era argument in favor of the mechanism. Proponents also touted the educative benefits that could be derived from the plebiscitary process itself. The initiative reinforced one of the Progressives' central pedagogical goals: the restoration of popular government through the reformation of the citizen. Many reformers viewed the process of citizen lawmaking as one of many ways to encourage citizens to become more actively engaged in the political process. By participating directly in policymaking decisions, Progressives thought the initiative could inculcate the citizenry with a sense of civic duty and participatory responsibility.[10]

Instrumental and Educative Justifications for the Initiative

Though not always sharply delineated, the instrumental and educative justifications of the initiative abound in the writings of Progressive Era direct democracy scholars, journalists, and practitioners. Progressives argued that the initiative served two interrelated purposes. In the words of Governor Wilson, the initiative could be an effective legislative tool, leading to successful outcomes without even "being called on to work at all." Irrespective of whether state legislatures passed Progressive reforms, advocates of the initiative viewed the process as an alternative means of adopting a wide array of substantive public policies. The initiative could directly or indirectly keep the legislature in check. Furthermore, in an age before instant polling of popular attitudes was possible, proponents of the initiative contended that citizen lawmaking could gauge the electorate's preferences. The popular vote on initiatives or even the qualification of measures for the ballot would approximate public opinion.

Progressive Era advocates and academics tendered a second—albeit more subtle—general principle for the adoption and implementation of the initiative, however. Procedurally, the initiative could have a positive educative value. Rather than emphasizing the substantive outcomes in keeping with public opinion that the plebiscitary device might produce, some reformers focused on how citizens would be empowered by the process of proposing and adopting their self-made laws and constitutional amendments. By directly involving citizens in debates regarding public policies, citizens and the commonwealth more generally might benefit from the pedagogical aspects of the process itself, which, Progressive reformers contended, could increase Election Day turnout, enhance individuals' civic engagement and political knowledge, and heighten citizens' political efficacy. The educative effects of the initiative would also help to mitigate the power of special interests and party bosses, relegating them to the political sidelines. While the instrumental defense of the initiative continues today to receive the preponderance of journalistic and scholarly attention, the educative defense of the device was equally important in the Progressive Era debate over direct legislation.

An Instrument for Substantive Change

The primary instrumental argument advanced during the Progressive Era was that citizen lawmaking could control unrepresentative or unresponsive legislatures. Lord James Bryce, an eminent British scholar and England's ambassador to the United States at the time, contended that direct democracy could help regulate the legislature. Summing up his argument in a revised edition of his tome, *The American Commonwealth,* Bryce stated,

> Reference [of ballot measures] to the people may act as a conservative force; that is to say, there may be occasions when a measure which a legislature would pass, either at the bidding of a heated party majority or to gain the support of a group of persons holding the balance of voting power, or under the covert influence of those who seek some private advantage, will be rejected by the whole body of the citizens because their minds are cooler or their view of the general interest less biased by special predilections or interests.[11]

Progressive politicians, most prominently Teddy Roosevelt and Woodrow Wilson, maintained that the initiative in particular could serve as an institutional check on unresponsive state legislatures. If legislators failed to recognize or respond to the public's wishes, citizens could resort to direct action by passing initiatives that either amended the state constitution or enacted a statute. By placing measures on the ballot for the electorate to consider, citizens could circumvent the legislature altogether. Deterring the usurpation of power by state legislatures, the device could supplement the representation of the electorate yet would not disturb the traditional operations of representative government. Serving as the "gun behind the door," in Wilson's words, the initiative would compel legislators to act. Indeed, most reformers contended that they did not want to supplant the legislative process with democracy by initiative. Most legislation would continue to be made via the legislative process.

Strong supporters of direct legislation, like William S. U'Ren of Oregon, argued that the initiative would reform the sickly system of representative government by forcing legislators to be more vigilant in protecting the public weal. U'Ren, the mastermind behind the "Oregon system," admitted that "it is not desirable that the Initiative shall be relied on as the principal and ordinary method of making laws. It will not be. But at present it seems to be the best means available for overthrowing government by plutocracy in the American states and cities and substituting Peoples' Power government."[12] Fellow Oregonian Jonathan Bourne Jr., a Republican U.S. senator and one of the leading national spokesmen for the spread of initiatives, argued that they would facilitate the adoption of popular Progressive reforms.[13] Bourne, who was formally appointed to the Senate by the Oregon state legislature after he won a plurality of votes in the 1906 primary election, emphasized that Progressives could use the initiative to bypass state legislatures to enact specific planks of the reform agenda, including the direct primary, the corrupt-practices act, and the recall of public officials.[14] As political scientist Delos Wilcox, an outspoken enthusiast for the initiative, joked half-seriously, "One of the most likely uses of the Initiative, would be to reconstruct the leg-

islative machinery in such a way . . . that the legislative mill may produce something for human consumption more digestible than
shredded straw."[15] Wilcox, whose numerous books chronicled the
corruption and patronage that ailed American city government,
sought salvation in the mechanisms of direct legislation, because he,
like other Progressives, saw as woefully inadequate the individual's
role in American politics at the turn of the twentieth century.

The other instrumental rationale advanced during the Progressive
Era for the adoption of citizen lawmaking was that the initiative
could link latent public opinion to substantive policies. Advocating
the adoption of the mechanism in the American states, Roosevelt,
perhaps the most nationally recognized proponent of the process,
argued that the initiative could provide "better and more immediate
effect to the popular will."[16] Other advocates of citizen lawmaking
claimed that it could ensure that the "pure" voice of the people
would be heard. Charles Zueblin, an activist scholar with an eye on
"municipal progress" (as he titled one of his many books), argued
that the initiative was a means by which citizens could "inform their
representatives of the current state of public opinion."[17] At the turn
of the century—with direct primaries, universal suffrage for women,
the Australian ballot, and the direct election of U.S. senators still on
the political horizon and hierarchical party machines under the
dominion of vested special interests—average citizens had little
opportunity to publicly voice their concerns. "A considerable part of
the population," Harvard professor William Munro once remarked,
"is made up of men and women who are neither capitalists, union
workers, nor politicians. Being unheard from they are likely to be
overlooked and forgotten. Direct legislation gives this silent section
of the electorate a chance."[18]

This instrumental defense of the initiative—that the mechanism
allows citizens to directly (or indirectly, by its mere threat) bring
about substantive public policies that approximate public opinion—
remains one of the chief rationalizations for the process. Several
scholars recently have tried to test empirically the claim first floated
during the Progressive Era that states with citizen lawmaking will
have legislatures that are more responsive to public opinion than

states without the process. Unfortunately, the scholarly findings on this question are mixed. In separate studies, political scientist Elisabeth Gerber and economist John Matsusaka find that the presence of the initiative influences policy outcomes.[19] But other political scientists, most notably Edward Lascher, Michael Hagen, and Steven Rochlin, along with John Camobreco, find that states with the initiative do not have public policies that conform to public opinion and that states with the initiative are no more likely to adopt policies closer to public opinion than are states without the process.[20] Furthermore, state legislatures in initiative states appear increasingly likely to overturn the will of the people through the passage of countermajoritarian legislation.[21] Still, defenders of the process continue to trot out the popular belief that initiatives can be used to gauge the public's opinions.

Both instrumental justifications for the initiative received sharp criticism during the Progressive Era. Well before celebrated columnist Walter Lippmann debunked public opinion in the 1920s, referring to it as the "phantom public" and questioning whether a pure democracy could be developed in a complex, modern society, several Progressive scholars dismissed the idea that citizen lawmaking could be used to gauge public opinion.[22] "Direct legislation," political scientist George Haynes wrote in 1911, "is not the spontaneous registering of the individual voter's matured judgment as to the best method of dealing with a given problem." In his far-reaching study of direct legislation in Oregon, Haynes observed that in some elections, "the voters simply say 'yes' or 'no' (or say nothing) to specific proposals originated, framed and phrased—and every step in the procedure is of consequence—for them by some one else. By whom? For what? These may at times prove disquieting questions." Haynes pointed specifically to three 1910 ballot measures dealing with taxation, saying that each "was drawn in such language as to make its intent clear and unmistakable."[23] Activist and author Mary Parker Follett similarly commented that it was a "mistake" to think that citizen lawmaking "is merely to record, that it is based on counting, on the preponderance of votes."[24]

Other critics challenged the instrumental assumption that controlling state legislatures through initiatives would lead to more representative and responsive public policy. Paradoxically, having a "gun behind the door" might create an environment in which the legislature becomes incapable of taking action, choosing instead to defer (or refer) particularly controversial measures to the people. Though he lauded how citizen lawmaking could potentially check governmental corruption, Walter Weyl, a Progressive educator, argued that the initiative might debase "the range and decision of our elected legislators." Weyl, whose synthetic treatment of emerging political and economic issues of the day was widely praised, feared that citizen lawmaking would transform state legislators "from representatives, possessed of personal, individual opinions (although elected because their opinions are in supposed accord with those of their constituents) into mere delegates; into mere mechanical forecasters and repeaters of popular deliverances; into parrot-like, political phonographs." Weyl warned that the results from direct legislation "may not always be good. A high-spirited statesman, placed in a position where he may be checked, halted, thwarted—often, most unreasonably—where an appeal lies from his every action, where even his tenure depends upon his 'giving satisfaction,' is tempted to withdraw from the impotent eminence of office; or, if he remain, he may suffer in initiative, courage, and self-esteem."[25] Other Progressives who were dubious about citizen lawmaking echoed Weyl's Burkean critique of citizen lawmaking. Historian Charles Beard, for example, noted, "The real danger [of direct democracy] is not that representative institutions will perish, but that law-making will not receive that critical deliberation and technical attention which it is supposed to receive in legislative assemblies."[26]

A Means of Educating Citizens and Political Organizations

Juxtaposed with the instrumental defense, Progressive Era reformers offered a second general defense for the adoption of the initiative. Though rarely articulated a century later, the educative effect of the initiative was widely touted in the early twentieth century and was in many ways equally important in the arsenal of the defenders of citizen lawmaking. The initiative's educative value was praised by a range of Progressives, some of whom saw education as secondary to the instrumental outcomes of the process, while others saw the process itself as paramount.[27] Scholars who were skeptical about citizen lawmaking's substantive outcomes, such as political scientist J. W. Garner, conceded as early as 1907 that voting on ballot questions offered several "educational advantages to the electorate."[28] Writing in his magisterial study of American politics, Bryce, also dubious about direct legislation, acknowledged the secondary impact of the process and its "educative effect on the people."[29] Even Weyl, a thorough skeptic of citizen lawmaking, acknowledged that with proper safeguards in place, it could be a real source of "democratic education."[30] Indeed, the educative by-products of citizen lawmaking were believed to reinforce the Progressive ideal of democratic participation, providing an institutional foundation to augment the electorate's turnout, civic engagement, and political efficacy while lessening the influence of special interests and party machines.

First and foremost, reformers contended that the initiative would have the secondary effect of bolstering turnout on Election Day. Many Progressives were deeply concerned about the American public's growing listlessness and indifference to political matters. Reformers saw direct legislation as a way to treat political apathy. The process, in Munro's words, promised "to increase [the voter's] serious interest in public affairs by giving him something more to decide than the party label of officeholders."[31] Writing in the 1930s of the Populist and Progressive promoters of direct legislation, political scientist Edwin Cottrell maintained that "direct legislation was adopted with the belief and confidence that the real cure for the ills of government was a more immediate participation by the average citizen in all governmental processes."[32] Supporters of citizen lawmaking pointed to Oregon's high voter participation levels—a sharp contrast to the downturn in other states—following the state's adoption of direct democracy in 1902. In the general elections of 1904, 1906, and especially 1908, Oregon experienced higher-than-normal turnout levels, which proponents of citizen lawmaking argued was directly attributable to the wide array of initiatives—including women's suf-frage, Prohibition, and the single tax—that citizens had placed on ballots through petitions.[33]

Second, promoters of the initiative claimed that it would have a positive impact on citizens' civic engagement—that is, that the process would help citizens enhance their knowledge of, interest in, and discussion of politics. In his reinterpretation of the Progressive Era, which casts a positive light on various reformers' community-building efforts, historian Kevin Mattson stresses how early-twenti-eth-century reformers "argued that before any other substantive political reform took place, citizens had to build institutions through which they could educate themselves for the making of binding polit-ical judgments."[34] Herbert Croly, for example, contended that public venues and processes needed to be created to foster citizens' political education. "The great object of progressives," Croly penned in his classic tome, *Progressive Democracy,* "must always be to create a vital relation between progressivism and popular political education."[35] While not uncritical of direct democracy, the founding editor of the *New Republic* contended that "pure democracy" was "one of a group of political institutions, whose object is fundamentally to invigorate and socialize the action of American public opinion." Whether the mechanisms would achieve the intended desire was by no means cer-tain, however. Discounting the fact that direct democracy was "still in its early youth," Croly envisioned that it could "invigorate and socialize the action of American public opinion" only if it was prop-erly subsumed in the context of a Progressive community.[36]

Other scholars stressed that the initiative process could inspire cit-izens to become more engaged in and knowledgeable about politics. Acting as citizen lawmakers, individuals would embrace the discus-sion of politics in an effort to cast informed votes on ballot measures. For Harvard's Munro,

> people who are called upon to vote upon measures will learn something about them before going to the polls. When the legisla-tors alone make the laws, the individual voter feels that he has no responsibility. But when the questions go on the ballot there is a

general public discussion of the arguments for and against. The newspapers devote whole columns to the issues. The questions are discussed, pro and con, before chambers of commerce, boards of trade, luncheon clubs, civic leagues, women's societies, on the radio—everywhere. In this way the whole body of the voters becomes informed on public problems.[37]

Alluding to the most discerning foreign observer of American political culture, Frenchman Alexis de Tocqueville, Garner argued that "the direct participation of the people in legislation" would make "them acquainted with the laws and instructed them in the art of government."[38] Zueblin contended that "citizens should enjoy the use of the initiative . . . in order that they may be educated to understand government."[39] Other scholars, such as Paul Reinsch, argued that voting on ballot measures would stimulate citizens to become more engaged in the legislative process. Reinsch claimed that "nothing will so train the electorate to see the difficulties and problems of legislation, and to form an intelligent opinion about them, as having to solve these problems itself at times. Moreover, it will increase the interest of the people in the legislatures as being organs which are constantly engaged in dealing with these important matters."[40] For these observers, a citizen's political knowledge was endogenous rather than exogenous; it was a function of the rules and processes of political institutions. Hence, the initiative could play a fundamental role in educating the public, thereby allowing all individuals to reach their full potential.

Not surprisingly, Progressives regularly pointed to the Oregon experiment when celebrating citizen lawmaking's positive effects on civic engagement. George Judson King, a lecturer with the People's Rule League of America, remarked that with citizen lawmaking, "the people of Oregon are at school, learning the lost art of self-government."[41] According to Haynes, one of the most trenchant observers of political life in the Pacific Northwest, "Oregon voters have had affairs of their own to think about, which have been quite as engrossing as the tariff or the new nationalism. There has been a vitality, a genuineness in Oregon politics sharply in contrast with the state campaigns in many of the eastern states." "With keen interest," Haynes wrote on the heels of the November 1910 election, when Oregonians faced 32 ballot measures (including 24 initiatives), "the voters have been grappling with the problems—political, industrial, educational, financial—of self-government within their own state. A genuine campaign of education has been in progress, which cannot fail to produce important and enlightening results."[42] Bourne also lauded the virtues of direct legislation in Oregon and the political knowledge possessed by the "citizen legislators" in his home state:

> In Oregon the farmer at his plow, the mechanic at his bench, devote a portion of their time to study of their government and methods of improving it. They have become the most intelligent, most progressive and most independent people in the world. They wear no intellectual halters. They cannot be led to the polls and voted on Election Day. They do their own thinking. They do their own voting. They acknowledge no human authority higher than a mandate legally recorded in a popular election.

Bourne appreciated the broader civic values of the process—what Robert Putnam and other contemporary political pundits might call social capital. "Possession and exercise of the power of direct legislation," Bourne argued, "has a strong educational influence upon the people," providing "a limitless field for the individual member of society and for society as a whole to develop through submission of new laws to the people." Once equipped with "the power to legislate," Bourne reasoned, citizens "will soon acquire a knowledge of public questions and demonstrate a degree of intelligence that will put opponents of direct legislation to shame."[43]

Third, early proponents of the initiative contended that the process might positively affect how citizens felt about the political system, in terms of both influencing governmental decisions (what political scientists refer to as internal efficacy) and seeing government as responsive to the people's interests (external efficacy). Rather than using the term *political efficacy*, however, Progressive Era reformers routinely used the word *sovereignty* to expound at length on how citizen lawmaking could help individuals have more of a say in public affairs as well as feel as though the government was being responsive to the people's wishes. This understanding of sovereignty as efficacy was propounded by numerous reform-minded academics. Direct legislation could "make the voter realize that he is a sovereign in fact as well as in name," Munro reasoned; the "psychological influence of popular cooperation in government upon the electorate must also be counted as one of the considerations in its favor, since popularly enacted legislation is likely to have a moral force back of it which renders its enforcement less difficult."[44] By voting directly on issues rather than for officials, Lewis Johnson, a proponent of the initiative, argued that voters would become more responsible citizens.[45] For still other devotees of the process, such as Wilcox, the initiative could "unlock for the uses of the state all the potential political capacity of the people."[46]

Finally, reformers thought that the initiative process might mitigate the power of political organizations—namely, interest groups and political parties—by helping to restore the voice of the people. In many states, party bosses colluded with a handful of corporate interests to control the legislative agenda. Progressive reformers such as Bourne argued for a "concentration of all efforts on *first* securing the initiative and referendum," because they "will absolutely establish and perpetuate the sovereignty of the people and make all public servants directly accountable to the people instead of to the irresponsible political machine, boss, or special interest."[47] Dominant corporations—from the infamous Southern Pacific Railroad in California to local public utilities and mining companies in Colorado, for example—had captured one or both political parties in many states at the turn of the century. In Colorado, "public utility corporations, banded together in an alliance defensive and offensive against the people, have for years ruled Denver," a muckraker noted in 1910, when both parties were "the private property of W. G. Evans, the president of the [Denver] tramway company" and the Republican party boss.[48] In California, reformers such as John Randolph Haynes, Meyer Lissner, Edward Dickson, and Franklin Hichborn decried the power over the legislative rank

and file held by the party bosses, who were in cahoots with the corporate monopolies, especially the Southern Pacific Railroad.[49]
"Unless the machine and its leader, the boss, could be broken, unless
the corrupt alliance between special interests and the machine could
be smashed," Richard Hofstadter reflected in 1955, "it seemed that
no lasting reform could be accomplished."[50] By serving as Election
Day legislators, citizens might break the special interests' political
stranglehold on the state legislatures and the parties.

Though not as acerbic or trenchant as the attacks on the instrumental justification for direct legislation, questions did arise about
the potency of some of the educative effects of citizen lawmaking.
Several scholars were uncertain about the initiative's indirect impact
on civic engagement. Some, like U.S. representative Samuel McCall
(a Republican who would later become governor of Massachusetts),
doubted that citizens, who are generally "so engrossed in [their] private business," would devote "attention to public questions."[51]
While admitting that every "initiative vote is educative," Haynes did
not think that the public debate would be evenhanded; rather, with
ballot campaigns, "the chances are that but one side will be fully presented."[52] Even Oregon, which received praise for its 1908 innova-
tion of mailing out voter guides to all registered voters, came under
attack for failing to stimulate enough public engagement. As George
Haynes wrote following the 1910 election, while "public speeches
and debates were frequent" and "the press from day to day published
editorials on the leading issues, together with lengthy letters from
interested citizens . . . to the majority of voters in Oregon—as in
every other state—politics is, of course, largely a game of 'follow my
leader.'"[53]

Similar criticisms concerned the process's possible educative
effects on political knowledge. One of the harsher critics, McCall, laid
the blame with voters for "political indifference." "There are far too
few of us who carefully study public questions and try to secure exact
information about them," McCall contended in 1912; citizens "are
attracted by sensational charges, by lurid headlines in the newspapers, and by generalities." Rather than "giving that serious attention

to the political issues which we bestow upon our private affairs," he complained, "we too often complacently accept the estimate that is placed upon our profound and exact political knowledge by the men who are asking us to vote for them."[54] Many others contended that the citizens predisposed to acquire knowledge would do so but that the majority of citizens were not competent enough to make complicated albeit binary choices. Haynes conceded that voters were not "fools" but challenged others to "deny that the great majority of us, when we go to the polls, have altogether inadequate information for forming a just opinion upon the men and measures there presented for our suffrage."[55] In some cases, prejudice against poor and uneducated voters informed this view. Analyzing Oregon's 1910 popular vote, scholar Burton Hedrick found that "the largest percentage of non-voters on proposed laws is found in the city slums, where the greatest percentage of ignorance and illiteracy prevails. . . . This new scheme of legislation seems to act automatically as a disfranchisement of the ignorant or careless."[56] As political scientist Robert Cushman observed following a 1914 wave of initiatives that attempted to regulate public utilities and ratify eminent domain procedures, "to submit these [technical] matters to popular vote is to strain the interest and intelligence of the citizen and invite the most haphazard results in the way of legislation."[57] Even in Oregon, a paragon of citizen lawmaking, some skepticism existed about average citizens' cognitive abilities. After considering the 32 measures on the ballot (in addition to the 131 candidates running for 45 offices), a policeman confessed on exiting the polls in 1910, "It's like voting a bed-quilt."[58]

Skeptics also claimed that having propositions on the ballot was not likely to spur citizens to vote. Doubting the democratic effects of the initiative, political scientist and Harvard president A. Lawrence Lowell alleged in 1912 that ballot measures would not increase electoral participation. Although he marshaled no empirical evidence to bolster his case, Lowell asserted that "the vote on measures is always less than that for the principal public officers to be elected at the same time."[59] Doubting the transformative power of the mechanisms of direct democracy, Croly too dismissed ballot measures' power to get out the vote, contending that ballot propositions were "disappointing as instruments of popular government" because they were "perfectly designed to facilitate minority rule in as far as the complex questions set before the voters in referendums could be passed with a distinct minority of total registration."[60]

A few critics also claimed that the process of initiated lawmaking would not augment citizens' political efficacy. In one of the earliest essays on the subject, Garner claimed that the process "produces an inefficiency which is out of all proportion to the resulting educational advantages to the electorate."[61] Garner feared that the inefficiencies of citizen lawmaking—that the process was too cumbersome and complicated—would overshadow its substantive merits. This perspective was reinforced by Professor Allen Eaton, who in 1912 published one of the most comprehensive and balanced appraisals of early initiative use in Oregon during the Progressive Era. Eaton, like later critics, found that the shortcomings of Oregon's initiative system ultimately outweighed the advantages, asking his readers,

> How would you like to live in a State where the people can and do amend their constitution in the most radical fashion by a minority vote; where one-third of the voters decides the fate of the laws affecting the other two-thirds; where one-twentieth of the voters can and do cripple the state educational institutions by holding up their funds; where special interests hire citizens to circulate petitions asking for the recall of judges who have found them guilty; where men representing themselves as the people, buy signatures with drinks, forge dead men's names, practice blackmail by buying and selling at so much per name, signatures for petitions needed to refer certain measures to the people; a State where the demagogue thrives and the energetic crank with money, through the initiative and referendum, can legislate to his heart's content.[62]

For Garner and Eaton, the system's inefficiencies—the low voter turnout, rampant corruption, and special interest involvement that plagued many ballot campaigns—certainly mitigated much of the political efficacy that might have been derived from the process of citizen lawmaking.

Finally, the initiative's detractors contended that the process would not prevent special interests or party operatives from shaping public policy. Rather, these observers argued that special interests and party leaders would simply use the new plebiscitary device to influence policy. Early critics of citizen lawmaking highlighted several special interests, including railroads, public utilities, mining operators, fishermen, schoolteachers, and even morticians, that had used the initiative and referendum to advance particular goals.[63] These scholars also exposed the fact that by the mid-1910s, special interests were employing legal talent to draft ballot measures and paying solicitors more than four cents per name to qualify narrowly tailored measures for the ballot.[64] Furthermore, critics provided evidence detailing how Progressive Era corporate interests spent exorbitant amounts of money to promote and oppose ballot measures. In California, for example, well over $1 million, largely from corporate coffers, was spent promoting seven measures on the 1922 ballot.[65]

Even some of the most diehard advocates of citizen lawmaking during the Progressive Era reluctantly conceded that special interests might use the process for their benefit, leading to an undesirable tyranny of the minority. In 1912, Wilcox admitted,

> It is to be expected that, in learning to use the Initiative as an instrument of direct government, the people will pass through a stage of experiment, in which they will have to rebuke not only public service corporations seeking to get favors from them, but also many other kinds of special interests having a pecuniary stake in legislation proposed by themselves. It may be the school-teachers, or the letter-carriers, or the policemen, proposing legislation for the increase of their own pay. It may be the brewers trying to knock holes through the liquor law. It may be the labor unions trying to outlaw the open shop. It may be any compact body or class of men, even though constituting a small minority of the people, offering some legislation for their own benefit or for the advancement of their pet ideas.[66]

The irony of special interests actively using the lawmaking device that had originally been designed to thwart their legislative clout was not lost on those who tried to stymie the spread of direct democracy. Cushman, reviewing the initiative activities of the previous decade, cautiously observed in 1916, "We have seen that the initiative and referendum petitions are being used more frequently, by an ever widening circle of groups and classes, for purposes vitally affecting the welfare of the community and in ways which directly concern the efficiency of the state government." According to Cushman, direct legislation was "a growing, not a diminishing phenomenon. It presents a problem ever more complex, ever more important."[67]

Similarly, critics charged that political parties would continue to exert their dominance by using the initiative process to their advantage. "Public-spirited citizens or associations may for a time attempt to set forth the records of candidates or to present the 'right' side of some burning issue," Haynes speculated, "but the party machine is equally active, and its activity is more persistent."[68] University of Pennsylvania professor Ellis Oberholtzer, in perhaps the most comprehensive and erudite study of direct democracy written during the Progressive Era, also raised concerns that citizen lawmaking would have little effect on political parties. He suggested that if citizen lawmaking was practiced in states and localities with strong party machines, the initiative would soon be co-opted by party bosses. Oberholtzer asked, "Does any experienced observer believe that 'machines' which assemble large majorities for candidates at the bosses' bidding could not pass and defeat laws [at the ballot] in the same manner?" After all, Oberholtzer concluded, "The history of the submission of measures to make loans and increase the debt of Philadelphia in the past few years, affecting, as they do, the pecuniary fortunes of every property-holding citizen, should be conclusive on this point. They are approved upon the order of the political managers without the slightest popular contest."[69] Scholars such as Haynes and Oberholtzer as well as reformers such as Follett expressed grave doubts that citizen lawmaking would function independent of the political party apparatus.[70]

☐ Adopting the Initiative: Populist and Progressive Underpinnings

Rebuffing Governor Wilson's repeated entreaties, the New Jersey legislature never did refer to the statewide electorate a constitutional amendment to create the initiative.[71] Activists in a host of other states, however, successfully promoted direct legislation during the apex of the Progressive Era. In 1912, political scientist Frederick Stimson of Harvard noted that direct legislation "seems to have completely taken possession of the imagination of the American people."[72] Indeed, between 1898 and 1918, voters in 20 states approved amendments that added the initiative to their constitutions. Most of the contagion occurred in the sparsely populated states west of the Mississippi River.[73]

The sudden surge of direct legislation altered the legislative landscape of these states. At the time, political observers were stunned by the rapid adoption of citizen lawmaking. In perhaps the most impartial exploration of the advent of direct democracy that was written during the Progressive Era, Munro observed that "there has been no more striking phenomenon in the development of American political institutions during the last ten years than the rise to prominence in public discussion, and consequently to recognition upon the statute-book, of those so-termed newer weapons of democracy—the initiative, referendum and recall."[74] Just a decade earlier, Professor S. Gale Lowrie noted that the push for direct legislation, "was scarcely looked upon as a permanent feature of our governmental system." According to Lowrie, during the 1890s, the campaign for citizen lawmaking "smacked of Populism and found its supporters chiefly among certain faddists who sought by this means to secure, at least in a limited degree, the adoption of their political nostrums."[75] By the 1910s, however, "a spontaneous uprising of the whole people" had occurred, as the electorate, in the words of California journalist John Works, experienced a "political awakening."[76]

Fundamentally, the philosophical underpinnings of direct democracy sprung from the Populist faith that government should be founded on the acquiescence of the governed. The initiative, more than the referendum and recall, symbolized the return of government to the people. Invoking the words of Thomas Jefferson, "whom the friends of the initiative and referendum never cease[d] to quote in support of their schemes," reformers sought to place faith directly in the hands of ordinary citizens.[77] But the desire to create a government of and by the people by devolving responsibility back to the citizenry also informed the Progressive movement. Although national reformers were primarily concerned with reigning in corporate power and breaking party machines, what sustained the Progressive Party's various platforms during the 1910s was the singular belief in the individual's abilities.[78] Many Progressives had an optimism regarding the advancement of the human condition that differentiated them from their Populist forbears. "It seems to me," Wilcox lamented in his treatise celebrating the adoption of the initiative, "that America's greatest governmental failure is its neglect to take full advantage of individual initiative in politics."[79] Though some scholars have tried to distinguish and separate the Populist and Progressive strands of direct democracy, the initiative's reliance on the involvement of individuals strongly appealed to leaders of both political traditions.[80]

Some Progressives especially placed abundant faith in what Hofstadter identified as "the intelligence, the self-restraint, the morality, the breadth of view of the average man, the emergent New Citizen."[81] For Kansas journalist William Allen White, the inexorable "drift toward democracy" during the Progressive Era would eventually shrink the influence of money in politics and sever the corrupting pressure of the political machine. With direct legislation, the party system would be rendered "mere political scrap iron by the rise of the people."[82] A generation later, rearticulating the programmatic aspirations of reformers, Hofstadter opined,

> What the majority of the Progressives hoped to do in the political field was to restore popular government as they imagined it to have existed in an earlier and purer age. This could be done, it was widely believed, only by revivifying the morale of the citizen, and

using his newly aroused zeal to push through a series of changes in the mechanics of political life—direct primaries, popular election of Senators, initiative, referendum, recall, the short ballot, commission government, and the like. Such measures, it was expected, would deprive machine government of the advantages it had in checkmating popular control, and make government accessible to the superior disinterestedness and honesty of the average citizen.[83]

As Hofstadter rightly noted, without a premise concerning the exalted abilities of the average citizen, "the entire movement for such reforms as the initiative, the referendum, and recall is unintelligible." Hofstadter saw the preeminent theme of the Populist-Progressive tradition as "the effort to restore a type of economic individualism and political democracy that was widely believed to have existed earlier in America and to have been destroyed by the great corporation and the corrupt political machine; and with that restoration to bring back a kind of morality and civic purity that was also believed to have been lost."[84] Hofstadter's revisionist interpretation of Progressivism—particularly his belief that the ratification of direct democracy reforms was "an attempt to realize Yankee-Protestant ideals of personal responsibility; and the Progressive notion of good citizenship was the culmination of the Yankee-Mugwump ethos of political participation without self-interest"—has received its fair share of criticism over the years, but the primacy of the individual was unquestionably a cornerstone of the Progressive movement.[85] In this sense, the educative mechanisms of direct legislation fit well within the early-twentieth-century Progressive ideal.

Though the diffusion of direct legislation across the states occurred largely during the Progressive Era, the underlying sentiment for the adoption of the mechanisms was clearly linked to erstwhile populist currents of the People's (Populist) Party rather than the Progressive Party.[86] With perhaps the exception of John Randolph Haynes of California, such notable advocates of direct democracy as James W. Sullivan and William U'Ren remained either nonpartisan or aligned themselves with the Populists.[87] In the late nineteenth century, Sullivan, a printer by trade, had worked closely with single-taxer Henry George in New York and was a close friend of Samuel Gompers of the American Federation of Labor, which endorsed the initiative and referendum in 1892.[88] In the same year, setting the print himself, Sullivan authored *Direct Legislation by the Citizenship through the Initiative and Referendum*. The book, which would soon become a classic, became the standard reference for adherents of the movement in favor of direct legislation. Drawing on firsthand research conducted in Switzerland, Sullivan's book was one of the first American texts espousing the theory and practice of direct democracy.[89] U'Ren, a Wisconsinite who traipsed through numerous professions, including blacksmith, miner, lawyer, and newspaper editor, was instrumental in bringing direct legislation to the Pacific Northwest. His dogged pursuit of the initiative was driven primarily by his desire to have the populace adopt his version of the single tax, which was modeled on George's proposals. The peripatetic U'Ren, who finally settled in Oregon, maintained that "there is no representative government in the United States now. There never has been."[90] For U'Ren, only direct legislation would permit citizens to be truly represented politically. Haynes, a prominent Los Angeles medical doctor and land speculator, was "the man most responsible for the adoption and retention of the initiative, referendum, and recall in California." Trained at the University of Pennsylvania, Haynes formed the Los Angeles Direct Legislation League in 1900 and was a major presence in the statewide organization, which led the extensive lobbying effort for the adoption of direct legislation. At times Haynes single-handedly financed the campaign that ultimately brought direct legislation to California in 1911.[91]

Through the yeoman's efforts of these and other maverick political entrepreneurs, working in tandem with a handful of elected Populists and Progressives, the adoption of direct legislation began to congeal. The movement was aided by several Republican and Democratic governors and state legislators who began to warm to the plebiscitary reforms. Reform governors such as Arizona's George Hunt, Arkansas's George Donaghey, California's Hiram Johnson, Colorado's John Shafroth, and North Dakota's John Burke helped to provide the legislative impetus to adopt a slate of direct democracy reforms in their states.[92] Typical was the case of Idaho. In 1911, a year before the state's voters approved the initiative, Democratic governor James H. Hawley threw his support behind the process. A self-described "conservative . . . in so far as radical changes in our governmental system are concerned," Hawley could not find "any tangible reason for opposing direct legislation." According to Hawley, "The powers of all governing bodies in this country are based upon the consent of those who are governed, and if in extreme cases the power to decide whether any given principle shall be formulated into a statute governing the people of the state, is exercised by the people themselves, it is simply restoring that delegated authority into the hands of those by whom it was delegated."[93]

Excitement about direct legislation also permeated the scholarly world. The rise of direct legislation paralleled the emergence of political science as a discrete discipline. Progressive Era academics devoted a copious amount of ink to celebrating and condemning plebiscitary devices. The journal *Political Science Quarterly*, published by the Academy of Political Science, was launched in 1886, and the American Political Science Association published its *Proceedings* between 1903 and 1914. The *American Political Science Review* began in 1906, and by 1920, it had published no fewer than a dozen articles on the mechanisms of direct legislation, including "notes" on ballot outcomes and updates on states that adopted the procedure. *Political Science Quarterly* also published nearly a dozen articles on direct legislation by 1920. Several trade presses, including stalwarts Macmillan and Appleton, published a flurry of volumes on the subject. By 1911, the Library of Congress deemed the subject worthy of its own index.[94]

When afforded the opportunity, citizens generally approved by large majorities the constitutional amendments that state legislatures placed on ballots. Between 1898 and 1912, voters in 15 states adopted direct legislation referenda with popular approval margins of at least two to one.[95] Supporters hailed the electoral success; the wide margins indicated widespread public discontent with the legislative condition. Calling on other states to adopt the initiative (and referendum), Governor Shafroth, a leading proponent of direct legislation, exclaimed, "The battle cry of 'the rule of the people' is spreading throughout the land without regard to political affiliations. States are adopting the initiative and referendum by overwhelming majorities."[96]

Despite the dominant trend, it is important to recall that citizens in several states chose not to approve direct legislation when their state legislatures referred constitutional amendments for popular consideration. In 1913, for example, the legislatures of seven states—Iowa, Michigan, Minnesota, Missouri, North Dakota, Texas, and Wisconsin—voted to place on the ballot for ratification constitutional amendments establishing the initiative. However, a majority of voters in four of the states (Iowa, Minnesota, Texas, and Wisconsin) rejected the constitutional amendments in general elections held the following year. Voters in Missouri (1904), Mississippi (1912), and Wyoming (1912) had previously defeated amendments that would have added the initiative to their constitutions.[97] Furthermore, in Massachusetts in 1918, a majority of voters in only two urban counties (Suffolk and Plymouth) approved the statewide referendum establishing the indirect initiative and referendum.[98] The legislative referendum nevertheless passed, although a majority of voters in the mostly rural counties had voted solidly against the constitutional amendment. The rapid adoption of the initiative during the Progressive Era obviously was more complicated than a "spontaneous uprising of the whole people"; nevertheless, this new political institution became diffused across the American states stunningly quickly, as table 1 shows.[99]

What caused the swift spread of direct legislation, especially in the West? According to historian Thomas Goebel's impressive account of the rise and adoption of the initiative during the late nineteenth and early twentieth centuries, an "opportunity structure" within the "antimonopoly tradition" enabled the spread of the mechanisms in the western states. Unlike eastern states, which were under the control of the party machines, and southern states, which were preoccupied by the dominant Democratic Party's efforts to keep the black population disenfranchised, the political agendas of most western states were under the spell of an "antimonopoly ideology that looked toward the initiative and referendum as the tools to free the political process from the dominance of corporations and bosses."[100] Seeing citizen lawmaking as a means to an end, bipartisan reform associations combined with temporary alliances of minor parties to push for direct legislation. In the West, the two major parties were relatively weak and often factionalized. Political reformers, including a handful of political entrepreneurs and the visionary leaders of a diverse set of mass constituency interest groups—including the Grangers, the Farmers' Alliance, single-taxers led by George, prohibitionists such as the Anti-Saloon League, organized labor (especially the Knights of Labor and the American Federation of Labor), and suffragists— tapped into the sentiments of a radicalized, antiparty electorate, much of which was suffering from the economic dislocation of the

TABLE 1.   Date of State Adoption of the Initiative

South Dakota	1898
Utah	1900
Oregon	1902
Montana	1906
Oklahoma	1907
Maine	1908
Michigan	1908[a]
Missouri	1908
Arkansas	1910
Colorado	1910
Arizona	1911
California	1911
Idaho	1912
Nebraska	1912
Nevada	1912
Ohio	1912
Washington	1912
North Dakota	1914[b]
Mississippi	1915[c]
Massachusetts	1918
Alaska	1959
Florida	1968
Wyoming	1968
Illinois	1970
Mississippi	1992

[a]Less restrictive version approved in 1913
[b]Less restrictive version approved in 1918
[c]Repealed by the state supreme court in 1922

late nineteenth century, for support of extralegislative policy-making reforms.[101]

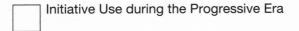

Initiative Use during the Progressive Era

In the states where voters approved the initiative during the Progressive Era, usage of the mechanism was striking. Between 1904 and 1920, the initiative was used as a "perpetual reform machine," with voters considering nearly 350 ballot initiatives in the 20 states that permitted the process.[102] Governmental reform was by far the most common subject during this period, comprising 36 percent of all initiatives that appeared on statewide ballots. Fiscal policy (taxation, spending, and bond issues) was the second-most-common subject matter, accounting for 22 percent of the total, and 15 percent of ballot initiatives concerned social policy. Somewhat surprisingly, only 6 percent of the initiatives on statewide ballots during the Progressive Era covered labor issues. The overall passage rate for initiatives from 1900 to 1920 was roughly 43 percent, only slightly less than the 1992–2000 approval rate for initiatives.[103]

Celebrating the substantive remedies the initiative process could introduce, proponents claimed that numerous reforms that intransigent state legislatures under the control of party bosses and corporate interests had blocked would be implemented if citizens could directly vote on public policies. Indeed, an array of salutary reforms with popular appeal were adopted via the initiative, including the enactment of an eight-hour workday, restrictions on child labor, workers' compensation, old-age pensions, Prohibition, and antitax measures. Some of the most notable "governance policies" brought about by initiative included the direct election of U.S. senators, the direct primary, home rule for municipalities, the secret (Australian) ballot, nonpartisan and at-large local elections, reapportionment, the merit system, professional city managers, and an end to the poll tax.[104] These as well as other substantive outcomes at the polls undoubtedly altered the political landscape in these states as initiatives resonated with and were routinely adopted by majorities of voters. Early reformers correctly understood the initiative to be a transformative instrument that could alter public policy by circumventing state legislatures, special interests, and party bosses.

Today, while differing in their assessments of the practice of direct democracy, many journalists and scholars continue to paint an overly exalted image of early initiative use. The underlying premise of most modern accounts of ballot measure activity during the Progressive Era is that the process was dominated by amateur, citizen-led groups. Journalists critical of the process draw heavily on the Progressive Era to justify how the increasingly corrupt practice of the initiative has deviated from its original intent and use. David Broder, for example, invokes an idyllic view of how the initiative operated nearly a century ago, writing nostalgically that "the initiative process has largely discarded its grass-roots origins" and is "no longer merely the province of idealistic volunteers."[105] Rather than citizen groups, Broder contends that narrow economic interests now dominate the initiative process, as corporations and unions pay signature-gathering firms thousands of dollars to circulate petitions and spend millions of dollars on 30-second television spots. In a nostalgic turn, Broder outwardly pines for the olden days when citizen groups used the initiative, as our Populist and Progressive forbearers originally intended.

But the Progressive Era image of an amateur-driven initiative process that encouraged the voice of the people is not entirely accurate. Scholars recently have begun to chip away at the gild of what Richard Ellis derisively calls the "mythic narrative" of direct legislation's "golden era."[106] The historical record, often conveniently forgotten or ignored (by both supporters and detractors of the initiative process), reveals how special interests and party machines in several states were just as quick and as savvy in utilizing direct legislation as Progressive forces were. Relying on the intended or unintended approval of the voters, special interests used the initiative (and referendum) to reverse a number of reforms passed by state legislatures. For example, in 1912, Colorado mining and public utility corporations placed deceptive business-friendly counterpropositions on the ballot in an effort to thwart Progressive measures. Colorado Fuel and

Iron, owned by industrialists Jay Gould and John D. Rockefeller, sponsored an initiative purportedly limiting the workday for miners to eight hours; in fact, the "joker" measure would have annulled a stricter measure passed by the state legislature just a year earlier.[107] Furthermore, voters rejected a great many Progressive initiatives placed on ballots by reformers. As is the case today, narrow economic interests during the Progressive Era had considerable success in defeating a series of initiatives that supposedly resonated with the general public. In 1914, for example, voters in California, Colorado, Oregon, and Washington all rejected eight-hour workday initiatives placed on the ballot by Progressive forces.[108] Voters in Oklahoma (in 1910) and Ohio, Missouri, and Nebraska (in 1914) defeated woman suffrage initiatives, maintaining the status quo.[109] And during the 1910s, voters in California, Colorado, and Washington rejected Prohibition initiatives as well as efforts to reform their states' public utilities commissions.

That special interests were able to defeat Progressive initiatives as well as advance narrow issues should not come as a surprise. The various ad hoc coalitions that shepherded the adoption of citizen lawmaking in the 1900s were not necessarily politically aligned concerning substantive issues. Thus, it would be unreasonable to expect that the Progressive coalitions comprised of issue minorities, which successfully championed direct democracy to alter the balance of power in initiative states, would have coalesced around each other's pet projects at the ballot box. Yet the facile (and inaccurate) perception that Populist and Progressive forces were singularly successful in transforming the political landscape by drawing on amateur forces to enact statutory and constitutional reforms only adds to the nostalgia of the era. A more accurate portrayal of early initiative use incorporates the not-so-progressive ballot measures advanced by the same special interests and party bosses that the process had been intended to hobble. As Goebel writes, "Direct democracy has been most importantly an addition to the repertoire of collective action enjoyed by an ever-growing array of interest groups."[110] Thus, political organizations quickly educated themselves to take advantage of the new plebiscitary mechanism.

The flurry of initiative activity (Progressive and otherwise) began to taper off following the aftermath of World War I, only to briefly reemerge during the 1930s. The drop in usage during the 1920s (and especially during the 1940s and 1950s) was partly attributable to the culmination of the prewar culture of Progressive reform. According to Mattson, the government's wartime "methods of manipulating the public—and the ideas informing this effort—had a devastating effect beyond the war" in that citizens were less likely to adhere to Populist rhetorical tropes and political efforts to undermine state authority.[111] Indeed, only a decade after the signing of the Treaty of Versailles, fans as well as detractors of direct democracy downplayed the significance of the mechanisms of direct democracy. Writing in 1931, Harvard's Munro noted that "progressives wonder why they ever based so much hope on these new devices, while the conservative business man marvels that he should have been afraid of them."[112]

Conclusion

During the adoption and early usage of the initiative, Progressive reformers and their critics substantially differed over the instrumental and educative merits and dangers of the process. Strident criticism of and praise for citizen lawmaking during the period emanated from diverse venues ranging from inside the White House to the editorial pages of the *New York Times*. In 1913, former president William Howard Taft quipped, "Could any system be devised better adapted to the exaltation of cranks and the wearying of electorate of their political duties than the giving of power . . . to the voters to submit all the fads and nostrums that their active but impractical minds can devise, to be voted on in frequent elections?" The *Times* opined, "This new method of handling the basic law of the state is advocated in the name of democracy. In reality it is utterly and hopelessly undemocratic. While pretending to give greater rights to the voters, it deprives them of the opportunity effectively and intelligently to use their powers."[113] Although the instrumental justification for the initiative advanced by Wilson and others was quite pervasive, the educative defense of the initiative was also widely articulated during the Progressive Era. As Munro summarized in his influential reader on direct democracy,

> Political thought and discussion can be best stimulated, it is sug-
> gested, by popular knowledge that these lead straight to action.
> The way to get voters interested in measures is to ask for their
> opinion upon measures, not for their opinion upon men. The way
> to educate the voter upon matters of public policy is to submit
> measures to him in person and not to some one who holds his
> proxy. The educative value of the ordinary ballot has long since
> been demonstrated; and friends of direct legislation now urge that
> this be enhanced by making the ballot a more elaborate political
> catechism.[114]

Seizing on the educative effects of citizen lawmaking, many proponents of the process heralded it as a palliative for what ailed American democracy at the dawn of the twentieth century.

A century later, questions about citizens' participation, civic
engagement, political knowledge, and political efficacy as well as
about the role of special interests and political parties in the political
process have once again reached the forefront of the public debate on
the crisis of American democracy. While proponents and detractors
continue today to disagree in their assessments of citizen lawmaking,
these combatants have largely ignored the process's possible educative aspects. Overshadowing its pedagogical facets, much of the contemporary debate continues to concern the substantive outcomes
resulting from successful ballot initiatives. Unfortunately, the
onslaught of recent studies documenting the merits and pitfalls of
citizen lawmaking has generally overlooked or greatly underesti-
mated the process's secondary, institutional effects. In the chapters
that follow, we reconsider the procedural side of the initiative,
empirically assessing the educative merits of citizen lawmaking in its
present form.

2 | The Education of Citizens
Voting

Of all the secondary effects that might be derived from citizen law-making, Progressive Era reformers most often singled out how the process could directly boost electoral participation. Following the strong-party era during the Gilded Age, when levels of voting participation reached historic heights, turnout began dropping precipitously at the start of the twentieth century. During what political historians alternatively refer to as the Fourth Party system or the postparty era, voter turnout outside the one-party, Democratic-dominated South fell by nearly 15 percent in presidential elections between 1896 and 1916. Structural barriers to participation—such as the abolition of party-line voting; party registration laws; the prohibition of fusion (listing candidates under multiple party labels); literacy tests; poll taxes; and the desynchronization of local, state, and national elections—were frequently blamed for the waning rates of voter turnout.[1]

A generation later, Progressive reformers took up the Populist mantle and began pressing for a series of institutional arrangements that could help forestall the decline in turnout among an increasingly disengaged electorate. Reform-minded scholars, such as Professor Delos Wilcox, lamented at the time, "The curse of our politics is apathy."[2] In addition to home rule and a commission form of local government, the short ballot, the direct primary, direct election of U.S. senators, and nonpartisan elections, advocates of good government touted the initiative and referendum as mechanisms that could generate excitement at the polls. Wilcox and other reformers of the day averred that the use of ballot initiatives would strengthen democracy

31

by encouraging a more engaged and participatory citizenry.[3] They were optimistic that the substantive nature of ballot measures would impel citizens to go to the polls, as the process enabled citizens to participate directly in the formulation of public policy.

A century after the adoption of the initiative process in 19 American states, participation has reemerged as an important theme in civic discourse, as policymakers and social commentators search for more democratic and collective mechanisms for sending signals to government.[4] U.S. voter turnout continues to decline, with only half of registered voters casting ballots in the 1996 and 2000 presidential elections and little more than a third casting votes in the 2002 midterm election. Voter turnout rates in the United States are among the lowest in the advanced industrialized nations.[5] Political observers are again turning to direct democracy mechanisms in hopes of increasing electoral participation. Boosting citizen participation is a primary goal of contemporary progressives, who propose to update our electoral system with such reforms as Internet voting, same-day voter registration, absentee and mail ballot voting, and motor-voter registration, among others.[6] Some reformers have suggested that states leading the way in ballot initiatives may well be the first to allow Internet voting and online voter registration.[7]

During the 1990s, with the explosion in the use of direct democracy, political observers began to note that the presence of initiatives on the ballot might positively affect turnout rates in the American states. Some referred back to the celebrated June 1978 case of Proposition 13 in California, where turnout of registered voters exceeded 69 percent in the primary election and more than 350,000 more ballots were cast for or against the tax-cutting initiative than the combined total received by all the Republican and Democratic gubernatorial candidates.[8] Other commentators, such as Republican insider Grover Norquist, the head of Americans for Tax Reform, a conservative, national, nonprofit organization, touted the puissance of initiatives, especially in turning out partisans for candidate contests.[9] Still others pointed worldwide, where the use of initiatives and referenda dramatically increased, partially in response to demands for more participatory models of governing consistent with the new information economy.[10] Proponents of citizen law-making, along with a host of democratic theorists, continue to contend that the act of voting directly on policy questions may increase citizen participation and turnout at the polls. They argue that allowing citizens to act as lawmakers heightens their interest in politics and the supply of information about elections.[11] Even staunch critics of direct democracy, such as *Washington Post* columnist David Broder and Peter Schrag, the former editor of the *Sacramento Bee,* concede that citizen lawmaking promotes electoral participation.[12] But does it?

We assess in this chapter the Progressive Era proposition that citizen lawmaking bolsters voter turnout. Drawing on both aggregate and individual-level data, we test whether states that allow citizens and interest groups to place policy questions on the ballot for a popular vote have higher voter turnout.

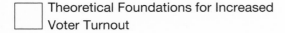 Theoretical Foundations for Increased Voter Turnout

Participation (or lack thereof) emerged as one of the dominant political themes of the 1990s, as advocates searched for more democratic and collective mechanisms to allow the electorate to send signals to and play a part in government.[13] Normative theorists, building on the foundational work of Progressive Era scholars, argued that direct forms of democracy could stimulate participation by energizing citizens with a sense of civic duty and political efficacy. Calling for more "discursive democracy," "strong democracy," "teledemocracy," "digital democracy," and "deliberation," scholars offered a variety of participatory models of decision making designed to make government function better by expanding the circle of voices heard in the policymaking process.[14] Expanding deliberations within the public sphere would allow public officials to tap into new sources of ideas and information when making decisions. The prescription is to foster greater individual and collective participation within segments of government organizations and to structure institutions to include mass citizen participation. Increasing government communication with citizens is of primary concern. In its simplest form, participatory government would function as a plebiscite, with the public being asked to decide public issues by a direct vote. These participatory models imply that the system of representative democracy is far from perfect in transmitting the wishes of the public into policy and that direct democracy procedures may improve the situation, even in a complex modern society.[15]

Journalists and supporters of direct democracy also commonly believe that ballot initiatives stimulate voter interest and, in turn, increase turnout on Election Day. Consumer activist Ralph Nader has claimed that direct democracy could mobilize "people who ordinarily would not be part of the political process."[16] In 1978, following the passage of Proposition 13, the *New York Times* editorialized, "Direct democracy offers another benefit: It is a powerful stimulus to political participation," while more recently, an article in *Congress Daily,* an outlet of the *National Journal,* claimed, "High-profile initiatives on statewide ballots could dramatically affect voter turnout in some House and Senate races [in the fall of 1998] and potentially influence who wins."[17] Direct democracy scholars have referred to this apparent increase in voter turnout in initiative states as a "spillover effect."[18] In states that frequently use the process, such as California, Colorado, and Oregon, some of the most controversial and important policies—taxation, government spending, education, health, environment, affirmative action, immigration, welfare, gun control, electoral reform—are now decided via initiatives and referenda.[19]

Despite the popular view, as well as claims by normative democratic theory scholars, empirical research conducted in the 1980s disclosed that voter turnout did not increase appreciably when initiatives were placed on the ballot. Two studies in particular downplayed direct democracy's positive effects on voter turnout. Using independent sample t tests, David Everson compared voter turnout in initiative and noninitiative states between 1960 and 1978 and found that in presidential and midterm elections, turnout is slightly higher in states with the initiative than in states without it. However, after removing from the equation southern states, which for cultural and historical reasons have had lower turnout, he showed that noninitiative states have higher turnout during presidential elections than initiative states do, with turnout during midterm elections staying roughly the same. Everson's analysis does not measure use of the initiative process, concurrent statewide races for political office (for example, governor or U.S. Senate), change over time, registration requirements, or other socioeconomic variations across the states.[20]

Building on Everson's findings, David Magleby, one of the foremost direct legislation scholars, suggests that on average, northern states with the initiative had no greater voter turnout than northern states without the initiative between 1960 and 1980. With respect to one aberrant year, 1978, when voter turnout was 3 percent higher in initiative states than in noninitiative states, Magleby speculates that voters in initiative states may have been responding to the stimulus of candidate contests rather than ballot measures. "In sum, over the last twenty years, turnout generally has been the same whether or not states had the initiative process," Magleby concludes; "no evidence exists for the claim that initiatives will increase voter turnout over time."[21]

Where this volume differs from previous studies, however, is in our use of multivariate regression. This common statistical method allows us to list a number of independent variables or possible explanatory factors for each result (for example, state institutional, economic, political, and demographic factors) and to identify which of these are statistically significant predictors of turnout. Such crucial statistical techniques are lacking in both previous formative studies, which did not control for other factors that might shape variation in electoral turnout across the states. In this chapter, we analyze the data using multiple controls that allow us to sort out which factors account for observed differences and which are statistically significant. Both previous studies also did not use statistical methods appropriate for time-series data. Furthermore, other research has measured only constitutional provisions for the initiative, not its usage over time.[22] Some initiative states, such as California, Colorado, and Oregon, have a large number of policies on the ballot every election, while other states, such as Illinois, Mississippi, and Wyoming, have used the process only sparingly.

Finally, scholars have not analyzed turnout rates in the 1990s, the period that saw the greatest direct democracy activity of the past century. In the realm of initiative politics, much has changed since the early 1980s, when Everson and Magleby conducted their studies. Not only has the amount of spending on ballot propositions increased exponentially, but usage of the process has exploded over the past two decades, reaching rates comparable only to the first two decades of the twentieth century. In the 1990s, for example, more than 300 statewide initiatives qualified for the ballot, an average of 60 per general election nationwide. The number of statewide initiatives on the ballot across the nation during the 1990s surpassed that of all other decades, including the 1910s, the previous high.[23] The increased usage of initiative process in the last two decades thus may have translated into higher levels of voter turnout.

Studying the effect of ballot measures on voter turnout is important for at least two reasons. First, turnout among the American electorate is low relative to turnout in other western democracies, especially among younger, less affluent, less educated, less partisan, and nonwhite citizens.[24] From a normative perspective, if citizen political participation is preferable in a democracy and ballot measures encourage voter turnout, then initiatives are indeed a good thing, independent of their policy content or outcome. Second, the impact of initiatives on voter turnout should be important to scholars of electoral studies, as there are more initiatives on state and local ballots today than ever before.

Do Ballot Initiatives Increase Voter Turnout in the States?

Reconsidering the indirect impact of the initiative on voter turnout in the states, we pool data for the 50 states over a 32-year period (1970–2002) to assess the impact of the number of initiatives appearing on state ballots on voter turnout. The data is analyzed using cross-sectional time series, which statistically controls for variation between states and over time. The dependent variable, or outcome to be explained, is average state voter age turnout (VAT). The data are measures of the votes cast for president or for U.S. representative in midterm years, divided by the state population older than age 18. There is considerable variation across the 50 states, with lower turnout in the South.

States with more frequent use of the initiative are hypothesized to have higher turnout rates over time. Thus, the key explanatory, or independent, variable is the use of ballot initiatives. In initiative states, citizens are accustomed to frequently voting on ballot propositions placed on the ballot by interest groups or the state legislature.[25] We anticipate that states with more frequent use of the initiative process will have higher voter turnout, measured by the number of initiatives appearing on the statewide ballot every two years from 1970 to 2002.[26]

Increased voter turnout in initiative states is hypothesized to be most pronounced in midterm elections, when ballot initiatives do not compete with presidential candidates for media attention. Thus, even if only one or two initiatives qualify for the ballot in midterm elections, this may be sufficient to stimulate increased participation, especially if the measures concern controversial policy questions. When ballot initiatives must compete with presidential candidates for media coverage, a larger number of initiatives may be required to increase turnout rates—that is, the threshold for the initiative process to have an impact on turnout rates may be higher in presidential contests than in midterm elections.

Another way of conceptualizing variation between midterm and presidential elections is in terms of voter information. Midterm elections are low-information elections with very few sources of mobilization, thus making the electorate more sensitive to those sources of mobilization that exist, such as ballot measures. Presidential elections, however, are high-information elections that have multiple sources of mobilization. As a result, one ballot initiative or referendum is unlikely to mobilize more voters, but the presence of several items on the ballot may be enough to bring out extra votes. We thus suggest that usage of the initiative process may have a different substantive impact in midterm and presidential elections.

A recent study by Mark Smith that uses different explanatory variables provides a useful comparison. Arguing that not all initiatives are the same, Smith measures the presence of "salient" initiatives and referenda—those with a high percentage of front-page newspaper coverage devoted to ballot issues on the day following the election— from 1972 to 1996. Smith finds that the presence of salient initiatives and referenda increases turnout in midterm elections by roughly 3 percent over states without direct democracy, but not in presidential election years. Without a presidential race on the ballot, voter and media attention focuses instead on state-level issues and candidate contests. Ballot measures that spark interest from a wide cross-section of the public appear to increase voter turnout. Because Smith's measure raises some questions of content validity, we use a more direct and simple measure of saliency: the number of initiatives on the ballot each election.[27]

Alternative Explanations for Variations in State Voter Turnout

What other demographic, political, and economic factors influence turnout rates across the 50 states? Following Everson's research, we control for southern states, which have traditionally had considerably lower turnout rates as a legacy of Jim Crow laws (poll taxes, literacy tests, and so on) and one-party dominance. We also measure the presence of statewide races—gubernatorial and U.S. Senate elections.[28] Previous research has shown that voter registration requirements have an important effect on statewide turnout—more stringent registration laws lead to lower voter turnout.[29] We measure registration requirements by the number of days before the election one can register to vote in each state: for example, states with Election Day registration or no required voter registration are coded zero, and states requiring registration a month before the election are coded 30.[30]

At the individual level, scholars and policymakers alike have long recognized differential voter turnout rates by socioeconomic status: individuals with higher income, education, and occupational status are considerably more likely to vote.[31] To control for the effect of an educated populace, we include a variable measuring the percentage of each state's population with a high school degree or higher.[32] States with higher income inequalities are also likely to have lower turnout rates. Yearly income inequality is measured by a Gini index for each state.[33] In addition, scholars such as V. O. Key and Rodney Hero have found that race plays a central if not defining role in subnational U.S. politics.[34] Using 50-state data, Kim Hill and Jan Leighley demonstrate that over the past half century, racial diversity is strongly associated with lower levels of voter turnout, weaker mobilizing institutions, and more restrictive voter registration requirements.[35] The sizes of state minority populations are measured with an index using 1980, 1990, and 2000 U.S. Census data and 1996 Current Population Survey data on the percentage of the Latino, African American, and Asian American populations.[36] In a multiple regression analysis, we control for these alternative explanations.

Findings from the Aggregate (50 State) Data

Previous research on voter turnout suggests that presidential and midterm elections must be analyzed separately, given the substantially higher turnout in presidential elections across states. In his study, Smith suggests that the presence of salient initiatives on the ballot may be particularly important in midterm elections.[37] We are interested in accounting for variation in turnout rates over time to see if the increased use of direct democracy has had a positive effect on turnout and across states to see if states that use the initiative process have higher levels of voter turnout.[38]

Presidential Elections

Our analysis reveals that states with frequent use of ballot initiatives have on average significantly higher turnout rates in presidential elections from 1972 to 2000. Table A.1 (see appendix) presents the impact of the usage of the initiative process using a multivariate regression model with panel-corrected standard errors. Consistent with our hypothesis, voter turnout rates are higher in presidential elections in states with more initiatives on the ballot, controlling for variation in other candidate races on the ballot, registration require-ments, state racial/ethnic composition, and economic conditions. The data indicate that states with more initiatives on the ballot have higher turnout rates in presidential elections than do states with low or no initiatives.

Scholars of direct democracy warn that too many initiatives on the ballot can decrease voter turnout.[39] To test this hypothesis, we exam-ine a nonlinear transformation by adding a square term for the num-ber of initiatives on the ballot. The quadratic model in the second column of table A.1 suggests that turnout levels off once a certain threshold of initiatives on the ballot is met. Our findings contradict previous research showing that states with the initiative process do not have higher turnout rates than noninitiative states and that higher turnout rates occur only in midterm elections. While Smith finds higher turnout rates in midterm elections in states with salient measures on the ballot, he does not detect higher turnout rates in presidential elections, as we have shown here.

How much does state turnout increase for every additional initia-tive on the ballot, holding other variations across the states con-stant?[40] (Controlling for the set of explanatory variables discussed ear-lier, we simulate average voter turnout in presidential elections using the quadratic model. We find that each additional initiative on the ballot raises turnout by one-half of a percentage in presidential elec-tions. Our findings suggest that multiple ballot contests encourage citizens to vote in presidential elections, lending support to participa-tory theories of democracy.

In contrast to previous research, our analysis distinguishes between states that have but rarely use the initiative (for example, Illinois, Mississippi, and Wyoming) and states that frequently use the process (for example, California, Colorado, and Oregon). The analy-sis confirms our hypothesis that ballot initiatives do increase state turnout rates, even in presidential elections, over the past quarter of

"What Matters"   BOX 1

Which states have higher voter turnout in presidential elections, 1972–2000?

Nonsouthern states with frequent initiative use, lower racial diversity, and lenient voter registration requirements.

Note: Only statistically significant differences are reported (see table A.1). When multivariate regression is used, these are the variables that matter, holding other factors constant.

What is the effect of each additional ballot initiative on state voter turnout?

	Turnout
No initiatives on the ballot	55.6%
One initiative on the ballot	56.1%
Two initiatives on the ballot	56.6%
Three initiatives on the ballot	57.1%
Four initiatives on the ballot	57.6%
Five initiatives on the ballot	58.1%

Note: Estimates are based on the assumption that there is a Senate and gubernatorial race on the ballot and that it is a nonsouthern state. State high school graduation rates, racial diversity, income inequality, number of initiatives squared, and voter registration laws held constant at their means. Estimated probabilities are based on coefficients reported in table A.1, column 2.

a century. Consistent with previous research, we find that southern states on average tend to have lower turnout rates than nonsouthern states and that states with more stringent registration requirements have lower voter turnout. We also find that states with higher racial diversity have considerably lower voter turnout rates in presidential elections over the past three decades, which confirms earlier research.

Midterm Elections

As with other studies of voter turnout, we find slightly different effects in presidential and midterm elections.[41] Corroborating Smith's research, our work shows that states with frequent use of ballot initiatives have higher turnout rates in midterm elections between 1970 and 2002, as reported in table A.2 (see appendix). As in presidential elections, usage of the process, measured by the number of initiatives on the ballot, is also positively related to higher turnout rates. States with more initiatives on the ballot have higher voter turnout in midterm elections.

But can too much of a good thing—that is, casting votes on ballot measures—lead to a decrease in turnout? In the quadratic model reported in the last column of table A.2, the coefficient for the squared number of initiatives on the ballot is inversely related to voter turnout. While more ballot initiatives lead to higher turnout, the increase in turnout eventually stabilizes as the number of measures on the ballot increases. This suggests that claims made by proponents of a pure (electronic) U.S. direct democracy—where voters would continually be asked to make public policy decisions—may actually have limited effects on democratic participation.[42]

How much does state turnout increase for every additional initiative on the ballot, all else being equal?[43] Simulating voter turnout in midterm elections, we find that each additional initiative on the ballot raises turnout by 1.2 percent.

As suggested earlier, midterm elections are generally low-information elections, with few sources of mobilization. Numerous ballot initiatives appear to transform low-information midterm elections into high-information elections, stimulating turnout.[44] Ballot propositions also appear to add information to already high-information presidential elections, increasing turnout.

Comparing Turnout in Initiative and Noninitiative States

The previous analysis suggests that there is a significant difference in turnout levels in initiative and noninitiative states in presidential and midterm elections. As figure 1 reveals, there is a significant gap in the percentage of voter turnout between initiative and noninitiative states

"What Matters"   BOX 2

Which states have higher voter turnout in midterm elections, 1970–2002?

Nonsouthern states with frequent initiative use, lower racial diversity, lower income inequality, U.S. Senate and gubernatorial elections, and lenient voter registration requirements.

Note: Only statistically significant differences are reported (see table A.2). When multivariate regression is used, these are the variables that matter, holding other factors constant.

What is the effect of each additional ballot initiative on state voter turnout?

	Turnout
No initiatives on the ballot	41.3%
One initiative on the ballot	42.5%
Two initiatives on the ballot	43.6%
Three initiatives on the ballot	44.8%
Four initiatives on the ballot	48.0%
Five initiatives on the ballot	47.1%

Note: Estimates are based on the assumption that there is a Senate and gubernatorial race on the ballot and that it is a nonsouthern state. State high school graduation rates, racial diversity, income inequality, number of initiatives squared, and voter registration laws held constant at their means. Estimated probabilities are based on coefficients reported in table A.2, column 2.

in midterm and presidential elections, not controlling for other factors. Figure 2 shows on average a 10 percent gap in voter turnout between initiative and noninitiative states in midterm elections, while figure 3 shows a 5 percent gap in turnout rates in presidential elections. Though a rough indicator, this is a nontrivial difference in voter turnout rates.

We also examine the impact of the number of initiatives on voter turnout in only those states with the initiative process.[45] Controlling for other factors, initiative states with more initiatives on the ballot have higher turnout in both midterm and presidential elections than states that use the process only rarely. This finding offers further

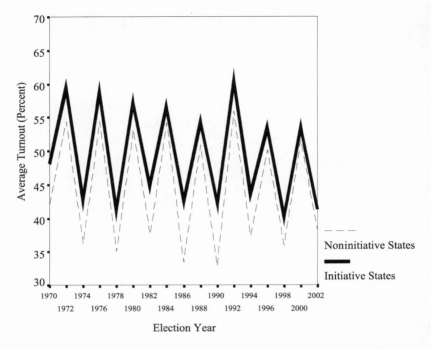

Fig. 1.   Turnout (voting age population) in initiative versus noninitiative states

confirmation of the positive impact of the initiative process on electoral participation rates in the states.

Although earlier studies by Everson and Magleby did not detect a
relationship between direct democracy and electoral participation,
higher voter turnout in initiative states should not come as a surprise.
Ballot initiatives can dominate media headlines, shape candidate
elections, and even affect national party politics. Some of the most
salient and emotional policy questions—taxes, gay rights, immigration, the environment, and affirmative action—are decided by voters
in initiative contests. In some states, ballot initiatives' salience among
voters has even eclipsed that of candidates running for office.[46]

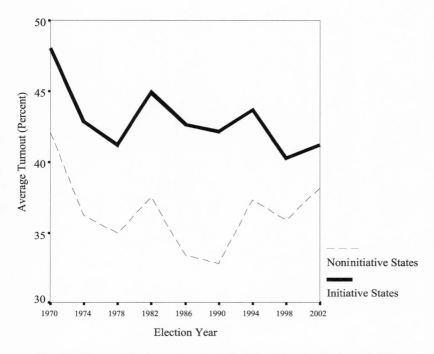

Fig. 2.   Turnout (voting age population) in midterm elections: initiative versus noninitiative states

☐ Does Exposure to Ballot Initiatives Increase the Probability of Voting?

To avoid the ecological fallacies to which the previous aggregate-level analyses are prone, we use American National Election Studies (NES) surveys for three recent election years—1996, 1998, and 2000—to conduct individual-level tests of whether exposure to ballot initiatives encourages voter turnout. We analyze the data separately for the three years (rather than pooling it) because of changes in survey questions and coding in 2000. We also use data from the 1992 Senate Election Study, which, unlike the NES surveys, contains samples of approximately equal size from each state. The dependent variable in

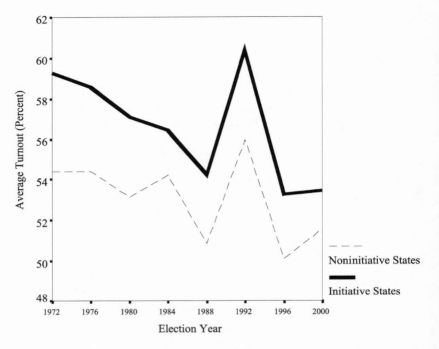

Fig. 3.   Turnout (voting age population) in presidential elections: initiative versus noninitiative states

our analysis is voting, measured by whether the respondent reported voting in the previous election. By merging the survey data with state-level data, we can test our hypotheses about the effect of ballot initiatives on the probability of voting. The key independent, or explanatory, variable is the number of initiatives appearing on the statewide ballot in each year. We expect this variable to be positively related to our dependent variable, voting.

We use several other independent variables to control for individual-level attitudinal and demographic factors that may also influence the probability of voting. As discussed earlier, research has long shown that socioeconomic factors, particularly income and education, influence participation in politics.[47] To control for the effect of income, we include a 24-point Likert scale measuring total family income. We control for the effects of education with a seven-point ordinal scale and for sex with a dichotomous variable coded one for females and zero for males. To control for race and ethnicity, African Americans, Latinos, and Asian Americans are coded one, with non-Hispanic whites as the reference group, coded zero. Age is measured in years. A series of dichotomous variables is used to account for partisanship, including strong Democrat, strong Republican, and pure independents, with moderate partisans as the reference group. We also measure whether the respondent had Internet access (yes coded one and no coded zero), since the Internet has become increasingly important in providing political news. Because Internet access was not included in the 1992 Senate Election Study, we use an ordinal measure of political interest measured by a Likert scale ranging from "very much interested" in the campaign to "not much interested."

As we argued earlier, higher state racial diversity is associated with increased barriers to voter participation and lower turnout. We again measure state racial context in our models with a racial and ethnic index created for the 50 states using data on Latino, African American, Asian American, and non-Hispanic white population percentages from the 1996 Current Population Surveys and the 2000 U.S. Census.

Findings from the Survey Data

Since the dependent variable is binary (voted is coded as one, did not vote is coded as zero), logistic regression coefficients are estimated. As shown in tables A.3 and A.4 (see appendix), after controlling for other factors, respondents living in states with frequent ballot initiatives were more likely to vote in the 1992 and 1996 presidential and 1998 midterm elections but not in the 2000 presidential election. These findings support the analysis based on 50-state data reported earlier and suggest that ballot initiatives may be particularly effective in stimulating political interest and participation in midterm elections when issue campaigns do not compete with presidential races and in noncompetitive, low-turnout presidential elections.

Also confirming previous aggregate-level research, individuals residing in states with higher racial diversity were significantly less likely to vote, controlling for other factors. The coefficients for the individual demographic variables in these models are in the expected direction and are relatively consistent over time. In each year, older people were more likely to vote than younger people. Consistent with previous research, strong partisans (Republicans and Democrats) and people with more education and income were more likely to vote in two of the three elections. Internet access also had a positive and statistically significant impact on voting in the two most recent presidential elections, suggesting that increased exposure to the Internet may enhance voter information about candidates and issues and thereby stimulate voting.[48]

A limitation of the NES surveys is that they do not sample by state. The surveys include respondents from more than 40 states, but they do not provide equal numbers of respondents in each state. We use a unique survey, the 1992 Senate Election Study, which contains samples of approximately equal size from each state, to estimate the relationship between initiative use and the probability of voting. Use of these data also expands our time frame to include the 1992 election.

What is the substantive magnitude of exposure to initiative contests on the probability of voting? Simulated probabilities suggest that each additional initiative on the state ballot increases the probability of an individual voting by 1 percent in the 1998 midterm election, holding all other demographic and political factors in the model constant.[49] Thus, an individual residing in a state with four initiatives on the ballot is estimated to have a 4 percentage point higher probability of voting than if the same individual resided in a state with no initiatives on the ballot, all else being equal. In the 1996 presidential election, the probability of voting increased by .5 percent for each initiative appearing on the statewide ballot, all else being equal. Many initiatives appeared on statewide ballots in 1992, increasing the probability of an individual voting by 4 percent for each initiative. This

"What Matters"   BOX 3

Who votes? Individual-level analysis

1992 Presidential election (competitive)
A voter who is exposed to ballot initiatives, a strong partisan (Democrat
or Republican), older, educated, affluent, politically interested, non-
Hispanic, and lives in a state with lower racial diversity.

1996 Presidential election (noncompetitive)
A voter who is exposed to ballot initiatives, older, affluent, has Internet
access, and lives in a state with lower racial diversity.

1998 Midterm election
A voter who is exposed to ballot initiatives, a strong partisan (Democrat
or Republican), older, educated, has Internet access, and lives in a state
with lower racial diversity.

2000 Presidential election (competitive)
A voter who is a strong partisan (Democrat or Republican), a partisan
(Democrat or Republican), older, educated, affluent, has Internet access,
and lives in a state with lower racial diversity.

Note: Only statistically significant differences are reported (see tables A.3 and A.4). When
logistic regression is used, these are the variables that matter, holding other factors constant.

estimate may be the most reliable, since it is based on survey data
with equal samples from all 50 states. While these probabilities may
seem modest for an individual, when multiplied by hundreds of
thousands or millions of voters statewide, direct democracy could
have quite a large effect on turnout rates.

Consistent with the previous analysis, we find that citizens in
states with more initiatives on the ballot are more likely to vote, after
controlling for the usual demographic and political variables. This
finding provides strong evidence that direct democracy fosters
increased political participation in the American states.

Conclusion

While numerous scholars continue to investigate the direct effects of ballot initiatives on policy outcomes and minority rights, we have begun to test claims regarding the process's indirect (or educative) effects on political participation. Lending support to arguments made by both Progressive Era reformers and contemporary normative scholars, our analysis indicates that states with more initiatives on the ballot had higher voter turnout in both midterm and presidential elections over the past quarter of a century, after controlling for alternative explanations for variation in turnout rates across the 50 states. Survey data substantiate this finding. We find that citizens with frequent exposure to ballot initiatives were also more likely to vote in the 1992 and 1996 presidential and 1998 midterm elections. Only in the 2000 election did we find no effect of initiatives on voter turnout. These are important findings, as the evidence contradicts previous research by Everson and Magleby, both of whom found the initiative process to have a negligible impact on voter turnout. Our analysis suggests instead that ballot initiatives can and do play a positive role in increasing electoral participation.

These studies suggest that the effect of the initiative on turnout is most pronounced in midterm elections and noncompetitive presidential elections, which are generally low-information, low-turnout contests with fewer sources of mobilization. In such elections, marginal voters may be especially sensitive to those sources of mobilization that do exist, such as propositions placed on the ballot. Ballot initiatives can provide information about and generate interest in elections and thereby lead to higher citizen participation. Presidential elections, in contrast, are generally high-information and high-motivation elections, which may weaken the mobilization influence of ballot measures. This research demonstrates that political context can affect initiatives' impact on political behavior.[50]

Ballot propositions may increase voter turnout by transforming low-information midterm elections into high-information elections and adding information to already high-information presidential elections. In high-information elections, such as presidential con-

---

"What Matters"   **BOX 4**

What is the effect of exposure to ballot initiatives on an individual's probability of voting?

1992 Presidential election
Each initiative appearing on the state ballot increases the probability of voting by 4 percentage points.

1996 Presidential election
Each initiative appearing on the state ballot increases the probability of voting by .5 a percentage point.

1998 Midterm election
Each initiative appearing on the state ballot increases the probability of voting by 1 percentage point.

Note: Estimates are based on a hypothetical respondent who is female, white, of independent partisanship with Internet access, with values for education, age, income, and state racial diversity, set at their mean. For the 1992 simulation, the respondent is interested in politics. We have calculated the probability of voting, holding other factors constant (see tables A.3 and A.4).

---

tests, a higher threshold appears to be operating, in which a larger number of ballot propositions is necessary to stimulate extra votes relative to low-information elections, when initiatives do not compete with presidential candidates for media coverage. The disparity in voter turnout rates among initiative and noninitiative states increased during the 1990s, when more propositions qualified for state election ballots than during any other period in the twentieth century.

As initiative elections gain in importance, they may play a growing role in presidential and midterm elections. As we have witnessed in California and several other states during the past decade, ballot measure proponents and opponents likely will continue to fuse their campaigns with the presidential, U.S. Senate, and gubernatorial candidates, and vice versa.[51] In the future, the initiative process and more participatory modes of governance, including mail or Internet voting, as well as national referenda may increase voter participation in both presidential and midterm election years. Given declining U.S. voter turnout, the presence of initiative questions on the ballot may indeed be a desirable way to mobilize voters. Our analysis lends support to the popular belief that initiatives mobilize voters, reshaping the electorate, which may have important ramifications for candidate elections. In light of the dramatic growth in the use of citizen initiatives and legislative referenda in the American states in the past twenty years, these moderate positive effects on voter turnout are important for any evaluation of the educative claims made by Progressive Era advocates of citizen lawmaking. In the following chapter, we examine whether the initiative process has similar positive effects on civic engagement.

3 | The Education of Citizens
Civic Engagement

Along with declining voter turnout, civic disengagement was one of the principal concerns voiced by advocates of direct legislation at the dawn of the twentieth century. Progressives, educators, and activists argued vociferously that direct forms of democracy would stimulate various types of political participation beyond voting.[1] Citizen lawmaking, these observers averred, would energize otherwise enervated citizens with a sense of civic pride and duty. Early proponents of direct legislation contended that ballot initiatives would help engender a more informed electorate. Senator Jonathan Bourne Jr. of Oregon, for example, stated that the initiative process (what he regularly referred to as "the system") would invigorate and edify the electorate:

> The system encourages every citizen, however humble his position, to study the problems of government, city and state, and to submit whatever solution he may evolve for the consideration and approval of others. The study of the measures and arguments printed in the publicity pamphlet is of immense educational value. The system not only encourages the development of each individual, but tends to elevate the entire electorate to the plane of those who are most advanced. How different from the system so generally in force, which tends to discourage and suppress the individual![2]

Pedagogically, then, reform-minded Progressives believed that citizen lawmaking would inevitably lead to higher levels of participation by citizens in myriad areas of civic life, as the process encouraged citizens to become well-informed consumers of the political process.

Nearly a century after the Progressive Era, the topic of civic engagement again constitutes a primary concern not only among scholars and political commentators but also among politicians and community activists. Contemporary American politics is distinguished by declining voter turnout as well as diminishing levels of civic and political engagement. In *Bowling Alone,* Robert Putnam contends that "political knowledge and interest in public affairs are critical preconditions for more active forms of involvement. If you don't know the rules of the game and the players and don't care about the outcome, you're unlikely to try playing yourself."[3] Other scholarly studies reflect Putnam's lament about the decline in civic engagement. Public opinion surveys reveal that recent college graduates know little more about public affairs then did average high school graduates during the 1940s.[4] Similarly, recent research based on a series of annual surveys shows that interest in politics among the electorate declined by one-fifth between 1975 and 1999. Daily newspaper readership among people under 35 dropped from two-thirds in 1965 to one-third in the 1990s; at the same time, viewership of television news among respondents in this same age group fell from 52 percent to 41 percent.[5] The decline in voting in America tracks closely the drop in the electorate's interest in public affairs and political knowledge. Does participatory democracy, in the form of citizen lawmaking, offer hope of reversing these disturbing trends in declining civic engagement?

Some contemporary advocates of direct democracy claim that use of institutions such as direct legislation can stimulate political interest and facilitate learning about politics. Democratic theorists such as Benjamin Barber and Carole Pateman argue that direct participation in policymaking can play a pedagogic role, allowing voters to learn considerable information on issues from referenda campaigns.[6] Similarly, constitutional scholar Bruce Ackerman argues that constitutional referenda help to engender civic participation because "apathy will give way to concern, ignorance to information, selfishness to serious reflection on the country's future."[7] For their part, political scientists have only begun to empirically test whether giving citizens a direct voice in lawmaking heightens their knowledge of, interest in, and deliberation about politics.[8]

Despite the claims of some democratic theorists who have built on the arguments advanced by Progressive Era scholars, Putnam contends that ballot initiatives cannot be taken as a reliable sign of widespread civic engagement.[9] Putnam agrees with the critics who contend that rather than institutionalizing a means of returning power to the people, the increased use of direct democracy merely reflects the professionalization of initiative politics.[10] The increased frequency of statewide ballot initiatives over the course of the twentieth century mirrors the decline in levels of civic engagement. As the number of initiatives that appeared on state ballots began to explode in the 1970s, citizen engagement in all forms of community and political life began its precipitous decline. As Putnam notes, "Although one might imagine that such ballot contests might spark widespread political discussion by ordinary citizens, studies show that most signers don't read what they sign. . . . [T]he opportunity for direct participation does not seem to have galvanized large numbers of voters."[11] Putnam concludes, along the lines of journalist David Broder and other critics of money's role in ballot contests, that the rise of direct democracy is more a measure of the power of well-financed special interests than some sign of augmented civic engagement.[12]

So, who correctly interprets the effect of direct democracy on civic engagement—Putnam or the array of Progressive Era reformers and democratic theorists? To answer this question, we use recent survey data to examine the initiative's secondary, educative purposes. In the previous chapter, we found that the likelihood of citizens turning out to vote increases with their exposure to initiatives. We continue the line of inquiry in this chapter, attempting to unpack the "black box" that encases direct democracy and increased political participation. Specifically, we assess the impact of citizen lawmaking on civic engagement in the American states by testing hypotheses concerning the relationships between exposure to ballot initiatives and political knowledge, interest, and discussion. An appreciable amount of

research links these aspects of civic engagement with the propensity
to vote. If direct democracy increases the probability of voting, does
it also lead to a more informed, engaged, and politically interested
electorate? Does more information about politics from ballot contests increase civic engagement?

This chapter explores whether ballot initiatives spark civic engagement by extending participation opportunities through the political
process. We hypothesize that information provided in direct democracy campaigns may increase knowledge of, interest in, and discussion of politics—questions that to date have been largely unexplored
in the literature.[13] We rely on American National Election Studies
(NES) data from 1996 to 2000, empirically answering these questions
by merging this information with state-level data on the number of
initiatives on state ballots. In the following section, we assess some
recent research examining factors associated with voter competence
and political interest. We then discuss and analyze the survey data to
test the relationship between citizen lawmaking and civic engagement. We follow with an exploration of the relationship between initiative use and social capital, a term popularized by Putnam and an
important measure of civic engagement aggregated at the state level.
We conclude the chapter with some brief comments about the
educative effects of the initiative process on civic engagement,
broadly understood.

Why Direct Democracy May Enhance
Civic Engagement

The effect of exposure to initiative campaigns on political knowledge
may resemble the effect of media exposure. Watching television news
has been found to be positively associated with political knowledge in
a variety of contexts. Media coverage of ballot measures may increase
information available to citizens about politics, potentially reducing
the costs of being politically informed.[14] Like the media, political
organizations such as parties may lower citizens' information-
gathering costs. In representative democracies, an essential role of

political parties is to reduce the complexity of voting in elections. Based on an ideological position, for example, voters can choose between a few parties and need not be well informed about the whole range of policies the parties' pursue. In a similar vein, Arthur Lupia as well as Shaun Bowler and Todd Donovan have shown that citizens can make rational voting decisions on initiative questions with simple cues from the media, elected officials, political parties, and interest group endorsements.[15] With few exceptions, however, scholars have not explored how initiative campaigns may foster citizens' broader political knowledge.

The media have long played an important role in lowering political information costs to citizens. While many researchers attribute lower voter turnout to media coverage, citing negative campaign ads and horse-race journalism, others find that media use (television and newspapers) is instrumental in increasing political knowledge. The agenda-setting literature reveals that citizens use the media to learn what issues are important. There is also evidence that voters use the media to acquire information with regard to candidate traits and candidate issue positions.[16]

The relationship between political knowledge and media use is mediated by interest. A number of studies show that individuals with low political interest are more vulnerable to media messages. People with higher levels of interest are more likely to receive political information from a variety of sources, thereby weakening the impact of any one source. These individuals are also more likely to seek out information from sources that provide more in-depth political coverage, such as the print medium. These kinds of sources may in turn allow interested voters to interpret, store, and utilize new political knowledge better then those who are less politically sophisticated.[17]

Despite these positive media effects, a host of scholars have found that by most standards, Americans possess little interest in or knowledge about politics.[18] However, some evidence shows that political learning is heavily influenced by the political environment.[19] Robert Luskin, for example, argues that political sophistication is endogenous to three broad factors: a person's ability to assimilate and organize political information; his or her motive or desire to follow political affairs; and his or her exposure to political information—that is, his or her information environment. Exposure to political information may be a function of the frequency with which such information is made available, communications technology, and media use.[20] Initiative campaigns may create additional opportunities for learning about politics, thus increasing political knowledge, interest, and sophistication.

Advocates of participatory democracy have argued for years that more "self-governance" would increase citizens' competence and interest in communal life.[21] Contemporary initiative campaigns may create additional information shortcuts for voters. Initiative elections usually involve extensive media campaigns (television, newspaper, radio) to persuade voters to approve or reject a proposed policy change.[22] The more costly an initiative campaign, the more information is provided to voters at a lower cost. As one campaign consultant noted, "most initiatives' campaigns really are processes of both one side and then the other side attempting to *educate* voters about different aspects of the measure. And as people get more information that tends to influence their attitudes about" the ballot measures.[23] Salient ballot initiatives should provide additional information to citizens, increasing their political knowledge and interest.

Recent research tends to support this claim. Political scientist Mark Smith maintains that initiatives and referenda are institutional arrangements that over time can encourage the development of skills that make for more informed citizens. Using the 1992 Senate Election Study, which contains samples of approximately equal size from all 50 states, Smith finds that citizens exposed to salient initiatives and referenda show an increased capacity to correctly answer factual questions about politics. That is, there is a positive relationship between salient ballot measures and political knowledge.[24] Similarly, two European scholars find that in Switzerland, citizens are better informed when they have more opportunities for direct political participation. Of the 26 Swiss cantons, some can be characterized as more "representative democratic," whereas others are more "direct democratic." Using an index that measures the degree of political participation in a canton on a scale of one to six, the authors find that

citizens are more politically informed and involved in political discussions in cantons with more extended direct democratic participation rights, after controlling for other factors.[25]

Data and Methods

To avoid the ecological fallacies to which aggregate-level analyses are
prone, we use NES data for three recent election years—1996, 1998,
and 2000—to conduct individual-level tests of whether exposure to
ballot initiatives leads to an informed and engaged electorate. We
examine data from three election years to consider change over time
and variation between midterm and presidential elections. As men-
tioned in the previous chapter, we analyze the data separately for the
three years (rather than pooling it) because of changes in NES survey
questions and coding in 2000. We examine each dependent variable
(political knowledge, interest, and discussion) in a separate model.

The dependent variable, or outcome to be explained, in the first
model is political knowledge, measured by the number of six general
political knowledge questions correctly answered. While questions
varied for the three elections, the 1998 questions, for example, were:
"What position does Al Gore hold?" "What position does William
Rehnquist hold?" "What position does Boris Yeltsin hold?" "What
position does Newt Gingrich hold?" "Which party had a majority in
the House before the election?" and "Which party had a majority in
the Senate before the election?" While we agree that the answers to
these questions per se are rather unimportant, they nevertheless serve
as adequate proxies for citizens' political information.

Closely related to an informed electorate is political interest.
Those who are interested in politics will seek out political information and become more knowledgeable. The dependent variable in the
second model is political interest, measured by a Likert scale ranging
from "very much interested" in the campaign to "not much interested." Because family and friends can be an important venue for
political information and attitudes toward politics, the dependent
variable in the third and final model is political discussion measured

by a dichotomous variable where one indicates that the individual regularly engages in political discussion and zero otherwise.

By merging the NES survey data with state-level data, we are able to test our hypotheses about the effect of direct democracy on citizens' behavior and attitudes. The NES data do not have the advantages of the 1992 Senate Election Study data used by Smith, with equal samples for all 50 states, but they do include large samples of respondents from more than 40 states. The key independent variable we use to test these hypotheses is the number of initiatives appearing on the statewide ballot in each year.[26] We expect this variable to be positively related to each of our dependent variables.

We use several other explanatory variables to control for individual-level attitudinal and demographic factors that may also influence political knowledge and interest as well as the frequency of political discussions. To control for the effect of income, we include a 24-point Likert scale measuring total family income. We control for the effects of education with a 7-point scale as well as sex with a dichotomous variable coded one for females. To control for race and ethnicity, African Americans, Asian Americans, and Latinos are coded one, with non-Hispanic whites as the reference group coded zero. Age is measured in years. Again, a series of dichotomous variables are used to account for partisanship, including strong Democrat, strong Republican, and pure independents, with moderate partisans as the reference groups.[27]

We also control for media consumption (television, newspaper, and Internet) and political efficacy, all of which are understood to be important influences on political sophistication and interest. We control for general media consumption by measuring the number of days the previous week that the respondent reportedly read the newspaper and watched the national evening news. We also include a dichotomous variable if the respondent viewed online election news, reflecting the Internet's increasing importance as a source of political information.[28] We control for political efficacy by combining the responses to two questions—"People don't have say in government" and "Public officials don't care about people like me"—that were measured on a 5-point Likert scale ranging from "strongly disagree" to "strongly agree." While a simple bivariate relationship (correlation) between exposure to ballot initiatives and voter information may exist, voter information may be higher among those who are educated, and states with direct democracy may have more educated voters. In a multiple regression analysis, such alternative explanations can be controlled for. We present the findings using multiple regression and including all the control variables presented in the last section.

 Findings

Political Knowledge

Since the dependent variable, political knowledge, is ordinal, measuring the number of six factual questions correctly answered, we use ordered logit to estimate the models' coefficients. The coefficients reported in table A.5 (see appendix) suggest that after controlling for partisanship, media consumption, and demographic and socioeconomic factors, citizens living in states with more exposure to ballot initiatives had greater political knowledge in 1996 than those who lived in states without the initiative. In this year only, exposure to ballot measures has a strong, positive, and statistically significant independent impact on political knowledge. The finding is consistent with recent research conducted using 1992 survey data from the American states as well as research on citizen competence in Swiss cantons and in Canada.[29] Every two initiatives appearing on the state ballot raises the probability of being knowledgeable about politics (answering five of six factual questions correctly) by 1 percentage point. While this effect may appear modest at the individual level, when multiplied by millions of voters in a state, the effect may be substantial. An individual residing in a state with no ballot initiatives had a 24 percent probability of answering five of six questions correctly. The same individual residing in a state with six initiatives on the ballot would have a 27 percent probability of being knowledgeable about politics, all else being equal.

"What Matters"   BOX 5

Who is more informed about politics?

1996 Presidential election
An individual who is exposed to ballot initiatives, watches television news, reads daily newspaper, is partisan (Democrat or Republican), older, male, white, educated, affluent, politically efficacious, and interested in politics.

Note: Only statistically significant differences are reported (see table A.5). When ordered logistic regression is used, these are the variables that matter, holding other factors constant.

What is the effect of exposure to ballot initiatives on political knowledge in 1996?

Every two initiatives appearing on the state ballot raises the probability of being knowledgeable about politics (answering five of six factual questions correctly) by 1 percentage point.

1996 Presidential Election	Political Knowledge
No initiatives on state ballot	24%
Two initiatives on state ballot	25%
Four initiatives on state ballot	26%
Six initiatives on state ballot	27%
Eight initiatives on state ballot	28%

Note: Estimates are based on a hypothetical respondent who is female, white, of independent partisanship, and has not been exposed to online political news, with values for education, age, income, TV news exposure, newspaper exposure, political efficacy, and attention paid to politics (interest) set at their mean. The respondent resides in a state with average racial diversity. We have calculated the probability of political knowledge, holding other factors constant (see table A.5).

As expected from previous research, people with higher incomes, political interest and efficacy, media consumption, and education also have greater political knowledge, while independents have less political knowledge than respondents with a partisan orientation. Thus, our research suggests that exposure to ballot initiatives not only increases political participation but also leads to a more politically informed citizenry.

This political information effect of direct democracy, however, was found only in 1996, not in the other elections analyzed. A closer look at the context of the 1996 presidential elections provides a potential explanation—the overlap of state ballot measures and the party platforms of the presidential candidates of the two major parties, Republican Bob Dole and Democrat Bill Clinton. As we document in chapter 6, the major party organizations have become involved in initiative contests for manifold reasons.[30] When state issue campaigns and federal election campaigns are intertwined, state ballot contests can have important implications for state and national politics.

In 1996, California voters adopted a controversial ballot initiative, Proposition 209, ending affirmative action in state college admissions and government employment and contracts. Both presidential candidates took strong positions on the issue of affirmative action in an attempt to split the opposing party's electoral base.[31] Dole supported Proposition 209 in his campaign speeches, promising to end affirmative action at the national level, while Clinton proposed to "mend, rather than end" affirmative action and opposed (albeit meekly) the controversial California ballot measure. In addition, the California Republican Party and the Republican National Committee promoted Proposition 209 and funded its sponsors in an effort to split Democratic support for Clinton.[32] The effects of ballot initiatives on political knowledge appear to vary with election context; in the 2000 election, for example, ballot initiatives were not central in the presidential contest between George W. Bush and Al Gore.[33] When initiatives are closely interrelated to the campaign issues of state and national elections, however, the process can increase the electorate's general political knowledge.

Political Interest

Because political interest is also measured on an ordinal scale, ordered logistic regression coefficients are reported in table A.6 (see appendix). Opportunity for direct participation in policy making has an important and more consistent effect on political interest than on political knowledge. Citizens residing in states with frequent ballot initiatives report higher levels of interest in both the 1996 and 1998 elections after controlling for media consumption, efficacy, partisanship, and socioeconomic factors. Every two initiatives appearing on the state ballot raises the probability of being interested in politics (measured by attention paid to political campaigns) by 1 percentage point in the 1998 election and .5 percentage point in the 1996 election. The effect of ballot initiatives on political interest is slightly stronger in the 1998 midterm contest than in the noncompetitive 1996 presidential election, but the findings from both elections are consistent with the analysis of voting, showing a greater positive effect of initiatives in low-information electoral contests. The data suggest that initiatives may enhance interest in politics by providing additional sources of political information, which is consistent with research conducted on the effects of a Canadian referendum on citizen politicization.[34] As we found with respect to political knowledge, exposure to ballot initiatives was not associated with an individual's political interest in the 2000 elections.

As expected, many of the control variables are also related to interest in politics and are consistent across time. The affluent and those with more education are generally more interested in politics. Media consumption is important, as individuals who watch more television or read a daily newspaper reported increased interest. In 1998, viewing online election news stimulated interest in the midterm election, but we did not find this effect in the 1996 presidential election, which may reflect the expanding number of people who had Internet access in the later election. Individuals with more political efficacy—that is, those who believe government is responsive to their needs—express more interest in politics, as do African Americans compared to whites. In the 1996 presidential election (but not in the 1998 midterm contest), we find that partisanship matters, with Democrats and Republicans more interested in politics than those with weak partisan identification. In general, the data show that citizens are more interested in politics when given opportunities to vote directly on policy questions, all else being equal.

Political Discussion

Closely related to an interest in politics is discussing the subject with friends or family. In fact, political discussion may be understood as a

Who is more interested in politics?

1996 Presidential election
An individual who is exposed to ballot initiatives, is a partisan (Democrat or Republican), watches television news, reads daily newspaper, is educated, politically efficacious, African American, and male.

1998 Midterm election
An individual who is exposed to ballot initiatives, watches television news, reads daily newspaper, reads online election news, is affluent, educated, and African American.

Note: Only statistically significant differences are reported (see table A.6). When ordered logistic regression is used, these are the variables that matter, holding other factors constant.

What is the effect of exposure to ballot initiatives on being interested in politics?

Every two initiatives appearing on the state ballot raises the probability of being very interested in politics (measured by attention paid to political campaigns) by 1 percentage point in 1998 and .5 percentage point in 1996.

1996 Presidential Election	Very Interested in Politics
No initiatives on state ballot	14.6%
Two initiatives on state ballot	15.1%
Four initiatives on state ballot	15.6%
Six initiatives on state ballot	16.1%
Eight initiatives on state ballot	16.6%

1998 Midterm Election	
No initiatives on state ballot	16.9%
Two initiatives on state ballot	17.8%
Four initiatives on state ballot	18.7%
Six initiatives on state ballot	19.7%
Eight initiatives on state ballot	20.7%

Note: Estimates are based on a hypothetical respondent who is female, white, of independent partisanship and has not been exposed to online political news, with values for education, age, income, TV news exposure, newspaper exposure, and political efficacy set at their mean. We have calculated the probability of political interest holding other factors constant (see table A.6).

precursor to an interest in government and policy. The dependent variable in table A.7 (see appendix) is coded so that higher scores are associated with increased likelihood of discussing politics. Because the dependent variable is the number of days during the previous week on which the respondent discussed politics, Poisson multiple regression coefficients are reported. We again find that exposure to ballot initiatives increases the frequency of political discussion, after controlling for traditional media consumption and individual-level factors, including socioeconomic status. Stated another way, citizens are more likely to discuss politics when given more opportunities to vote directly on policy issues, but only in the 1996 election, not in 1998 or 2000. Every two initiatives appearing on the state ballot raises the probability of an individual discussing politics one day a week by 1 percentage point. While modest at the individual level, the effect may loom large in an election. Similar to the models estimating political knowledge and interest, we find that the impact of initiative use on discussing politics varies with electoral context and is not consistent across election years.

We do find, however, that media consumption and partisanship are consistently important in predicting the likelihood of discussing politics. Similarly, the affluent and educated are more likely to discuss politics, as are non-Hispanic whites. Ironically, African Americans are more likely to report an interest in politics but less likely to discuss politics with friends and family. Overall, the findings suggest that initiative campaigns promote political interest, knowledge, and interpersonal communication (discussion) by providing supplementary political information in relatively low information (noncompetitive presidential or midterm) electoral contexts.

Ballot Initiatives and Social Capital in the American States

In addition to our analysis of direct measures of individual civic engagement—political interest, discussion, and knowledge—we are interested in whether citizen lawmaking influences states with higher

"What Matters" BOX 7

Who is more likely to discuss politics?

1996 Presidential election
A voter who is exposed to ballot initiatives, watches television news, is partisan (Democrat or Republican), non-Hispanic, white, and educated.

Note: Only statistically significant differences are reported (see table A.7). When Poisson regression is used, these are the variables that matter, holding other factors constant.

What is the effect of exposure to ballot initiatives on the frequency of political discussions?

Every two initiatives appearing on the state ballot raises the probability of an individual discussing politics one day a week by 1 percentage point.

1996 Presidential Election	Frequency of Political Discussions
No initiatives on state ballot	62.0%
Two initiatives on state ballot	63.2%
Four initiatives on state ballot	64.3%
Six initiatives on state ballot	65.5%
Eight initiatives on state ballot	66.7%

Note: Estimates are based on a hypothetical respondent who is female, white, of independent partisanship and has not been exposed to online political news, with values for education, age, income, TV news exposure, newspaper exposure, and political efficacy set at their mean. We have calculated the probability of discussing politics, holding other factors constant (see table A.7).

civic engagement (what Putnam calls social capital). Putnam argues that rich, dense networks of social interaction are central to U.S. democracy; indeed, his social capital thesis has become highly influential in contemporary studies of American and comparative politics and democracy more generally. Social capital especially involves and works through face-to-face interactions and social networks. The most common type of nonoccupational and extrafamilial social capital in America is church attendance. Social capital is formally defined by generalized reciprocity—"I'll do this for you with-

out expecting anything specific back from you." A society characterized by generalized reciprocity is more efficient, according to Putnam, than a distrustful society.[35] We use Putnam's measure of state
social capital as a proxy for civic engagement.

Putnam's overall social capital index for the states (in 1990) com-
prises 14 specific variables.[36] The index measures civic engagement
and includes 5 specific components measuring community organizational life, engagement in public affairs, community volunteerism,
informal sociability, and social trust.[37] Putnam derives some of data
from the DDB Needham Life Style surveys (1975–99), aggregating
them to the state level. The dependent variable in our analysis is
aggregate state social capital. States ranking highest in social capital,
according to Putnam's index, include North and South Dakota, Ver-
mont, Minnesota, Montana, and Nebraska. States ranking lowest in
terms of social capital include Nevada, Mississippi, Georgia,
Louisiana, Alabama, and Tennessee.

Our primary explanatory variable is the average annual number of
citizen initiatives appearing on state election ballots from 1970 to
1992.[38] This variable is chosen to measure usage of the process over
time, not merely constitutional provisions for the initiative. Several
variables were added to control for variations across the 50 states that
could affect levels of social capital. Demographic (racial and ethnic)
diversity is measured by the size of Latino, African American, and
Asian American populations from the 1990 census.[39] We control for
whether the state has open primaries (coded one if yes, zero otherwise) as well as political party competitiveness as measured by an
index of district-level competition.[40] We also control for state ideology using a public opinion (liberal/conservative) index.[41] Finally, we
account for economic variations across the states, including the percentage metropolitan (urbanization), the percentage of high school
graduates (education), and the median household income.[42]

The multiple regression coefficients from the model reported in
table A.8 (see appendix) indicate that states with frequent initiative use
have higher social capital, after controlling for political and socioeconomic factors. Direct democracy and social capital tend to "go
together," to borrow a phrase from *Bowling Alone*. The substantive

impact of direct democracy is large, with each initiative appearing on a state's ballot increasing the state's score on the social capital index by 20 points, all else being equal. Just four initiatives on the statewide ballot in any given election boost the state from a low score on the social capital index to a very high score, holding other factors constant. Despite Putnam's valid concerns about the professionalization of initiative campaigns, the data analysis suggests that citizen lawmaking may foster the accumulation of social capital and civic engagement. Frequent initiative use may also be a sign of a healthy polity with higher levels of social capital. Social capital is thus related to direct democracy, and as chapter 5 will show, the use of the initiative process is also associated with a greater density of citizen groups. Since a standard measure of social capital is joining groups, the evidence seems to strongly point in the direction that ballot initiatives increase levels of social capital—that is, community and civic engagement. These findings are consistent with the survey analysis reported previously.

In addition, we find that other variables included to account for state demographic and electoral environments are important (and statistically significant). States that are relatively homogeneous (that is, white), tend to have higher social capital, all else being equal. States with open primaries and more electoral competition also have higher levels of social capital. Rural states with higher median household incomes also have higher levels of social capital, as do those states with more liberal public opinion. In sum, we find that states that allow citizens to directly participate in policy decisions via the initiative have higher levels of social capital, after controlling for other factors.

Conclusion

Despite Putnam's pessimistic conjecture concerning citizen lawmaking, our findings are generally consistent with Progressive reformers' claims concerning citizen lawmaking's benefits for civic engagement. While numerous scholars continue to investigate the direct effects of ballot initiatives on policy outcomes and minority rights, we have

"What Matters"   BOX 8

Which states have higher social capital?

States that are affluent and rural with frequent ballot initiatives, less racial diversity, open primaries, more electoral competition, and more liberal public opinion.

Note: Only statistically significant differences are reported (see table A.8). When multivariate regression is used, these are the variables that matter, holding other factors constant.

What is the effect of ballot initiatives on levels of state social capital (Putnam's overall indicator)?

	Putnam's Social Capital Index
No initiatives on state ballot	.21 (low social capital)
One initiative on state ballot	.42
Two initiatives on state ballot	.64
Three initiatives on state ballot	.85
Four initiatives on state ballot	1.06
Five initiatives on state ballot	1.27 (very high social capital)

Note: Estimates are based on a hypothetical state with open primaries and with values for racial diversity, median household income, political ideology/public opinion, high school graduation rates, percentage metropolitan, and electoral competition set at their means. We have calculated the level of state social capital, holding other factors constant (see table A.8).

begun to test direct democracy proponents' claims about the process' *educative* effects on civic engagement. Lending support to arguments made by both Progressive Era reformers and contemporary normative scholars, our analysis indicates that people in states with frequent ballot questions are more informed about politics in the 1996 presidential election, more interested in politics in the 1996 and 1998 elections, and more likely to discuss politics in the 1996 presidential election. Consistent with the previous chapter on voting, we find that ballot initiatives may have the most impact in low-information elections, such as midterm elections and noncompetitive presidential elections, providing voters with additional political information. As we have discussed, ballot initiatives' positive effects on civic engagement—specifically, increases in political knowledge, interest in politics, and political discussions—are consistent with previous research on voter competence. Unlike previous research, however, our longitudinal analysis reveals that participatory democracy's effect on various expressions of civic engagement varies with the electoral context. The research is unique in reporting citizen lawmaking's positive (though mixed) impact on political discussions, a critical ingredient in participatory democracy.

Building on our individual-level findings, we draw on Putnam's social capital data and discover that over time, states with frequent ballot initiatives have higher levels of social capital after controlling for economic, social, and political variations across the states. Overall, our results suggest that citizen lawmaking has a positive (though contextually constrained) impact on a critical set of factors that shape participation and engagement in the political system. In keeping with the findings in the previous chapter, which demonstrate a positive relationship between initiative use and voting participation, we find that citizen lawmaking may stimulate other forms of civic life. In light of the dramatic growth in the use of ballot initiatives (as well as legislative referenda) in the American states over the past 30 years, these educative effects of citizen lawmaking on civic engagement are important to incorporate in any evaluation of the overall merits of direct democracy. In the following chapter, we assess whether the initiative process has a positive effect on citizens' attitudes toward government.

4 | The Education of Citizens
Confidence in Government

One of the distinguishing features of American politics in the late twentieth and early twenty-first centuries is a pervasive sense of public distrust of, frustration with, and alienation from government from Washington, DC, to state capitals. A mid-1990s Gallup Poll, for example, revealed that only 20 percent of respondents said that they trusted the federal government all or some of the time—half the percentage during the Watergate scandal of 1974.[1] Stated differently, during the 1990s, approximately three of four Americans did not trust the government to do what is right most of the time. The public's expressed confidence in government and elected officials is at an all-time low, falling every year since the late 1970s. In 1966, with the Vietnam War raging and race riots in major U.S. cities, two-thirds of Americans trusted government and elected officials and rejected the view that "the people running the country don't really care about what happens to you." In 1997, in the midst of the longest period of peace and prosperity in the twentieth century, almost two-thirds of Americans *endorsed* this view.[2] Low public confidence in government and elected officials is related to perceptions that government is unable to solve problems, to spend money in an effective and efficient manner, or to represent average voters' interests and policy preferences.[3]

In response to the current political malaise, there have been calls to "reinvent" government, to increase its efficiency and effectiveness, and to provide opportunities for direct participation in government decision making.[4] This refrain is not new. As with modern proponents of the initiative, many Progressive Era reformers suggested that the initiative process could help to improve citizens' communication with government and mitigate their apathy and distrust. A common sentiment voiced by Progressive Era proponents of direct democracy was that the initiative's populist underpinnings could help make government institutions more responsive and representative to the citizenry at large. Rather than using the expression *political efficacy*, Progressive Era Reformers routinely used the term *sovereignty* to expound on how citizen lawmaking would help individuals have more of a say in public affairs as well as feel as though the government was being responsive to the people's wishes. Direct legislation, as political scientist William Munro put it, would "make the voter realize that he is sovereign in fact as well as in name."[5]

The ability to make decisions on ballot measures, Progressives argued, would bring the voter "into closer touch with great affairs," in the words of direct democracy advocate Lewis Johnson, allowing the voter to "begin to assume the stature of a man, to become a sovereign in fact as well as in fancy."[6] U.S. senator Jonathan Bourne Jr. contended that the foremost solution to the problem of the corruption and nonaccountability of government bodies was to return power—albeit not all of it—to the people and thereby keep elected officials working for citizens' benefit. Harkening back to a rhetoric celebrating "reasoned deliberation, republicanism, and civil virtue," the Oregon senator declared in 1912 that the initiative was a necessary tool "to restore the sovereignty of the people."[7] Progressives demanded accountability, insisting that government become more responsive to citizens' opinions.[8] Serving as a safety valve, the process would ensure that government decisions mirrored citizen interests. By positively reflecting the views of citizens, direct legislation was widely thought to engender popular sovereignty and, as a result, to enhance citizens' political efficacy.[9]

Has contemporary use of direct democracy lived up to Progressive reformers' expectations? Do citizens living in states with frequent ballot initiatives perceive government to be more responsive? Political efficacy refers to people's belief that they understand politics and can influence government decisions. External efficacy, our focus here, is the term that political scientists use when an individual feels that the government is responsive to the individual. Research has shown that citizens who believe they can influence government and that government officials care about the people will be more likely to vote and participate in the political process. If Progressive reformers were correct, we would expect that citizens given the opportunity to directly make policy decisions should display increased political efficacy. By exploring citizen lawmaking's indirect impact on individual attitudes toward the political process, we hope to contribute to a more complete understanding and assessment of direct democracy's educative effects.

Why Direct Democracy May Enhance Confidence in Government

Recent research has examined attitudes toward government, with a major focus on explaining declining trust in government.[10] Such analyses increasingly have incorporated the effects of institutional contexts, examining the link between voter trust and attitudes and outcomes—that is, whether the voter "wins" or "loses" under differing government arrangements. Institutions may thus shape perceptions of the political process by affecting the extent to which an individual wins or loses on policy questions.[11] Direct democracy is an alternative to state legislatures for making laws and amending state constitutions and an alternative to representative government as a form of decision making. As a state-level political institution, then, the initiative may shape general attitudes about government.[12] Does a more participatory process of decision making affect citizen evaluations of government?

Because the initiative enables voters to directly adopt policy (such as tax cuts or term limitations) even over the opposition of elected officials, citizens living in initiative states might be expected to perceive government as more responsive. Hence, a potential consequence of direct democracy concerns political efficacy. While the degree to which government policy reflects citizens' desires is a matter of debate, evidence suggests that policy more closely matches mass preferences in American states with direct democracy.[13]

Normative theorists such as Benjamin Barber and Carole Pateman emphasize the importance of process, arguing that direct forms of democracy can motivate participation by energizing citizens with a sense of civic duty and political efficacy.[14] Proponents tend to adhere to the tenets of participatory democracy, which expects meaningful participation to transform citizens into civic-minded actors in communal life. Adherents to this view argue that the more people participate in self-governance, the more competent, interested, and satisfied they will feel.[15] Robert Putnam finds that individuals who are more engaged in community life are both more trusting and trustworthy.[16] Based on this logic, if the opportunity to make policy by voting on ballot initiatives increases voter turnout and civic engagement, as we report in chapters 2 and 3, it should also increase political efficacy.

Recent research by John Hibbing and Elizabeth Theiss-Morse suggests that satisfaction with both policy outcomes and the political process play an important role in governmental approval.[17] The gap between policy preferences and the perceived policy offerings of various parties, institutions, and governments has been an important variable in previous research.[18] Policy-related discontent may be an important source of political cynicism. According to political scientist Jack Citrin, an acute observer of the initiative process and voter behavior, "Political elites produce policies; in exchange, they receive trust from citizens satisfied with these policies and cynicism from those who are disappointed."[19]

Hibbing and Theiss-Morse caution, however, that attitudes toward government relying solely on policy satisfaction are likely to be incomplete. Rather, they find that "attitudes toward the processes of government, as apart from the policies, constitute an important free-standing variable that has serious implications for the health of democracy."[20] The literature shows that attitudes about government process are important components of public opinion. Stephen Weatherford finds that citizen complaints about government could result from problems with representational linkages, including access, or with the elite policymaking process.[21] Dissatisfaction with government is highest among those individuals who expect elected officials to be honest, caring, and altruistic but perceive them to be otherwise.[22] Televised debates of the U.S. Congress exposing an often combative process have been found to be a major reason for its consistent low public approval.[23]

To measure these important attitudes, Hibbing and Theiss-Morse use a national Gallup survey to measure attitudes about the political process. One end of the ordinal scale (or spectrum) is labeled "direct democracy," reflecting the perspective that people themselves should make policy decisions through town meetings, digital democracy, or direct democracy. The other pole is labeled "institutional democrat," meaning support for a trustee style of government where public opinion does not directly influence the determination of public policy and elected officials make most important decisions. A location on the index close to the direct democrat pole could indicate support for participatory democracy, or ballot initiatives. The authors find that people's process preferences, while not at the direct democratic pole, are to the left of what they perceive to be the processes employed by the federal government—that is, most Americans believe that government dominated by elected officials is insufficiently sensitive to ordinary citizens' views. While most people hold a centrist position and want elected officials to be involved in decision making, the data show that public beliefs about an out-of-touch government have more to do with process than with policies, "with the way decisions are made rather than their specific content."[24]

Using multivariate regression and controlling for the usual demographic and political variables, Hibbing and Theiss-Morse find that both policy and process expectations shape approval of government. Individuals who are pleased with policy are more likely to approve of the government than those who are displeased. The further governmental policies are from a person's preferences, the less that person is satisfied with government. More importantly, however, process matters. Even after controlling for other factors, a process that matches a person's preferences for how the process should work increases approval of government.[25] Because the average American prefers a political process that more regularly includes citizens in government decisions (that is, leans toward the direct democracy pole), it follows that citizens should be more content with government when residing in states that offer opportunities to make direct policy decisions (ballot initiatives and referenda). This research tests this hypothesis.

If the ability to have a say encourages citizens to take a more sanguine view of their place in the political system, individuals from states with ballot initiatives might be expected to express a different level of efficacy than people from states without initiatives. Little empirical research has addressed the question of ballot initiatives and citizen attitudes toward government, particularly efficacy, in the United States. Previous research on this question is inconclusive or is limited to studies conducted in a single election year. One of the few studies to examine the relationship between direct democracy and trust in government found no difference in trust in government across states with and without direct democracy; this study examined attitudes aggregated at the state level and measured the presence rather than the use of the initiative process.[26] Using more sophisticated statistical methods and data (the 1998 American National Election Study [NES] survey merged with aggregate state data), Martin Gilens, James Glasser, and Tali Mendelberg found that the presence of state ballot propositions did not impact levels of political efficacy (internal or external) but that "salient" ballot measures have a positive effect.[27] They measure direct democracy using two different explanatory variables: (1) a dichotomous variable for constitutional provisions for the initiative process; and (2) a measure of the average number of initiatives that have appeared on the state's ballot in each election cycle since the initiative process was instituted. In both cases, they fail to find a relationship between the presence and number of initiatives on a state's ballot and citizen efficacy.[28]

In contrast, Shaun Bowler and Todd Donovan, two of the most astute scholars of public opinion and direct democracy, find that exposure to direct democracy gives citizens a greater sense that they can influence government. Utilizing 1992 NES survey data merged with the total number of initiatives that have appeared on state ballots, Bowler and Donovan find that more frequent ballot initiatives are associated with higher levels of political efficacy. Citizens living in states with more initiatives tend to have more positive views of individuals' political abilities (internal efficacy) and look more favorably on the responsiveness of government (external efficacy), after controlling for other state contextual variables and individual-level factors. Indeed, the effect of exposure to direct democracy on internal and external political efficacy rivaled the effects of formal education. Thus, state-level institutions may contribute to democratic practices by instilling in citizens the belief that they can shape what their governments do.[29]

Because of the conflicting results of previous research, we seek to further explore whether citizens living in American states with extended opportunities to participate in policymaking exhibit higher levels of efficacy and confidence in government. We improve on the previous research based on single election years by examining this question over a 10-year period, including three midterm and three presidential elections. The extended time frame protects against idiosyncratic variations in one election or an unrepresentative survey from biasing the results.

 Why Direct Democracy May Not Enhance
Confidence in Government

Other observers argue that direct democracy may not affect or may even undermine civic orientations and confidence in government. Public distrust has been strongly expressed in ballot initiatives that have fundamentally changed the way some states conduct elections and develop public policy.[30] Particularly in California, political distrust is so ingrained that many voters have lost faith in the abilities of their state and national officeholders to spend taxpayers' money in an effective and efficient manner.[31] Voters have made it extremely difficult for state and local governments to increase existing taxes or to create new ones. Voters have also required elected state officials to spend a certain amount on education each year and have punished them by restricting the number of terms they may serve in office. Thus, a loss of public trust may create a vicious cycle in which ballot initiatives further undermine representative institutions, the capacity of state and local elected officials, and governance.[32]

Another reason why direct democracy may not lead to increased political efficacy involves racial and ethnic minorities. As a majoritarian decision-making process, majorities may be more likely to "win" in direct democracy elections, whereas minority groups—such as Latinos in California—may be more likely to lose on ballot initiatives targeting their own group interests.[33] Although racial and ethnic minorities (African Americans, Latinos, and Asian Americans) constitute a majority of California's population as of 2000, with Latinos representing the largest ethnic group, amounting to almost a third of the state's population, California's electorate is still majority white.[34] If a particular institution, such as the initiative process, is associated with highly visible political losses, perhaps this shapes racial and ethnic minorities' general attitudes toward government as well as those of nonminorities. The passage of initiatives targeting minority interests may stigmatize these groups, leading to decreased efficacy and more negative attitudes about politics and government.[35] If ethnic and racial minorities are more likely to lose in initiative elections, this may be linked to reduced political efficacy.

While not directly addressing the question of political efficacy or trust, some research suggests that ballot initiatives will fail to engage citizens in the political process because the process does not fulfill its intended purpose; rather than grassroots populism, it is "faux populism."[36] The number of ballot propositions has risen not because of the actions of the citizenry at large but primarily because well-funded interest groups or wealthy entrepreneurs have learned to use the process for narrow proposes. The process of placing measures on the ballot and campaigning on their behalf is so costly that it is beyond the reach of ordinary citizens and has become the purview of an "initiative industry."[37]

No matter who sponsors an initiative, we hypothesize that ballot measures provide additional political information to citizens, increasing civic engagement and confidence in government. In addition, envisioning initiative campaigns as a fight between narrow professional interests who use the industry and broad-based amateurs who do not may be too simple. Most groups (both broad-based citizen and business) require assistance in qualifying and operating successful ballot measures campaigns; rather than something new, this professionalism has marked the use of the process since its inception at the turn of the twentieth century.[38]

Other scholars contest the hypothesis that business interests have captured direct democracy, although these observers generally agree that the initiative process provides a structural advantage to groups that are well mobilized and have adequate financial resources. While citizen groups appear to do better than industry interests in passing direct legislation, economic groups appear to be more successful in defeating ballot propositions. Even if state-level direct democracy does not resemble grassroots populism, the policies that emerge from the process typically serve broad constituencies.[39] Both proponents and critics of the initiative process make persuasive appeals. Here, though, we are interested in how exposure to direct democracy affects citizens' perceptions of government responsiveness.

Research Questions

Political efficacy is a complex concept, especially since it may partly be a function of environmental effects, including political institutions. But most research on political trust and efficacy has focused on individual effects, such as the media and attitudinal and demographic factors. We are interested in exploring the institutional context that may shape political efficacy. To examine this issue, we use cross-level data on individual attitudes about government responsiveness and state contextual factors. Our sample is constructed from pooled NES postelection surveys for 1988–98, relevant state-level census data, and data on the number of ballot initiatives appearing on statewide ballots.[40]

A primary hypothesis is that experience with direct democracy will improve attitudes about government responsiveness for the general population. In 24 American states, the initiative process allows citizens to draft new laws or to amend the constitution by collecting a specified number of voter signatures. Because of the stringency of petition requirements and judicial review, some states where the institution exists rarely use the process (for example, Illinois, Mississippi, and Wyoming), while in California and Oregon, among others, ballot initiatives are a common means of lawmaking. In these states, the institution not only shapes policy outcomes but could also affect the nature of the democratic process as well as perceptions of government. We measure the average number of initiatives appearing on state election ballots rather than using a dichotomous variable coding for states with and without the initiative process, as in other studies.[41] This measurement captures variation in use of the process over time. If exposure to direct democracy affects political attitudes, we would expect the frequency of initiative use in a state to explain some of the variation in individual-level attitudes about political efficacy.

Survey Data

We pool data from six NES postelection surveys from 1988–98.[42] The same questions were asked in these surveys as in the 1992 NES survey used by Bowler and Donovan, thus providing a longitudinal data set spanning a 10-year interval with which to assess direct democracy's impact on citizen attitudes about government.[43] The pooled surveys also provide a sufficiently large sample of minority respondents to include separate coefficients for racial and ethnic groups (Latinos, African Americans, and Asian Americans) rather than only a non-white-white comparison.

The national survey data permit us to measure political efficacy with a variety of measures. Earlier research on political efficacy produced inconsistent findings, in large part as a result of the indicators used to assess efficacy and the fact that only one year at a time has typically been studied. Beginning in the 1970s, scholars came to view political efficacy as having two major components, internal and external efficacy.[44] Here, we focus exclusively on external efficacy because of its close relationship to political trust.

The dependent variable, or outcome to be explained, measures external efficacy, or government responsiveness. The NES surveys asked respondents (1) "if people like you have any say in what government does," and (2) if they "think that government officials care about what people like you think." The variables were measured on a five-point Likert scale and indicate increased external efficacy as the scale increases. The scores from these two questions were added to obtain an overall measure of external efficacy. The NES survey data are merged with state-level data to explore the impact of exposure to statewide initiative campaigns on individual-level attitudes. Because statewide ballot propositions affect all residents of a state, the state is the appropriate level for measuring institutional context. Frequency of direct democracy use is measured by the average annual number of initiatives appearing on state election ballots over the period 1970–92.[45]

Based on previous research focusing on voter turnout, we expect citizens residing in states with sizable minority populations to have lower political efficacy than people residing in more homogeneous states.[46] State racial environments are an important control variable in our analysis and are measured by an index of racial and ethnic percentages based on the size of Latino, African American, and Asian American populations using 1996 Current Population Survey data and U.S. census data from 1980 and 1990.[47] To control for the overrepresentation of minorities residing in California and acknowledging that the experience of California may bias the results, a dichotomous variable for respondents living in California is included (coded one, residents of all other states coded zero). The variable measures the effect of being in California, a unique state with high racial diversity and frequent use of direct democracy. Following Bowler and Donovan's research, we also control for the degree of divided government in the state for the period 1988–98, because split party control of state government may affect citizen perceptions of government responsiveness.[48]

A number of individual-level variables were used to control for demographic and attitudinal factors. The effects of race and ethnicity are controlled for with dichotomous variables for Latino, African American, or Asian American respondents, with whites (non-

Latino) as the reference (omitted) group. To create the Latino variable, data were merged from two survey questions—one asking respondents to identify their race and the other asking if respondents were of Hispanic origin. The pooled NES surveys include large enough samples of Latino, African American, and Asian American respondents to allow for separate analyses of each group. This differs from Bowler and Donovan, who considered only "nonwhite" respondents (white versus African American, Asian American, Native American) and grouped Latinos with whites. We also include a control for the size of the state minority population (as discussed earlier).

Because numerous studies find that perceptions of the economy influence attitudes about government responsiveness, we include an attitudinal factor related to the economy.[49] Perceptions of the national economy were measured by variables in which higher scores reflect worse economic evaluations. A retrospective evaluation of the state economy question was not asked in a number of the surveys and was thus excluded. A series of dichotomous variables are used to account for partisanship, including strong Democrat, strong Republican, and pure independents, with moderate partisans as the reference groups.[50] We also control for age (measured in years), education (measured on a seven-point scale), and gender (female respondents coded one, male respondents coded zero). Furthermore, dichotomous variables for election years are included because of the pooling of midterm and presidential elections, with 1988 as the baseline (reference) year.

Findings from the Survey Data

Does citizen lawmaking affect citizens' confidence in government responsiveness? External political efficacy, our dependent variable, is coded so that higher scores are associated with a more efficacious response. Because external efficacy is an ordinal variable, ordered logistic regression coefficients are reported in table A.9 (see appendix). We find strong evidence that citizens living in states with fre-

---

"What Matters"   **BOX 9**

Who has more external efficacy or confidence in government responsiveness, 1988–98 elections?

A voter who is exposed to ballot initiatives, is partisan (Democrat or Republican), perceives an improved economy, is younger, educated, and white.

Note: Only statistically significant differences are reported (see table A.9). When ordered logistic regression is used, these are the variables that matter, holding other factors constant.

---

quent use of direct democracy are more likely to claim that government is responsive to their needs, after controlling for other factors. This is consistent with earlier research, which drew on survey data from only one year.[51] The coefficient for frequency of initiative use is positive and statistically significant over the 10-year period. Citizens given more opportunities to directly make policy decisions are more likely to perceive that "people like me have a say about what the government does" and are more likely to claim that "public officials care about what people like me think." Given the extended time frame, large sample size, and extensive control variables, our findings offer strong evidence that direct legislation may improve citizen attitudes about government responsiveness.

Among the other individual-level variables, the data indicate that regardless of state institutional context, African Americans have lower political efficacy than whites, after controlling for other factors. Similarly, Asian Americans report lower levels of external efficacy than do whites. In contrast, Latinos report levels of confidence in government responsiveness that are similar to those of white non-Hispanics, which is consistent with survey data examining Latino political behavior.[52] At the same time, there is a significant relationship between economic attitudes and external efficacy. Individuals who believe the national economy is strong report higher political efficacy, all else being equal. Strong Republican partisans are generally more efficacious than independents or those with only weak partisanship, consistent with previous research. Also, higher education is consistently associated with improved perceptions of government responsiveness. After controlling for other factors, there is no difference in political efficacy between men and women. The young report more political efficacy, which may be explained by the fact that the elderly tend to be more attentive to politics and more affected by the media's negative portrayals of the government.

Divided government at the state level also does not appear to affect attitudes regarding government responsiveness. The California variable, included to measure "California exceptionalism" (because initiatives provide an especially important form of policymaking in that state), is also not statistically significant. Thus, living in California does not affect external efficacy. This finding puts into context recent survey data from California showing low levels of governmental approval.[53] The signs for the dichotomous variables measuring years are consistent with fluctuations that might be expected as a result of changes from midterm to presidential elections, with increased efficacy reported in presidential election years.

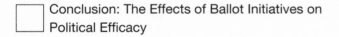

Conclusion: The Effects of Ballot Initiatives on Political Efficacy

This chapter has considered direct democracy's impact on attitudes about government responsiveness—what political scientists commonly refer to as external political efficacy. Consistent with the aspirations and expectations of Progressive Era proponents of citizen lawmaking, we find evidence that state-level institutions may contribute to American democracy by instilling greater confidence in government: citizens residing in states with frequent exposure to ballot initiatives are more likely to believe that government is responsive. Citizens living in states with extended opportunities for participation in policymaking (ballot initiatives) not only are more likely to participate in politics and express an interest in and knowledge of politics but also express more general confidence in the political process. Unlike the previous chapters, where electoral context was found to be important, direct democracy's beneficial effects on political efficacy occurred across midterm and presidential elections.

Regardless of state environmental contexts, African Americans and Asian Americans have less confidence in government responsiveness than do whites and Latinos. Because political efficacy is an important predictor of broader political participation, reduced efficacy among African Americans and Asian Americans may affect turnout rates and representation in the political process. Despite being the most frequent "losers" in California initiative elections directly targeting minority groups, Latinos have confidence in government that is similar to that of white non-Hispanics. This may result from the fact that in absolute terms at least, Latinos end up on the winning side of initiative votes most of the time.[54]

In addition, because we rely on a nationwide sample of respondents over a 10-year period, the analysis contrasts not only initiative and noninitiative states but also a largely legislative process and a process consisting of both initiatives and representative institutions. The data suggest that citizens have more positive views of American democracy when governed by both ballot initiatives and legislatures. Matthew Mendelsohn and Andrew Parkin argue that there is a single system rather than two systems; they call this unified system "referendum democracy," and it emphasizes a connection between direct and representative institutions.[55] Ballot initiatives' broader beneficial effects on citizens' attitudes toward government responsiveness support Bowler and Donovan's research, which was based on a single year.[56]

In the following two chapters, we examine the initiative's educative effects on political organizations—namely, interest groups and political parties. Rather than focusing on how the initiative process indirectly shapes citizens' attitudes and behaviors, we assess how interest groups may be adapting to the institutional opportunities presented by the adoption and increased usage of citizen lawmaking in the states. We first turn to direct democracy's educative effects on interest groups.

5 | The Education of Special Interests

Progressive Era reformers expressed high hopes that the initiative process would help eliminate or at least curtail the power of special interests, particularly within the legislative process. At the time, the corrosive influence of corporate interests was visible in many state legislatures, as party bosses and their legislative minions frequently succumbed to the pressures of the business lobby.[1] In his seminal treatise, *Direct Legislation by the Citizenship through the Initiative and Referendum,* James W. Sullivan partially justified citizen lawmaking on the grounds that "Congress and the legislatures have each a permanent lobby, buying privileges for corporations, and otherwise influencing and corrupting members."[2] In particular, state legislatures were "so discredited," in the words of University of Wisconsin–Madison professor Paul Reinsch, "that they offer no field for political action of a high type, and so they naturally became the instruments of the 'great interests.'"[3] Direct legislation, reformers such as Sullivan and Reinsch claimed, would help dispel the legislative clout of lobbyists doing the bidding of vested economic interests.

By the 1910s, numerous elected officials had jumped on the direct democracy bandwagon. One of the most visible elected Progressives, Republican governor Hiram Johnson of California, coasted to victory in 1910 on a sweeping platform that included his support of the initiative and referendum. At the turn of the century in California, corporate lobbyists, especially those doing the bidding of the Southern Pacific Railroad (dubbed the Octopus in a 1901 novel by Frank Norris), had a stranglehold on the state legislature.[4] In his 1911 inaugural address, Johnson asked rhetorically, "How best can we arm the people to protect themselves hereafter?" He responded that "the first step in our design to preserve and perpetuate popular government shall be the adoption of the initiative, the referendum, and the recall" because "the first duty that is mine to perform is to eliminate every private interest from the government, and to make the public service of the State responsive solely to the people." While the initiative was not a "panacea for all our political ills," Johnson viewed it as essential to "place in the hands of the people the means by which they may protect themselves."[5] Other reform-minded politicians like Johnson, who ran as Teddy Roosevelt's vice presidential candidate on the Bull Moose (Progressive) ticket in 1912, contended that citizen lawmakers would be empowered to shape public policy directly, bypassing special interests.

Not all reformers shared Governor Johnson's certitude, however. A handful of Progressive Era scholars doubted that only citizens would use the initiative. By 1916, in a review essay, Professor Robert Cushman cautioned that interest groups were increasingly using the process to promote measures that negatively affected the workings of state government and "the welfare of the community."[6] Cushman's concern that the initiative could become easily co-opted by the same interests it was intended to eliminate continues to be articulated today. Many contemporary observers perceive that special interests have "derailed" citizen lawmaking, with "special interest groups using and abusing the initiative process" with relative impunity.[7] As Thomas Goebel, a historian of the development of the initiative in America, laments, "As a tool to create a government able to withstand the influence of corporate interests, [the initiative] has been a conspicuous failure."[8]

Rather than probing the instrumental effects of citizen lawmaking by examining the substantive impact interest groups have had on public policy via the initiative, we reverse the causal flow of inquiry. We take a critical look at how the process of citizen lawmaking has shaped—and continues to shape—interest group activity in the American states. We consider four aspects of how citizen lawmaking effects the terrain of state politics as it pertains to interest groups. First, contrary to the expectations of Progressive reformers, we amass evidence of how the initiative process has led to vigorous interest group participation in the financing of ballot campaigns in the two dozen states that permit the process. Second, using comparative state data, we examine the extent to which citizen lawmaking has led to larger and more diverse interest group systems than are found in states lacking the process. Third, we investigate the initiative process's impact on an individual's propensity to give money to interest groups. Finally, we inquire how the initiative process itself has become an electoral tool of interest groups interested in altering political power in the states. Although Progressive Era advocates of direct democracy had hoped to use the initiative to eliminate interest groups' clout, we find that many political organizations have adapted to the presence of the initiative, educating themselves to use the process to advance their agendas.

The Effect of Citizen Lawmaking on State Campaign Financing

Before looking back at the role played by special interests in early initiative campaigns, we first inspect the contemporary landscape of the campaign financing of ballot measures. Again, we are not concerned here with normative arguments about whether money spent on ballot campaigns is beneficial or detrimental to the public interest or with instrumental questions about whether initiatives sponsored by special interests are more or less successful at the polls than measures sponsored by citizen groups. Rather, we are interested in how interest groups have adapted their strategies, using citizen lawmaking to advance their causes. Interest groups clearly could give their money to candidates or political parties instead of spending money on ballot campaigns, but many groups deem spending money on ballot initiatives a way to transform the political landscape. The heavy presence of interest groups in ballot campaigns belies the expectations of Progressive Era reformers, who had envisioned the initiative as an unspoiled setting in which the voice of the people could be heard.

Recent Spending on Ballot Initiatives

The jury continues to deliberate about whether campaign spending is a major determinant of the success or failure of ballot measures. Some observers argue that big money from vested interests distorts citizen lawmaking.[9] Other commentators discount the role of money, arguing instead that increased spending on ballot measures helps to better inform the electorate about the issues.[10]

Keen observers of the initiative process, however, would admit that money currently plays a significant if not decisive role in ballot initiative campaigns. In 1998 alone, issue committees across the country spent a record $400 million promoting and opposing ballot initiatives and referenda in 44 states. In comparison, during the 1997–98 election cycle, the national Republican and Democratic Parties raised *only* $193 million in soft money, with federal congressional committees raising another $92 million in soft money contributions.[11] Thus, more than $100 million more was spent on ballot initiative elections than both national parties spent in soft money that election cycle. In 2002, though the number of initiatives on the statewide ballots declined by nearly 40 percent from 2000, spending levels on ballot measures remained high, with more than $140 million spent on initiatives and referenda. Backers of three gaming measures in Arizona spent more than $37 million promoting their initiatives, and 11 corporations contributed more than $4 million to defeat an Oregon initiative that would have required the labeling of genetically modified food.[12]

With the largest population of any state in the Union, California not surprisingly continues to lead the pack of initiative states in the campaign financing of ballot measures. In 1998, for example, issue committees in California spent roughly $250 million on 12 general election and 9 primary ballot measures, approximately the same amount spent by all the political candidates running for the California General Assembly and statewide offices. The amount spent on ballot measures was double the $118 million that gubernatorial candidates doled out during the primary and general elections, by far the most ever spent in the state for the governorship. The $250 million spent on the 21 ballot measures broke the previous all-time state record of $141 million, set just two years earlier. More than $88.6 million was spent on a single November 1998 ballot initiative, Proposition 5, a successful measure that allowed Native American tribes to operate casinos on reservations.[13]

During the past three decades, spending on ballot campaigns in California has grown exponentially. In 1996, for example, groups supporting and opposing measures in California spent an average of $8 million per ballot measure, up from $3 million in 1976. In addition, by 1988, spending on ballot measures in the Golden State for the first time exceeded the amount of money special interests spent on lobbying state legislators. In 1976, interest groups lobbying state legislators spent $20 million in California, double the amount spent on ballot measures. Just 12 years later, issue committees expended nearly $130 million on ballot measures, a third more than the total amount spent on lobbying in the state. Indeed, as the California Commission on Campaign Financing stated in its 1992 report, *Democracy by Initiative*, "today . . . money often dominates the initiative process even more than it does the legislative process."[14]

Big spending on ballot measures is by no means limited to California. Following the adoption in 1968 of the initiative (which permits constitutional amendments only), Florida was a relatively low-use initiative state: between 1976 and 2002, Floridians passed 16 of only 21 initiatives on the ballot. While the initiative process in the Sunshine State began innocently enough with a 1976 clean-elections initiative, special interests quickly learned that they could sponsor initiatives to alter the state constitution. In 1996, for example, nearly 70 percent of Florida's voters backed a statewide tax-limitation measure, Amendment 1. While the measure appeared to be sponsored by a grassroots group, the Tax Cap Committee, state campaign disclosure records revealed that Florida's powerful sugar industry bankrolled the measure. Over a three-year period, the Tax Cap Committee raised more than $4.7 million, with the sugar industry contributing $3.5 million, roughly 75 percent of the total.[15]

Less populous states also witnessed a dramatic rise in the spending levels on initiatives at the turn of the twenty-first century. While past spending on ballot measures would occasionally exceed the total spent on races for political office, in Colorado during the 1990s spending on ballot initiatives regularly surpassed that of all candidate races. According to veteran Colorado political analyst Floyd Ciruli, the initiative process became the state's "new growth industry." With no contribution or expenditure limitations on ballot campaigns, more than $10 million was spent in Colorado's eight 1998 ballot initiatives, nearly doubling the total spending on all statewide races, including the race for governor, and easily surpassing the previous spending record on ballot measures, $8.8 million in 1994. In 2000, contributions to the issue committees organized for and against the six initiatives on the ballot skyrocketed, exceeding $24 million, with proponents and opponents spending more than $7 million on just five 2002 ballot initiatives.[16]

The rise in ballot initiative spending in Colorado is hardly unique among smaller initiative states. In Montana in 1996, opponents of Initiative 122, a measure that would have required tougher water treatment standards in mine operations, spent nearly $9 per vote to defeat the measure. The proponents of Question 2, Massachusetts's 1998 "clean money" and public financing measure, spent upward of $1 million promoting it. In Washington in 1998, proponents and opponents of five ballot initiatives spent more than $5.6 million. And in Nebraska, AT&T spent $5.3 million in its successful campaign to defeat a single 1998 initiative that would have lowered long-distance access charges.[17] Initiative campaigns are increasingly drawing on national interest groups for their financial support. According to a recent study by the Ballot Initiative Strategy Center (BISC), a non-profit based in Washington, DC, the majority of the money raised by 10 issue committees in 2000 in seven states (Arizona, Colorado, Maine, Massachusetts, Missouri, Oregon, and Washington) came from out-of-state interest groups and wealthy benefactors.[18] National interest groups have learned that the initiative process affords them the opportunity to systematically alter public policy by going directly to the people, shunning state legislatures.

In aggregate amounts, interest groups' large financial contributions to issue committees tend to dwarf smaller contributions. The

BISC study of the 2000 election examined the contributions made to the issue groups advancing and opposing 78 initiatives on the ballots in seven states in 2000. The study found that "79,023 individual and institutional donors contributed to 175 different issue committees," with aggregate contributions totaling more than $109 million. However, the seemingly large number of contributors is misleading. The bulk of the $109 million came from relatively few sources: contributions of $1,000 or more comprised nearly 96 percent of the money raised, with contributions of $50,000 or more making up more than 57 percent of the total. Not ordinary citizens but corporations, labor unions, and wealthy individuals are the major financiers of current ballot campaigns.[19]

With the passage of the Bipartisan Campaign Reform Act (BCRA, also known as McCain-Feingold) in 2002, which banned soft money contributions to federal political parties and eliminated the electioneering broadcasting of so-called issue ads two months before a general election, the amount of special interest money funneled into ballot campaigns is likely only to escalate. BCRA effectively closed the parties' soft money spigot. As a result, interest groups are looking strategically at alternative ways to influence public policy, including using the initiative process to subtly promote or oppose candidates running for state and federal offices by linking these individuals to ballot measures.[20] Although big money in initiative campaigns is no guarantee that a ballot measure will succeed on Election Day, interest groups are actively taking the initiative, which includes using the process as part of their arsenal for shaping public policy.

Big Money and Early Ballot Measures

Big money in ballot campaigns is not a new phenomenon. The historical record suggests that even in its formative years, the initiative was not solely the province of grassroots, citizen-led operations run by amateurs. While the special interests and wealthy individuals who sponsor ballot measures certainly do not always succeed, these actors have been inextricably involved in the making and thwarting of direct legislation since the Progressive Era. Despite the good intentions of Progressive reformers, who hoped that the initiative would help circumvent the power of well-heeled individuals and economic interests, these forces quickly learned how to use the plebiscitary process to advance their interests.[21]

Some early advocates of the initiative freely admitted that special interests would inevitably try to influence the outcomes of ballot measures. Writing in 1912, Professor Delos Wilcox, an ardent supporter of the initiative, stated that he fully "expected" that "the people . . . will have to rebuke not only public service corporations [public utilities] seeking to get favors from [the people], but also many other kinds of special interests having a pecuniary stake in legislation proposed by themselves." Wilcox predicted that schoolteachers, postal carriers, policemen, brewers, and labor unions would in all likelihood try to use the initiative to offer "some legislation for their own benefit or for the advancement of their pet ideas."[22] He realized that no institutional safeguards would prevent these and other vested interests from using the initiative to advance or protect their private agendas. As a result of their considerable financial resources, special interests—certainly more than the venerated but often ephemeral "citizen legislators"—would overcome barriers to collective action and thus successfully employ the initiative.

Economic historian Charles Beard examined in some detail the November 1910 South Dakota ballot campaigns, in which voters rejected 11 out of 12 propositions. Beard contended that the defeat of the measures, which included a popular referendum invoked by the railroads to overturn a law requiring electric headlights for locomotives and a referendum regulating embalmers, could be directly attributed to the "activity of certain parties, especially interested in the defeat of one or two propositions, who filled the newspapers with advertisements and plastered the fences with billboards advising the electors to 'Vote No.'"[23] Two years earlier in Oregon, rival fishing interests made substantial expenditures during the months leading up to the June election. Upstream and downstream fisherman each placed an initiative on the ballot that would effectively eradicate the other group's right to fish for salmon on the Columbia River.[24] In his provocative book, *Democratic Delusions,* Richard Ellis documents that special interest money was so rampant in Oregon ballot measures that the state's newspapers frequently editorialized about how the initiative process was becoming corrupted. In 1913, the *Eugene Register* warned, "Any person with sufficient money knows that he can get any kind of legislation on the ballot," with the *Portland Oregonian* opining, "The corporation, the 'vested interest' or 'big business,' when it takes a hand in law-making, dips into a well-filled cash box and never misses the money."[25] Special interests were similarly involved in early ballot campaigns in Colorado. In 1912, the year of the state's first initiative and referendum election, citizens voted on 32 ballot measures: 20 initiatives and 6 popular referenda placed on the ballot by citizens, and 6 referenda placed on the ballot by the state legislature. Several of the initiatives were sponsored by special interests. Most notably, mining and smelter operators sponsored a successful eight-hour workday initiative that gutted a Progressive law passed by the state legislature a year earlier, and public utility companies offered a deceptive initiative that would have stripped the state public utilities commission of virtually all power to regulate its industries.[26]

Evidence of special interest ballot initiative activity in California during the 1920s and 1930s is particularly striking. A California Senate committee issued a 1923 report that unearthed "startlingly large expenditures in [ballot initiative] campaigns." The committee reported that more than $1 million had been spent on seven measures on the 1922 ballot. In an effort to defeat the Water and Power Act, proponents and their opponents (led by the powerful Pacific Gas and Electric Company) spent more than $660,000. By the 1930s, the process of direct democracy in California was becoming even more centralized and capital-intensive. Clem Whitaker and Leone Baxter, a husband-and-wife partnership, led this "industrialization" of the initiative process. Whitaker and Baxter joined forces in 1933 to work as campaign managers for candidates and ballot initiatives. The two public relations specialists experimented with radio and television ads, direct mail solicitation, and the use of "gimmicks" in ballot campaigns. A few years later, Whitaker and Baxter were running as many as five or six ballot campaigns per election. In 1936, special interests spent $1.2 million fighting for and against a referendum taxing chain stores, and groups battling an initiative on a retirement life payment proposal spent almost $1 million. In 1956, Whitaker and Baxter were hired by Pacific Telegraph and Telephone, Standard Oil, Pacific Gas and Electric, and Southern Pacific Railroad, which collectively had raised $3.45 million to fight Proposition 4, an oil conservation initiative.[27]

The exorbitant amount of money spent on ballot measures by special interests is nothing new; such spending is deeply rooted in California's political history as well as that of other states. As such, the eye-opening amount of money that interest groups currently spend on campaigns certainly needs to be placed in historical context. Adjusting for inflation, spending on ballot measures today in California and in other states is only marginally higher than expenditures during the 1930s, the first decade during which reliable campaign finance figures were recorded.[28] Though not always successful in their endeavors, special interests since the Progressive Era have waged expensive campaigns to advance their political agendas. As such, the initiative process has helped condition interest groups' campaign financing practices.

The Initiative's Effect on the Size and Diversity of State Interest Group Systems

If the initiative affects the campaign finance environment in states permitting citizen lawmaking, is it possible that the process has an effect on the structure of state interest group systems? A widespread belief expressed during the Progressive Era, after all, was that citizen lawmaking could counteract the influence of special interests, especially corporate interest groups, by giving citizens a mechanism for altering public policy at the polls. In this section, we assess whether direct legislation has a measurable impact on the size and diversity of interest group systems in the American states.

In an innovative comparative analysis, Fredrick Boehmke finds that American states allowing citizen lawmaking have larger and

more heterogeneous interest group systems than those states pro-
hibiting the process. Boehmke argues that the institutional "threat"
of the initiative may encourage groups, especially "citizen" groups, to
form to influence public policy. Pooling Virginia Gray and David
Lowery's data sets of interest group representation in the states for
three years (1975, 1980, and 1990),[29] Boehmke finds that states permitting the initiative have on average 17 percent more interest
groups than states without the process, after controlling for other
factors that might lead to interest group growth. More importantly—and seeming to reflect Progressive Era reformers' expectations—he finds that initiative states have 29 percent more "citizen"
groups than noninitiative states, whereas the difference between
"economic" interest groups in initiative and noninitiative states is
only 12 percent. Following the line of inquiry advanced by Elisabeth
Gerber, Boehmke reasons that direct democracy increases not only
the aggregate size but also the diversity of interest group representation in states. Lending support to the educative aspect of direct legislation, Boehmke observes, "If access to the initiative process
increases the number of groups active, particularly citizen groups,
then the consequences of the initiative process cannot be measured
solely by initiatives observed on the ballot."[30]

We update Boehmke's study using Gray and Lowery's 50-state
interest group lobbying registration figures from 1997.[31] Rather than
using Boehmke's dichotomous typology of citizen versus economic
groups, we instead use Gray and Lowery's alternative categories, for-
profit and not-for-profit organizations.[32] If Boehmke's empirical
findings are valid, we too should find significantly more not-for-
profit organizations in initiative states than in those without the
process, as citizen (that is, not-for-profit) groups, in Boehmke's
words, should be "disproportionately mobilized by access to the initiative."[33] We also divide state interest group systems in 1997 into
three different subpopulations using another typology devised by
Gray and Lowery that categorizes interest groups variously as membership (that is, organizations with individuals as members, such as
the Sierra Club, AARP, and the League of Women Voters), associations (business organizations whose members are institutions, such

as the Sugar Cane Growers Association or the Association of Washington Business), or institutions (entities with no members, such as corporations, banks, universities, and cities).[34]

A limitation of Boehmke's analysis is his use of a simple dichotomous measure of whether a state permits or does not permit the initiative to approximate the impact of citizen lawmaking on a state's interest group system. This limitation found in other research has been noted in earlier chapters. Even the most casual observer of initiative politics will find this measure suspect, as the use of the process varies considerably across the two dozen states allowing citizen lawmaking. It is problematic to assume that the potential impact of the initiative on interest group mobilization is equal in all states that permit the process. For example, Illinois technically has citizen lawmaking, but it is constitutionally limited to a narrow set of substantive uses. Since 1970 (when Illinois adopted the process), citizens have voted on only one statewide ballot initiative. Thus, it makes little theoretical sense to assume that the initiative in Illinois—or in Wyoming and Mississippi, other extremely low use states—provides a nurturing institutional framework in which interest groups might become mobilized. Yet Boehmke's model does not control for differences in the usage of citizen lawmaking across initiative states.

Rather than treating identically all states that permit citizen lawmaking, it is essential to place initiative states in their historical context. A better measure of citizen lawmaking's possible effect on the structure of interest group populations is the number of initiatives on the ballot. If the theory of interest group mobilization is accurate, states with long track records of initiative use, such as Oregon, California, and Colorado, should have substantially more interest groups than noninitiative states and considerably more groups than initiative states with low usage rates.[35] Using Gray and Lowery's 1997 registration data, we test whether a state's recent initiative usage (measured by the number of statewide initiatives on the ballot from 1990 to 1996) positively affects the size and diversity of the state's interest group population (and subpopulations).[36] If ever there was a year in which the educative effects of the initiative should have mobilized interest groups to register with states, it should have been 1997; the previous year broke all records for the number of initiatives (93) on statewide ballots.[37]

Following Boehmke, we also control for several alternative explanations of interest group growth and diversity in the states using multivariate regression. Based on the "density dependency" hypothesis advanced by Gray and Lowery, whereby they find that interest group systems are constrained by environmental factors, we expect a state's 1997 real gross state product (GSP) will positively affect the size and diversity of a state's interest group system. Second, we include the square of the GSP, which takes into consideration the nonlinearity of state wealth and the size of the interest group system. Third, we control for the effects of divided government, expecting, as Boehmke does, that states without united government in 1996 will have higher numbers of and levels of diversity of interest groups. Finally, following Boehmke, we use updated data from Robert Erikson, Gerald Wright, and John McIver to control for a state's political ideology. We expect that states with more liberal political ideology will have more diverse and larger interest group populations.[38] Unlike Boehmke's study, in which he uses a dichotomous measure of initiative/noninitiative state as his key independent variable, we use the recent historical initiative usage (1990–96) to examine the effects of citizen lawmaking on interest group size and diversity.[39]

Our updated models are consistent with many of the findings reported by Boehmke. As reported in table A.10 (see appendix), we find that recent initiative use has a positive effect on the number of membership, association, and not-for-profit organizations registered to lobby in a state. In other words, as states have more initiatives on the ballot, they have more registered membership (citizen) and not-for-profit interest groups. At the same time, having more initiatives on the ballot is not associated with having more registered for-profit or economic interest groups. Thus, despite the extensive spending on initiative campaigns, as discussed in the previous section, the usage of the initiative does not appear to lead to more for-profit interest groups registering in a state but does appear to promote the representation of citizen interests. The data suggest that the initiative process encourages some kinds of economic interests, since states with high levels of citizen lawmaking have more associations registered, controlling for other factors. States with frequent initiatives on the ballot, however, do not have more institutional interest groups than noninitiative states. Contrary to Boehmke, though, we find that citizen lawmaking does not affect the total number of interest groups registered in a state, as the total number of initiatives on the ballot during the preceding seven years had no effect on the total number of interest groups registered with a state in 1997.

Our models also reveal that a state's wealth affects the size and diversity of state interest group systems. The quadratic model of GSP confirms Gray and Lowery's macro-level theory of interest group growth, which stipulates that as competition for resources among organizations increases with interest group systems becoming more dense, the expansion rate of an interest group system slows. Consistent with Boehmke's research, we find no evidence that the diversity of interest group systems is spurred by divided government or liberal state ideology.

To better understand the magnitude of the effect of ballot initiatives on the diversity of state interest groups, we calculate the expected number of membership, association, and not-for-profit interest groups based on the regression models presented in table A.10. We compute the expected value estimates by setting the independent variables to their mean values while adjusting the number of initiatives on the ballot from 1990 to 1996 to 0, 4, 8, 16, and 40. More than half of the states (26 without the process and Illinois) had zero initiatives on the ballot between 1990 and 1996; at the other extreme, California and Oregon each had 47 initiatives on the ballot during the seven-year period.

Recent initiative use had the biggest impact on the registration levels of not-for-profit organizations. Controlling for other factors, the addition of just 1 initiative on the ballot every two years increases by 11 the overall size of not-for-profit groups registered in a state. The number of not-for-profit groups in a state is 67.5 percent higher (268 to 160) in states with 40 initiatives on the ballot from 1990 to 1996

"What Matters"   **BOX 10**

What is the impact of initiative use on the number of interest group organizations (in 1997) in the states?

Number of Statewide Initiatives on the Ballot, 1990–96	Number of Registered Interest Groups		
	Membership ("citizen")	Associations ("economic")	Not-for-Profit
No Initiative/0 on the Ballot	127	148	160
4 Initiatives on the Ballot	133	153	171
8 Initiatives on the Ballot	139	158	181
16 Initiatives on the Ballot	150	168	203
40 Initiatives on the Ballot	187	197	268

Note: Only statistically significant differences are reported (see table A.10). When multivariate regression is used, these are the variables that matter, holding other factors constant. Expected value computed by setting the independent variables GSP, GSP^2, government expenditures as % of GSP, divided government, and state ideology/public opinion to their mean values and adjusting number of initiatives on state ballot to 0, 4, 8, 16, and 40.

---

than in states with zero initiatives on the ballot over the same period. Similarly, states with heavy initiative usage (40 measures on the ballot between 1990 and 1996) have 47.2 percent more membership organizations than states with no initiatives on the ballot. Finally, with peak associations, we found that states with 40 initiatives on the ballot over the period have 33.1 percent more registered associations than those states with no measures on the ballot. While the number of registered associations increases as states become more frequent users of the process, the number of interest groups does not increase at a rate comparable to the rise in not-for-profit and membership interest groups. This is strong evidence that direct democracy increases the representation of citizen interests in the democratic process, which is consistent with Progressive Era expectations about the process.

Initiative use seems to clearly impact the diversity if not the overall size of interest group populations in the states and therefore advantages citizen interests. This makes intuitive sense, as the initiative, when utilized, clearly can spur into action membership and not-for-profit groups as well as economic peak associations that promote or oppose ballot measures. Regardless of whether initiatives are frequently used, economic interests are likely already to be registered to lobby the state legislature. The mobilization of "potential groups," in the words of interest group scholar David Truman, seems to be actuated by the deployment of ballot measures.[40]

In sum, we find that interest group systems seem to be dynamically shaped by the use of citizen lawmaking rather than by its mere institutional presence. In other words, to influence state interest group systems, the initiative must be used. Using Gray and Lowery's 1997 data, we find that initiative states do not have more interest groups overall than noninitiative states. However, when controlling for other factors in our multivariate analysis—the size of the economy, government expenditures, ideology, and divided government—we find that the usage of the initiative process is a significant factor in explaining the diversity of state interest group populations in 1997. States with more initiatives on the ballot have more registered not-for-profit, membership, and economic associations, providing evidence of the mobilization of both citizen and economic interests in states with direct democracy.

Progressive reformers had hoped that the initiative process would help dissipate the power of interest groups in the states by opening up the political system and making interest groups less hierarchical. It is important to recall that during the Progressive Era, the initiative was most welcomed by reformers in the states that had the most powerful economic interest groups and the weakest political parties.[41] While the diversity of interest groups registered in the American states appears to be positively affected by citizen lawmaking, the evidence is mixed about whether initiatives have mitigated the power of economic interest groups.

The Effect of Initiative Use on an Individual's Contributions to Interest Groups

The initiative appears to shape the macro-level realm of campaign financing in the states that permit the process as well as the structure of state interest group systems. But has citizen lawmaking also altered the micro-level behavior of individuals with regard to interest groups? In this section, we inquire whether any differences exist in individuals' financial contributions to interest groups in initiative and noninitiative states. Specifically, we are interested in whether citizens living in states with frequent exposure to initiative campaigns are more likely to donate money to interest groups than are people living in states without direct democracy. Since interest groups are often major players in ballot initiative contests, we might expect that citizens living in initiative states would be more likely to contribute money to interest groups than citizens living in states without this institutional mechanism would be. After all, the mechanism of the initiative, in theory at least, offers citizens an alternative venue for influencing public policy.[42]

Drawing again on National Election Studies (NES) survey data from 1996, 1998, and 2000, we examine the effect of initiative use on an individual's propensity to give to interest groups. By merging the NES survey responses with state-level data, we can explore the state institutional environments in which individuals make choices about contributing to interest groups. As with our analysis in previous chapters, we use the number of initiatives appearing on the state election ballot in each year as our primary independent variable.[43] We analyze the data for the three years separately; they are not pooled because of changes in NES survey coding in 2000. Based on the findings in the previous section using aggregate 50-state data, we anticipate that respondents living in states with higher levels of initiatives on the ballot will report an increased probability of contributing to interest groups. The binary dependent variable in our model, coded one if yes and zero otherwise, is whether the respondent gave money to an interest group. We also discuss findings regarding whether an individual living in a state with citizen lawmaking was more likely to give campaign contributions to political parties and political candidates.

We control for a number of attitudinal and demographic factors commonly used in individual-level studies. Previous research, including what we report in earlier chapters, finds that socioeconomic factors, particularly income and education, influence decisions about whether to vote, or participate, more broadly defined.[44] To gauge income, we use a 24-point Likert scale measuring total family income for the three years in the study. We control for formal education, measuring it with a 7-point scale, and provide a dichotomous variable for female respondents. To control for race and ethnicity, African Americans and Latinos are coded one, with non-Hispanic whites as the reference group (coded zero). Age is measured in years. A 7-point Likert scale also measures partisanship, with possible responses ranging from 1 = strong Democrat to 7 = strong Republican. A series of dichotomous variables is used to account for political attitudes, including strong Democrat, strong Republican, and pure independents, with moderate partisans as the reference (omitted) groups.[45] We also use dichotomous variables to control for union membership (coded one if the respondent is a union member and zero otherwise), and ideology, with self-identified liberals and moderates coded one and conservatives as the reference group (coded zero).

In addition to the other individual-level controls, we measure whether a respondent had Internet access. A question about Internet access was first asked in 1996. Since that time, candidate Web sites have become increasingly important in providing election news and a forum for political contributions that may reinvigorate interest in the political process.[46] This may be particularly important in midterm elections, when there is no presidential race to arouse public interest, and in low-stimulus elections, such as many initiative contests. Previous research also shows that social context is an important factor in understanding voter turnout in the American states: between 1950 and 1998, states with higher racial diversity have significantly lower turnout rates, after controlling for other factors.[47] As in previous chapters, we measure state racial context by an index of racial and ethnic percentages created for the 50 states using 1996 and 2000 demographic data on the size of the Latino, African American, Asian American, and non-Hispanic white populations.[48] We expect that citizens in states with higher racial and ethnic diversity will be less likely to make political contributions.

Corroborating the previous analysis examining voter turnout in midterm and presidential elections (chapter 2), we find that citizens living in states with frequent ballot initiatives were significantly more likely to contribute money to interest groups in the 1998 midterm election. (Regression coefficients for the model are reported in table A.11 [see appendix].) However, we find no relationship between the two factors in the two years with presidential elections. The data suggest that ballot initiatives stimulate political participation above and beyond voting, in terms of campaign contributions. The strength of the relationship in the midterm election but not in the two presidential elections again points to the importance of citizen lawmaking in low-stimulus elections.

Individual citizens, of course, are more likely to contribute money to nonprofit and membership groups than to business (or economic) interest groups. Findings from the survey data are consistent with the aggregate analysis reported in the previous section that not-for-profit and membership groups are more common in states with more initiatives on the ballot. Holding other factors constant, we find that every two initiatives appearing on the state ballot raises the probability of an individual contributing money to interest groups by 1 percentage point. A citizen residing in a state with four initiatives appearing on the ballot has a 2 percent higher probability of contributing money to an interest group than a similarly situated individual residing in a state with no initiatives on the ballot. This effect multiplied by the voting age population of a state can result in significant financial support for nonprofit and membership interest groups. This mobilization of citizen groups can provide a significant counterbalance to economic interests, consistent with Progressive Era intentions for the process.

As previous chapters have demonstrated, when a person lives in an environment where statewide ballot questions are a common occurrence, the individual's electoral, attitudinal, and behavioral responses are affected by the process of citizen lawmaking. We even find, with additional analysis, that citizens living in states with frequent exposure to ballot initiatives were not more likely to give

---

"What Matters"   **BOX 11**

Who contributes to interest groups?

1998 Midterm election
An individual who is exposed to ballot initiatives, affluent, Hispanic, of liberal ideology, and lives in a state with lower racial diversity.

Note: Only statistically significant differences are reported (see table A.11). When logistic regression is used, these are the variables that matter, holding other factors constant.

What is the effect of exposure to ballot initiatives on contributing money to interest groups?

Every two initiatives appearing on the state ballot raises the probability of an individual contributing money to interest groups by approximately 1 percentage point.

No initiatives on state ballot	2.5%
Two initiatives on state ballot	3.1%
Four initiatives on state ballot	3.7%
Six initiatives on state ballot	4.6%
Eight initiatives on state ballot	5.6%

Note: Estimates are based on a hypothetical respondent who is female, white, a union member, of independent partisanship, moderate ideology, with Internet access, with values for education, age, and income set at their mean. The respondent resides in a state with average racial diversity. We have calculated the probability of contributing money to interest groups, holding other factors constant (see table A.11).

---

money to political parties or political candidates in any of the three elections (analysis not shown). That is, the effect of ballot initiatives on increased campaign donations appears to be limited to interest groups and not to include other actors in political campaigns.[49] In sum, then, we find that individuals living in active initiative states are more likely than those living in states with inactive (or no) citizen lawmaking to make financial contributions to interest groups in midterm elections, after controlling for a range of socioeconomic and political attributes.

☐ The Effect of the Initiative on Interest Group Electoral Strategies

In line with Progressive reformers' hopes, citizen lawmaking appears to have brought about some structural change in the diversity (if not the aggregate size) of interest group populations in the states. Furthermore, the presence of the initiative appears to increase the likelihood of individuals contributing money to interest groups. In this final section, we examine how the mechanism of the initiative affects interest groups' electoral strategies. Institutionally, citizen lawmaking adds another dimension to the dynamics of interest group politics in the American states. As such, some organizations have tried to use the process of citizen lawmaking to alter the political equilibrium of initiative states, independent of any substantive outcomes that may result from a successful ballot measure. Growing evidence demonstrates that in an effort to tip the balance power in a state, some interest groups are using the initiative process intentionally to drain their competitors' resources.

Not all interest groups become involved in the initiative process primarily to pass laws or to amend state constitutions. Citizen lawmaking affords interest groups the opportunity to make mischief. During the 1990s, a handful of interest groups began advancing ballot measures that were not designed specifically to pass substantive laws or amendments but were intended to disrupt the balance of a state's interest group system. Typically, national interest groups are behind such initiatives designed to drain the resources of the targeted groups, which are expected to oppose the measures. Rather than a way to enact substantive laws or amend state constitutions, citizen lawmaking in this case is a means by which interest groups can transform the balance of the state's interest group system. While Progressive Era scholars never envisioned this use of citizen lawmaking, it is yet another indirect effect of the process.

Republican insider Grover Norquist, the executive director of the not-for-profit Americans for Tax Reform, pioneered this devious yet legal use of citizen lawmaking. His scheme was to use the initiative process to drain the resources of organized labor, thereby depriving

Democratic candidates of campaign funds. Stuffing his organization's coffers in 1996 with than more than $4.5 million courtesy of
the Republican National Committee, Norquist led the effort to place
several conservative initiatives on statewide ballots.[50] Norquist funneled a substantial amount of the committee's money to issue groups
in California, Colorado, and Oregon to promote antitax and "paycheck protection" ballot measures. In 1996, for example, Norquist's
Americans for Tax Reform contributed $509,500 to Oregon Taxpay-
ers United, the sponsor of Measure 47, a tax-limitation initiative. The
successful measure, which reduced property taxes and limited annual
tax increases, had the direct effect of downsizing state and local governments in Oregon. While he certainly backed the initiative for its
substantive value, Norquist's support for the measure also stemmed
from the fact that it would weaken organized labor and the Democratic Party. "Every time you nick the budget," Norquist crowed following the antitax victory in Oregon, "somewhere a Democratic
precinct worker loses his job."[51]

In 1998, Americans for Tax Reform sponsored other measures in
an effort to weaken organized labor by strategically using citizen lawmaking. The group transferred $441,000 to the Campaign Reform
Initiative in California, the official sponsor of Proposition 226, a paycheck-protection measure. Unions in California (aided by contributions from labor organizations across the country) spent more than
$23 million fighting June 1998 primary initiative, which they dubbed
"paycheck deception."[52] A similar situation occurred in Oregon in
November of that year, with unions fighting off another Americans
for Tax Reform–sponsored paycheck-protection initiative. Had the
two measures passed, they would have required unions to obtain
annual authorizations from their members to collect dues to be used
for political campaigns. Despite losing both initiatives, Norquist's
tactic nevertheless paid dividends, as organized labor's efforts to
defeat the measures resulted in unions having significantly less
money to pour into the November candidate elections. At a 1999
conference in Washington, DC, Norquist stated with pride, "Even
when you lose, you force the other team to drain resources for no
apparent reason."[53]

Norquist's strategy for utilizing citizen lawmaking as an offensive weapon to alter the balance of power among interest groups in a state has been replicated elsewhere. Gary Boyce, a Colorado rancher in the San Luis Valley, took a page from Norquist's playbook in 1998. Boyce and his California-based Stockman's Water Company financed two ballot initiatives, Amendments 15 and 16, both of which dealt with water rights in the valley's Closed Basin. Although the Colorado electorate easily defeated the two initiatives—each received less than a quarter of the total vote—the measures served their tacit purpose. The widespread coalition of opponents—including the Colorado Water Congress, San Luis Valley businesses and farmers, Trout Unlimited, the Colorado Farm Bureau and the Cattlemen's Association, the Sierra Club, and the Rio Grande Water Conservation District—was forced to spend more than $1 million to defeat the measures. This was perhaps Boyce's primary motivation for placing the two ill-fated measures on the ballot. A million dollars was nothing to Stockman's Water, but fighting the initiative bled the financial resources of San Luis Valley ranchers and farmers. The real battle over water rights in the valley would be decided in water courts. Boyce revealed to a reporter that his initiatives were designed in part to render his opponents as weak as possible—"to make sure the playing field is level" in upcoming legal battles. Indeed, Boyce admitted that although he did not intend to bankrupt the Rio Grande Water Conservation District, "if that happened as a result, I wouldn't shed a tear."[54]

Most recently, in 2000, the Association of Washington Business informed its members that it would begin aggressively using the initiative to pursue public policies it favored that were languishing in the state legislature. The association had previously promoted ballot measures, including a hazardous waste cleanup initiative in the late 1980s and a state spending limitation initiative in 1993, and had spent several million dollars opposing initiatives lowering taxes on car registrations and banning affirmative action. But in an internal memo to its members, the organization's rationale for the use of the initiative went beyond merely an instrumental justification to enact public policy by circumventing the state legislature. The business association argued that by sponsoring ballot initiatives, it could sub-stantially weaken its labor counterparts by forcing them to spend money fighting initiatives.[55]

 Conclusion

The call for direct democracy gained momentum during the early twentieth century as a result of the widespread popular concern that moneyed special interests were controlling the legislative process. Ironically, far from eliminating the clout of special interests, as many Progressive Era advocates of the initiative had hoped, both citizen and economic interest groups quickly adapted to the new institu-tional process. Since direct democracy was first adopted in the states more than a century ago, interest groups have played a major role in ballot measure campaigns. Responding to changing institutional structures, interest groups have educated themselves, using the plebiscitary process to increase or consolidate their relative strength.

In this chapter, we demonstrate that the process of citizen law-making affects both macro- and micro-level aspects of interest groups. Going beyond the question of whether the mere institutional presence of the initiative affects the overall size of interest group sys-tems, we find that the number of initiatives on state ballots affects the profile of interest group populations. States with higher usage of the initiative have more not-for-profit and membership groups, which enhance the power of citizens. However, we also find that states with high initiative use have more associational organizations than states with low or no initiative use. These are important findings, providing some evidence that Progressive Era reformers were correct in think-ing that direct democracy would increase the power of citizen voices in the political process but that economic interests could also benefit. At the micro-level, we find that exposure to ballot initiatives posi-tively affects individuals' propensity to give money to political orga-nizations. National survey data show that individuals who live in states that permit the initiative are more inclined to give money to interest groups (but not parties or candidates) than residents of states without citizen lawmaking. The initiative seems to provide individuals with yet another financial avenue for becoming involved in political life.

Progressive Era reformers' targets continue to utilize the process of citizen lawmaking, however. Despite the cries from some camps that citizen lawmaking is under attack, efforts under way in several states to retard the number of initiatives on the ballot have done little to curb the activity of economically powerful interest groups.[56] While economic interest groups by no means win all their direct legislation endeavors, the historical record provides little indication that vested interests will voluntarily lessen their involvement in direct democracy. A growing number of economic interests view the initiative process not only as an avenue to substantively shape public policy but also as a political tool in and of itself. Furthermore, the practice of economic interests secretly funneling contributions to ballot campaigns through stealth education committees, 527s political organizations, 501(c)(3) and (c)(4) nonprofits, and limited-liability corporations may very well become more common in direct democracy campaigns since the U.S. Supreme Court's decision in 2003 upholding federal campaign finance reforms banning soft money contributions to the national parties.[57]

Our findings suggest that the process of citizen lawmaking does have an educative effect by altering the strategies and composition of interest groups as well as individuals' behavior toward interest groups. Independent of the substantive issues on the ballot, then, the initiative itself is another arena in which political conflict occurs. Richard Ellis rightly observes, "The initiative process does not offer a respite from interest group politics but rather a new venue in which most of the same old interest groups contest for power."[58] As the following chapter will demonstrate, the effect of citizen lawmaking is felt not only by interest groups but also by political parties and their candidates.

6 | The Education of Political Parties

Political parties represented one of Progressive reformers' principal targets, second only to the problem of economic interests unduly swaying elected state officials. Many Progressives offered vociferous criticisms of how party bosses routinely disregarded public opinion. The "wishes" of the political machines, scholar William B. Munro noted bluntly in 1912, "do not usually run parallel to those of the electorate."[1] John Shafroth, a reform-minded Democratic governor of Colorado, complained that rather than promoting the public good, party machines were doing the bidding of the "combinations of capital."[2] Shafroth, California governor Hiram Johnson, and other reformist public officials routinely denounced the corruption and "representative turpitude" that accompanied the two major parties' spoils systems.[3] By the first decade of the twentieth century, Progressives had reached a broad consensus that party machines were too powerful. "Control of political parties," as professor Walter Weyl succinctly observed in 1912, "is the very beginning of political democracy."[4]

Progressive Era reformers envisioned that the initiative process, through its educative involvement of citizens directly in policy decisions, could effectively weaken political parties. By petitioning measures onto the ballot, citizens could circumvent state legislatures controlled by the party machines. Nathan Cree, an early proponent of direct democracy in the United States, conjectured that the initiative would "break the crushing and stifling power of our great party machines, and give freer play to the political ideas, aspirations, opinions and feelings of the people."[5] Drawing on Cree's work, the influential *Oregonian* newspaper opined in 1906, "The method of initiative and referendum permits each voter to express his individual opinion upon every question standing entirely by itself and without admixture of personal or partisan bias."[6] Party elites would no longer control the message, much less the machinery to make policy. The following year, William U'Ren, the father of the Oregon system of direct democracy, maintained that "party political organizations are in failing health" in that state. For U'Ren, citizens' "absolute power . . . to decide many questions at one election and each separately on its own merits appears to be fatal to the perfection of party discipline and organization."[7] In Oregon, as in other states, even critics of direct democracy conceded that it occasionally allowed citizens to stifle "the selfish and the dishonest who would use the government to enrich themselves personally and the class which they represent, the 'Boss' and his men who are the curse of the system in America."[8] "Unless the machine and its bosses could be broken, unless the corrupt alliances between greedy corporate interests and the machines could be smashed," political scientist Thomas Cronin summarized, "it seemed that no lasting improvement could be achieved" during the Progressive Era. Yet according to Cronin, the reformers did not intend to create "a revolution, merely a restoration. The remedy would be the initiative, referendum, and the recall."[9]

In this chapter we explore political parties' involvement in the initiative process, arguing that a symbiotic relationship has emerged between parties and citizen lawmaking. Drawing primarily on examples from California and Colorado, two trendsetting states that are among the leaders in terms of the number of initiatives placed on their ballots both recently and since the advent of process, we call attention to the partisan nature of direct democracy campaigns. Interviews with state party officials reveal how the initiative has educated them. We find that party officials are interested not only in the substantive outcomes that ballot measures may produce but also in the partisan advantage that initiative campaigns may generate. We also test the partisan underpinnings of votes cast in recent initiative elections in California. While it is widely accepted that political parties in the United States have not been major players in most statewide ballot contests, our empirical findings challenge this assumption. In the analysis that follows, we demonstrate not only that political parties are engaged in citizen lawmaking—as they use ballot measures to stimulate voter turnout, drive wedges into the opposing partisan coalition, and generate campaign contributions— but also that party officials' efforts to use citizen lawmaking can pay real dividends, as voters often respond to ballot questions along partisan lines.

Party Avoidance or Involvement in the Initiative Process?

The idea that during the Progressive Era, direct legislation "strictly limited, more or less by design," the power of political parties continues to inform scholarship on the relationship between political parties and the initiative process. Some scholars have argued that by subverting the party's traditional electioneering function and providing "the opportunity for private (i.e., nonparty) organizations to offer advice and conduct campaigns," citizen lawmaking has obviated the role of political parties in the initiative process.[10] In his classic work, *Direct Legislation,* David Magleby reported in the early 1980s that, "parties are excluded from participation in drafting the measures and therefore may not play much of a role in interpreting them to the voters." Parties generally shunned the initiative process, Magleby reasoned, because the success or failure of initiatives rarely translated into "any payoff to the electoral fortunes of the party candidates in the election."[11]

It is true that American political parties, unlike those in European Union countries, only occasionally endorse ballot questions.[12] Yet American parties at the state as well as national levels are more involved in citizen lawmaking than is generally assumed. Unfortunately, few scholars have probed empirically political parties' involvement in the initiative process.[13] In keeping with the sentiments expressed by many Progressive Era advocates of the process, scholars generally assume that political parties avoid initiative campaigns because ballot issues transcend traditional partisan cleavages.

A closer inspection of the historical record, however, reveals that not all Progressive Era scholars celebrated the curative properties of direct legislation with regard to party machines. A few critics voiced concerns that political parties would not necessarily be undone by the practice of citizen lawmaking. Buried beneath the nearly ubiquitous praise for how the initiative would emasculate party machines, one social reformer and political commentator, Mary Parker Follett, anticipated the political parties remarkable ability to adapt the initiative for partisan advantage. In 1918, the waning days of initiative use in the early twentieth century, Follett warned in her prescient book, *The New State,* that without community institutions to foster and facilitate public deliberation of ballot issues, direct legislation would fail.[14] For Follett, "The faith in direct government as a sure panacea is almost pathetic when we remember how in the past one stronghold after another has been captured by the party. Much has been written by advocates of direct government to show that it will destroy the arbitrary power of the party, destroy its relation to big business, etc., but we see little evidence of this." She challenged the position of scholars such as A. Lawrence Lowell, the president of Harvard University, who had argued that direct legislation "tends in a variety of ways to lessen the importance of parties" because it "entails a decision only on the special measure under consideration, and hence the people are never called upon, either at an election or a referendum, to judge the conduct of the party as a whole."[15] Follett, in contrast, argued that the party machine was "quite able to use 'direct government' for its own ends. Direct government worked by the [party] machine will be subject to much of the same abuses as representative government." Explicating her unique version of group theory, Follett argued that direct democracy would work only "if accompanied by the organization of voters in nonpartisan groups for the production of common ideas and a collective purpose. Of itself direct government can never become the responsible government of a people."[16]

The 1990s: Parties Take the Initiative

Though often subtle, growing evidence indicates that many state and national party organizations are becoming more than bit players in ballot campaigns, raising anew the fears first articulated by Follett nearly a century ago. That party organizations—whose political power has been diminished by a variety of institutional changes as well as by the rise of interest groups and candidate-centered campaigns—are not visibly involved in most initiative campaigns does not mean that parties are absent from the process. State party organizations, the Democratic National Committee (DNC), and the Republican National Committee (RNC) do not sit idly by as ballot measures become more prominent features of state policy-making. From a rational-actor perspective, this engagement by party organizations seems perfectly logical. As ballot measures become more important vehicles for policy change, it is rational that party organizations will try selectively to use initiatives to advance political agendas as well as candidates for public office. Parties' strategic (including financial) participation in ballot measure campaigns also has the potential to offset the parties' depreciated influence in the legislative arena. Although the initiative process continues to be used primarily by citizen and special interest groups to circumvent partisan state legislatures, party organizations clearly acknowledge the power of direct democracy even if they are not terribly fond of it.

Some observers suggest that the level of party activity may be limited by the type of initiative that is on the ballot. Using a fourfold typology to classify recent California initiatives, a group of scholars finds that "majoritarian" ballot measures (those in which the groups promoting and opposing a ballot measure tend to be large and diffuse, as opposed to narrow economic interests) tend to encourage party participation. The authors find that "candidates and political parties dominate the campaign discourse" of majoritarian ballot contests dealing with social and moral questions because proponents of these measures often "welcome the adoption of their issue by other groups, political parities, or politicians."[17]

There is good reason to expect that party involvement in citizen lawmaking will extend beyond majoritarian initiative campaigns. Political parties in several states have become involved in "entrepreneurial" initiative contests with broad support and narrow opposition and even "interest group" initiatives with narrow support and opposition, which is not typically expected.[18] Three factors appear to motivate the major parties to become involved in the initiative process. First, a party may become involved if a ballot measure has a chance of promoting voter turnout for the party's candidates for elected office. Second, a party may become engaged in initiative politics if a proposed measure can serve as a wedge issue against the other party. Third, a party may choose to support (or oppose) a proposition to garner financial contributions from the sponsoring (or opposing) issue committees. Recent developments in California and Colorado indicate that party officials consider all three of these reasons when determining whether to become directly or indirectly involved with initiatives.

Bolstering Voter Turnout

As chapters 2 and 3 document, ballot initiatives can increase Election Day turnout and stimulate voter interest in politics. Candidates for political office often use ballot measures to advance their campaigns and turn out the partisan vote. This strategy was most recently employed in 2002 by Ohio governor Bob Taft. The Republican visibly opposed Issue 1, a constitutional amendment that would have allowed drug treatment in lieu of jail time for eligible first- and second-time nonviolent drug offenders. According to a study by the nonpartisan Ballot Initiative Strategy Center, roughly one-fifth of the contributions to the opponents of Issue 1 came from donors who had "also contributed generously to Taft's re-election effort." Taft made his opposition to the ballot initiative central to his reelection bid, "instruct[ing] his supporters to contribute to the No on 1 effort in a June 2002 fundraising letter."[19] Perhaps Taft's opposition to the initiative did not arise from substantive grounds but rather for hereditary reasons, as his great-grandfather, President William Howard

Taft, was a determined detractor of direct democracy.[20] Whatever his motivation, Bob Taft's direct involvement in the anti–Issue 1 campaign was rewarded, as conservative voters were mobilized to vote against the ballot measure and to support Republican candidates. Not only was Issue 1 soundly defeated, but Taft won reelection by a landslide and Republicans swept every major statewide office.

The practice of candidates using initiatives to advance their campaigns and partisan ideology is a well-established tradition in California. According to journalist Peter Schrag, a sage observer of the state's political process, "embracing and demagoguing hot-button [ballot] issues" enables candidates to "showcase" their credentials.[21] Using ballot issues to bolster candidacies dates to the gubernatorial runs of Secretary of State Jerry Brown and Attorney General John Van De Kamp. In 1974, Brown cosponsored a campaign finance ballot measure to strengthen his credentials in his run for governor. In 1990, Van De Kamp cosponsored three ballot initiatives in an attempt to energize support for his campaign for governor.

More ubiquitous was former governor Pete Wilson's well-documented use of initiatives. Beginning in 1990, with Proposition 115, a tough-on-crime measure, Wilson campaigned for numerous majoritarian ballot measures in an effort to promote his candidacy. For example, when running for reelection in 1994, the governor actively supported two measures that were popular among the party faithful: Proposition 184, a harsh three-strikes measure for repeat criminal offenders, and Proposition 187, a punitive anti-illegal-immigration measure. Wilson spent $2 million of his campaign funds on advertisements in favor of Proposition 187 and became the campaign's point man.[22] As in Ohio, the governor's involvement paid off, as both of his initiatives succeeded at the polls and helped to energize California conservatives to turn out for Republican candidates, including Wilson.

Wilson did not exploit the initiative process only for personal gains during his repeated quests for political office during his eight-year tenure as governor; he promoted ballot measures to advance the cause of the Republican Party more generally. Prohibited from serving a third term, Wilson actively backed two California ballot initiatives that the party calculated would promote voter turnout for the GOP's slate of candidates in the 1998 elections. During the June primary, Wilson contributed not only his name but also more than $1 million from his personal campaign fund to help place Proposition 226, dubbed "paycheck protection," on the ballot.[23] Until Election Day, when the measure was defeated at the polls, Republican support for the initiative remained consistently strong, never dipping below 57 percent.[24]

In Colorado, three-term governor Roy Romer actively campaigned for several ballot measures during his tenure in office to help turn out the vote for the Democratic Party. As de facto head of the state's Democrats between 1986 and 1998 (and head of the DNC in 1997–98), Romer publicly endorsed a measure dealing with the funding of public education and opposed antiabortion and tax and spending limitation measures.[25] The Colorado Democratic Party chairman from 1992 to 1994, lawyer Howard Gelt, indicated that although the party worked closely with Romer on several initiatives in the early 1990s, the parties had no "overt involvement" in the initiative process: the coordination between the party and public officials was "incredibly covert."[26] In 1992 and 1994, according to Gelt, the Democratic Party's coordinated campaign committee met regularly with organized labor interests and the groups supporting and opposing the initiatives to talk strategy, arrange literature drops, send out direct mailings with slate cards and sample ballots, and plot television advertising. In 1992, for example, Romer was not up for reelection. Nevertheless, in an effort to get out the Democratic vote, the governor worked closely with the state party to oppose Amendment 2, a successful anti-gay-rights measure, and to support Amendment 6, an unsuccessful initiative that Romer sponsored to increase the state sales tax to fund public education.[27]

In addition to individual candidates or elected officials using initiatives, the two major parties have also become important power brokers in the process. In California and Colorado as well as in other states, parties often take public stances on ballot measures. By endorsing and promoting initiatives, the parties hope to stimulate partisan voter anxiety or excitement about the measures, which the parties hope will translate into increased across-the-board support. According to a California GOP official, "get out the vote" (GOTV) was one of the main reasons why the party supported Proposition 187 in 1994. Backing the measure represented a "calculated effort on our part" because the measure was very "popular" and seemed like it was "going to pass." Governor Wilson supported the initiative because it was "good" and would "help him and the party."[28] In 1998, the state Republican Party, headquartered in Burbank, voted in its September party convention to support or oppose each of the eight initiatives on the general election ballot. The California Democratic Party also took a formal position on all of the measures, except for Proposition 5, the Indian gaming measure (for reasons discussed later in this chapter).[29]

In Colorado, the state Democratic Party did not officially endorse or oppose any of the eight statewide measures in 1998. Bylaws permit the party to take a public stance on an issue with the approval of either the party's executive committee or the chair. Unlike previous party heads, Phil Perington, the boss in 1997–98, was not about to "stick his neck out" on any of the issues. He did not recommend any party endorsements because he saw no electoral payoff for Democratic candidates.[30] However, while Perington was out of town, the topic of supporting or opposing issues came up at a meeting of the party's executive committee. In Perington's absence, the committee, against party rules and defying his will, decided to send out an absentee ballot mailing with the party taking a position against Amendments 11 and 12, the two antiabortion measures. In contrast, Colorado's state Republican Party, which had similar bylaws regarding the taking of positions on initiatives, supported or opposed all eight of the 1998 statewide initiatives as well as the three statewide referenda. For Steve Curtis, the chairman of the Colorado GOP from 1997 to 1998, "it's the responsibility of the parties to come out and advocate issues. . . . Sitting on the fence doesn't excite people."[31] According to Curtis, the party wins "when we turn the base out." The party came out strong against Referendum B, a statutory measure placed on the ballot by the legislature to retain excess taxes to spend on education and transportation needs. The party placed "No on B" yard signs and bumper stickers in its office for activists to pick up, and Curtis spoke out in favor of the referendum, which was defeated by a two-to-one margin on Election Day.

In an effort to get out the vote, parties are increasingly contributing money to issue committees that sponsor or oppose ballot initiatives if the parties think the measures will help bolster base-voter turnout. In California, the two major parties count as contributions to issue groups any money spent on direct mailings to party members in support of or opposing ballot propositions. For example, in the 1998 primary election, the state GOP, in late contributions alone, reported in-kind contributions of $1,100 to five issue committees sponsoring propositions on the statewide ballot. In addition, the party contributed $14,740 to the opponents of Proposition 223 (which limited school spending on administrative costs) and $29,740 to the proponents of Proposition 226 (the paycheck-protection initiative).[32] More substantially, Governor Wilson and the California Republican Party in 1998 were the top two contributors to Proposition 8, Governor Wilson's public education "reform" measure. Wilson contributed $499,485 and the California Republicans anted up $175,878 after Wilson came to the party and said, "I'd like you to kick in some money" for the campaign.[33] On the other side of the partisan divide, the Democratic State Central Committee of California, based in Sacramento, reported making in-kind and monetary contributions to issue committees in both the primary and general elections. A few weeks before the primary election, the state Democratic Party contributed $13,046 to the group opposed to Proposition 226, the antiunion paycheck-protection measure. The state party also spent $21,000 in the 1998 general election opposing Proposition 8 and more than $25,000 fighting Proposition 9, which would have recaptured costs from the utility industry.[34]

After the November 1998 election, a small controversy engulfed the Colorado Democratic Party over the DNC's role in two statewide issue campaigns. On October 27, 1998, the DNC, cochaired by Governor Romer, who was nearing the end of his term, funneled $60,000 to the issue committee supporting Referendum B and $20,000 to the opponents of Amendment 17, which would give tax credits for private education. Even though the state Democratic Party took no official stance on the two measures, during the campaign Romer pushed for Referendum B and fought against Amendment 17 in an effort to indirectly bolster turnout of registered Democrats. Perington disagreed with this strategy, commenting after the election that he "would rather have seen that money go to a get-out-the-vote effort," which "would have helped with a lot of candidates."[35]

There is clear evidence that elected officials and candidates—and, more importantly, political parties—are heavily involved in citizen lawmaking campaigns in California, Colorado, and other states. Political parties and top ticket candidates not only have contributed financially to ballot initiatives but also have sponsored and opposed measures as part of an electoral strategy to help mobilize the party faithful. Both the Republican and Democratic Parties understand that certain issues generate great interest from the electorate. As a result, the parties have strategically utilized citizen lawmaking to turn out their voters.

Exploiting "Wedge" Issues

Political parties may also promote ballot initiatives if it appears that they might help to split the opposing party's electoral base of support. During the 2002 elections in Florida, for example, Kendrick Meek, a Democratic state senator from Miami who was running for the U.S. House of Representatives, sponsored a ballot initiative, backed strongly by the Florida Democratic Party, that called for smaller class sizes in public schools. Beyond the substantive issue at hand, Meek and the Democrats hoped his initiative, Amendment 9, would raise doubts in the minds of traditionally Republican voters about Governor Jeb Bush's record on education during his first term in office. Bush's Democratic challenger, attorney Bill McBride, latched onto Amendment 9 in an effort to bolster his uphill campaign. The state Republican Party's executive board voted to "strongly oppose" the initiative. Governor Bush and other prominent Republicans, including retired U.S. senator Connie Mack, campaigned vigorously against the measure. For their part, Democrats enlisted the help of Vice President Al Gore, the 2000 Democratic presidential candidate, to call voters to support Amendment 9.[36] Although the initiative narrowly passed, with 52 percent of the vote, Bush easily won reelection, as McBride was unable to articulate a broader plan of education reform.[37] As a result, Amendment 9 failed to act as the Democrat's magic wedge issue to derail Bush's reelection bid.

Ballot measures' success as wedge issues has differed in California and Colorado. In California, there is evidence that the Republican Party aggressively promoted ballot measures as part of its effort to split the Democratic Party's base of support during the 1990s. These divisive initiatives, some of which were documented in the previous section, tend to receive extensive media coverage. But state parties (and their candidates) have not frequently used ballot measures for this purpose because they bring potential risks, as in the case of McBride's dogged effort to align himself with Amendment 9, which voters clearly perceived as not genuinely being his ballot measure.

What still remains the single-best example of a political party trying to exploit a ballot initiative to split its opposition's core supporters is the GOP's 1996 backing of Proposition 209, a divisive anti-affirmative-action measure officially known as the California Civil Rights Initiative. Proposition 209's resounding passage created shock waves that continue to reverberate across the country. Journalist Lydia Chavez's extended case study of the measure details how the Republican Party provided essential funding to Ward Connerly's organization in an effort to split Democratic support for President Clinton's reelection.[38] Disavowing his long-standing support for affirmative action, Governor Wilson and the California GOP offered financial support to help save the floundering campaign to end affirmative action. Wilson and his party envisioned the measure severing moderate Democratic supporters (particularly white men) from Clinton, turning them to Dole's camp. In a teleconference call with Newt Gingrich, Wilson claimed that Proposition 209 was "a partisan issue . . . that works strongly to our advantage [and] has every bit the potential to make a critical difference" to defeat Clinton.[39] For his part, Clinton did his best to shy away from the measure, discussing its substance only when prodded by the media. The Democrat's chief political strategist, Harold Ickes, strongly advised the president not to discuss affirmative action, a hot-button issue that might disaffect Clinton's white, ethnic, male supporters in California. While the relationship with the state GOP was never cozy, Connerly and his fellow backers of Proposition 209 received extensive direct funding from the state Republican Party and indirect support from the RNC. At Wilson's behest, the California Republican Party contributed $997,034 to the Yes on 209 campaign, with the Senate Republican Majority Committee contributing an additional $90,000. At the federal level, the RNC, in a noncoordinated effort, made substantial "independent expenditures" to produce and air television ads that championed Proposition 209.[40]

In Colorado, recent state party officials had a hard time recalling any recent initiatives that the parties tried to use as wedge issues in races for political office.[41] Don Bain, the state GOP chairman from 1994 to 1996, personally took a strong stance against party activity in ballot campaigns during his tenure, maintaining that, "the party should not get involved in issues at either the legislative or issue level." For Bain, the costs of the party becoming involved in citizen lawmaking clearly outweighed any gains because the process "brings out opposing special interests who galvanize against the issue or candidates."[42] The Colorado parties are less likely than those in California to become heavily invested in ballot contests as a result of the state's relatively weak levels of party identification; since the 1960s, more than one-third of the electorate has been registered as "unaffiliated."[43] Yet on rare occasions, Colorado parties are tempted to use ballot contests to drive a wedge into their opposition's base. The Republican Party, for example, actively promoted several socially divisive ballot measures in 1998—including two abortion measures and a school-choice-voucher measure—in an effort to draw conservative independents and Democrats to the polls. Party stalwarts such as Bain denounced the effort, saying that it would result in a backlash. Indeed, party leaders criticized the Republican involvement, which had been orchestrated by the party's outgoing chair, Steve Curtis, as mobilizing Democratic, independent, and even moderate Republican voters against the initiatives and, in turn, against Republican candidates.

Nevertheless, state as well as national parties may continue to try to exploit wedge initiatives for partisan advantage. During the 1990s, the two national parties made significant soft money transfer payments to nonpartisan 527 political organizations and not-for-profit corporations, which then funneled the contributions to issue groups promoting or opposing state ballot measures. While these payments are extremely difficult to trace, as they are not required to be reported to state election commissions or the Federal Elections Commission, the RNC, as documented in the previous chapter, transferred more than $4.5 million to Grover Norquist's "nonpartisan" organization, Americans for Tax Reform, for the explicit purpose of promoting statewide ballot measures in 1996.[44] The temptation for parties to use ballot initiatives as wedge issues seemingly will remain strong in states with strong, competitive parties and partisan electorates.

Raising Party Funds

In addition to lending financial support to committees sponsoring or opposing ballot measures to increase turnout or split the opposing party, the two major parties have found that taking positions on ballot measures that ideologically complement the parties' platforms can raise funds for their organizations. The California Republican Party aggressively pursued this strategy during the 1990s. In 1998, the party sent out more than 13 million pieces of direct mail to registered voters. Before several of the mailings, party officials approached the leaders of issue committees and explained the party's official position regarding the ballot measures. The party officials then asked, "Would you like to buy some support . . . at cut rates . . . in our mailing?" According to a high-ranking state GOP official, this was "a relatively new practice" for the party.[45] Issue committees that opposed the regulation of electric utilities (Proposition 9) and the tobacco tax for early childhood programs (Proposition 10) placed ads in the Republican mailers and "donated" money to the party to "offset" the cost of mailing. In addition, according to one high-placed party operative, the party has "netted money from proposition campaigns" by endorsing measures opposed by narrow special interests.[46]

In contrast, the California Democratic Party found that it could raise funds by avoiding an official stance on a measure. At its August 1998 ballot endorsement meeting, the Democratic Party backed seven of the eight issues to be decided at the general election; the lone exception was Proposition 5, the high-stakes initiative that allowed gaming on tribal lands. According to Democratic officials, "tons of Indians and union" members attended the meeting and voiced their respective support and opposition to Proposition 5. The party chairman refused to allow the 300-member executive board to vote on the matter because it was potentially a divisive issue for two core constituent groups. The decision to avoid voting on the measure was viewed largely as a "victory by the Indians," which led several tribes to contribute money to the state party.[47] But like California's Republicans, the Democrats also garnered contributions by endorsing ballot initiatives. The party officially opposed Proposition 9, the measure sponsored by progressive groups to recapture costs on electricity suppliers, and Proposition 8, Governor Wilson's public education reform measure. In return, the party received substantial contributions from several utility companies and the California Teachers Association.[48]

In Colorado, the parties have been less aggressive in courting contributions from initiative proponents or opponents. In 2002, however, executives overseeing the party's coordinated campaign voted to include the backers of Amendment 30, an Election Day registration ballot initiative, as part of the party's grassroots outreach to bring voters to the polls. As a result, the "Yes on 30" campaign slogan was prominently displayed on the party's GOTV literature, including its slate mailers and door hangers, as part of the effort to turn out core supporters. The inclusion of the ballot measure in the party's coordinated campaign came at a cost: the issue committee sponsoring Amendment 30 was required to kick in $25,000 to the state party's "pay to play" coordinated campaign.[49]

State party organizations in California and to a lesser extent in Colorado have become involved in the promotion and opposition of ballot measures for three interrelated reasons. Contrary to the expectations of several scholars, U.S. state (and even national) party organizations are entangled in the complex web of direct democracy. Party organizations are neither as impotent nor as irrelevant in the initiative process as it might at first seem. As they turn to the initiative to regain their strength, it is evident that initiatives are not "beyond party politics," as Shaun Bowler and Todd Donovan maintain.[50] In both direct and indirect ways, parties in California, Colorado, and a handful of other states utilize the initiative process to increase base turnout on Election Day, drive a wedge into the opposition's constituency, and raise financial contributions.

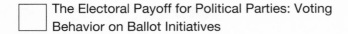

The Electoral Payoff for Political Parties: Voting Behavior on Ballot Initiatives

Although there is compelling evidence that parties are becoming more involved in ballot contests, does this heightened involvement translate into an electoral payoff for the parties? In other words, do citizens vote along party lines on ballot measures? Previous empirical evidence is decidedly mixed. In his seminal study, David Magleby found that voters tend to support or oppose propositions independent of their partisan leanings, relying instead on "ideological self-classification."[51] More recently, other scholars have reinforced the conventional wisdom that voting behavior on ballot initiatives is nonpartisan. Some scholars have argued that in direct legislation elections, "partisan cues are usually absent" because "campaigns are typically run by organizations that have different incentives than traditional political parties."[52] But research by Jack Citrin and his collaborators demonstrates that support for an "official English" initiative in California in 1986 was "strongly related to party and ideology." Registered Republicans were 27 percent more likely to vote for the measure than were registered Democrats.[53]

With respect to voting behavior on ballot questions, growing evidence indicates that political parties provide important cues for voters in many ballot measure elections. Recent empirical research finds that voters are capable of making rational decisions in direct democracy elections, even with limited information.[54] Scholars such as Arthur Lupia and Bowler and Donovan have found that voters can make decisions consistent with policy preferences in initiative elections by relying on available voter cues—such as the support or opposition by political parties, elected officials, political elites, interest groups, and the media.[55] Voters with higher education rely on more varied and diverse sources of information and thus are capable of making the most rational decisions, but even voters with less income and education can make informed decisions in initiative elections with very minimal information by relying on voter cues. For example, Bowler and Donovan find that with governance-related ballot measures, such as term limits for elected officials, partisan voters are particularly able to "respond to their party's interest over the course of an initiative campaign."[56]

To answer the question of party influence on voting behavior in issue elections, we examine initiatives on the California ballot between 1994 and 1998. California, the nation's largest and most diverse state and perhaps the pioneer in citizen lawmaking, provides a useful test case for the partisan nature of direct democracy elections. Historically, California has been a leader in the use of direct democracy, with more initiatives qualifying for the ballot over the past century than in any other state except Oregon.[57] The dramatic rise in the use and importance of ballot initiatives in the past three decades has altered the democratic process, with candidates and state and national parties increasingly compelled to debate divisive issues during elections.[58]

We explore the role of political parties in initiative elections by using both aggregate and individual survey data. Because we are interested in the political context in which voters make choices, we draw on the vast amount of aggregate data available to measure political, economic, and social context. Aggregate county-level data allow us to examine patterns of political party registration and voting on a series of ballot measures. We then use survey data to examine the relationship between self-identified political party affiliation and voter policy preferences at the individual level. While previous research on state politics and policy has relied on aggregate data or survey data, we gain theoretical leverage by combining these two levels of analysis.

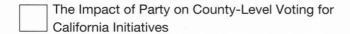

The Impact of Party on County-Level Voting for California Initiatives

As administrative arms of the state government, counties provide a useful unit of analysis for partisan behavior on ballot measures. In California, counties are also the direct providers of social services, with significant discretion over public policy. Historically, counties represent important political jurisdictions and voting blocs in California legislative politics. From 1930 to 1968, the California Senate was apportioned geographically, with roughly one vote per county. Counties have thus played an important role in California politics, comparable to the identity of states in the U.S. Senate. California counties today remain remarkably cohesive in their partisan composition. While studying counties has limitations, we believe it provides a useful lens for analyzing the impact of party politics in the initiative process.[59]

We analyze county-level voting patterns for the 13 statewide initiatives appearing on the June 1998 primary and November 1998 general election ballots. (We exclude referenda placed on the ballot by the legislature.) These initiatives cover a range of substantive policy issues, from political reform (term limits, political donations by unions), tax policy and bond issues, environmental policy, and animal-rights legislation to social policy, such as ending bilingual education in the public schools and child development. In each model, the dependent variable is the popular vote (measured as a percent) for the ballot initiatives at the county level. We examine whether support for the ballot initiatives is related to political party composition, measured by percent of registered Republicans (1998) at the county level. The models control for two competing explanations for policy adoptions. Economic conditions have been found to be important in initiative voting on tax and bond issues.[60] We measure prevailing economic conditions with 1998 county unemployment rates. Other research illustrates the importance of racial and ethnic composition in explaining public policy decisions.[61] To measure the demographic composition of a county, two indexes are created at the county level. One measures the size of the Latino, African American, and Asian American populations, and the other measures "white ethnic" diversity, using the size of the self-reported Greek, Hungarian, Italian, Polish, Portuguese, Russian, and Irish populations.[62]

A statistically significant relationship between Republican Party affiliation and voting for 11 of the 13 initiatives is found using bivariate correlations (data not shown). Based on these correlations, in 85 percent of the 1998 California initiative contests, political party affiliation is associated with county-level voting patterns. A series of ordinary least squares regressions are used to estimate the impact of Republican Party affiliation on the county-level vote in the 1998 ballot initiatives. As reported in tables A.12 and A.13 (see appendix), we find that party registration affects ballot initiative outcomes across a range of policy issues. The data show that political party registration is associated with the vote for 77 percent of the initiatives appearing on the 1998 California ballot, even after controlling for unemployment rates and racial diversity. Ten of the 13 initiatives have a statistically significant relationship between political party affiliation and the vote. Based on these findings, we conclude that at the aggregate level, partisanship within the electorate appears to be strongly related to the popular vote for a series of policies decided at the ballot box in California.[63]

Of the 10 propositions in which political party is a statistically significant predictor of the popular vote, the regression coefficient for registered Republicans is positive in 4 cases and negative in 6. Thus, 60 percent of the initiative contests in which party affiliation is important were "liberal" policies, and 40 percent were "conservative" policies. These findings emphasize the partisan nature of citizen-initiated measures on the ballot, which runs contrary to much of the literature on direct democracy. As expected, Republican Party affiliation at the county level is positively related to the vote for a limit on school district spending for administrative costs (Proposition 223), a U.S. constitutional amendment to limit congressional terms (Proposition 225), a limit on unions' political contributions (Proposition 226), and an end to bilingual education programs in public schools (Proposition 227). Also as expected, the percentage of registered Republicans is negatively related to the county-level vote for a ban on the use of traps and poisons in hunting animals (Proposition 4); gaming on Indian reservations (Proposition 5); tax credits to encourage pollutant-emission reductions (Proposition 7); a prohibition on the assessment of taxes, bonds, and surcharges to pay the costs of nuclear power plants borne by electric companies (Proposition 9); an additional tobacco surtax for state and county childhood-development programs (Proposition 10); and the authorization of local governments to enter into sales tax revenue-sharing agreements with local jurisdictions (Proposition 11).

The aggregate findings from California are not unique. In other states, party registration is a strong predictor of voting patterns on ballot measures. In 1996, for example, party registration was a significant and salient aggregate predictor of ballot measure voting in Colorado, Idaho, Michigan, and to a lesser degree Washington.[64] Using the same models to estimate the impact of Republican party registration on the county-level vote (data not shown), we find that party registration shapes the vote on 10 of the 18 initiatives on the November ballot in these four states. In Colorado, party registration was a significant predictor of the vote for 5 of the 8 ballot measures. Counties with high Republican registration were significantly more likely to oppose ballot measures banning trapping, regulating campaign finance, creating a state land trust, and allowing gambling in Trinidad, Colorado. Conversely, Republican-leaning counties were more likely than those with large numbers of registered Democrats to support a parental rights ballot measure that would have empowered parents to direct the upbringing and education of their children.[65] In Idaho, counties with higher levels of registered Republicans were statistically more likely to oppose an initiative banning the hunting of black bears with bait or hounds as well as a measure outlawing the disposal of nuclear waste. Interestingly, however, party affiliation did not help to predict the countywide vote on two seemingly partisan initiatives, one to limit property taxes and the other to limit congressional terms. Counties with heavy Republican registration in Michigan were less likely than Democratic strongholds to support an initiative calling for casino gambling in Detroit. Finally, in Washington, party registration was a significant predictor on 2 of 5 measures. Counties with a sizable number of registered Republicans were less likely than counties that were heavily Democratic to support an animal-protection ballot initiative as well as an initiative allowing gaming on Indian reservations. Party registration, however, was not a significant predictor for county voting patterns on a term-limits initiative or on two measures dealing with school vouchers and charter schools.

Political Party Affiliation and Initiative Voting Behavior

Is political party affiliation an important cue for voting on ballot initiatives at the individual level? Are political parties endorsing or even funding state ballot measures that are ideologically consistent with their party platform to increase turnout of partisan voters? We use exit poll survey data conducted by the Voter News Service in California to measure the importance of political party affiliation on support for a series of ballot initiatives and candidates on the ballot in the 1994 and 1996 California general elections.[66] We measure the impact of Democratic support for four ballot measures (and two candidate races), controlling for personal economic conditions, race/ethnicity, income, education, and gender. To measure how economic conditions affected vote choice, the survey asked respondents to rate their financial situation compared to one year previously. Those responding "worse" were coded as five, those responding "the same" were coded as three, and those responding "better" were coded as one. We used dichotomous variables to measure respondents' race/ethnicity and gender. We measure income by the total family income and education with an ordinal scale reflecting the highest degree received. The dependent variable in the statistical models is dichotomous and coded one for a vote in favor of the candidate or issue and zero otherwise.

We use separate logistic regression models to test voter support for two 1994 ballot initiatives, Proposition 186 (creating universal health care) and Proposition 187 (ending social services for illegal immigrants), and one candidate election (the vote for Governor Wilson). We also analyze two 1996 initiatives, Proposition 209 (ending affirmative action) and Proposition 215 (legalization of medical marijuana), and one candidate race (the vote for President Clinton). By analyzing voting in two consecutive elections, we examine the impact of partisan affiliation in a presidential or midterm election. By comparing across initiative and candidate races, we gain a better understanding of political parties' role in shaping voter preferences across election types, and by comparing across a series of diverse (liberal and conservative) ballot initiatives, we examine the impact of political party along a continuum of public policies.

In keeping with previous research, we find that political party affiliation in California appears to be the most salient predictor of voting behavior in direct democracy elections as well as in candidate races.[67] As table A.14 (see appendix) reveals, partisanship informs voting on ballot initiatives. In every candidate and issue election, self-reported Democratic Party affiliation is a statistically significant predictor of individual-level voting behavior. Democratic partisans were considerably more likely to vote for universal health care, legalization of medical marijuana, and President Clinton and were less likely to vote for ending affirmative action programs, ending social services for illegal immigrants, or Wilson's reelection, even after controlling for other factors. The consistency in the saliency of political party as a predictor of vote choice across candidate and issue elections provides evidence that partisanship and voting behavior on ballot measures are increasingly intertwined.

Conclusion

In 1918, Mary Parker Follett commented that "direct government will never succeed if operated from within the party organization."[68] Follett's observations mirrored those of other skeptics of the initiative process, including political scientist George Haynes. While "public-spirited citizens or associations may for a time attempt to set forth the records of candidates or to present the 'right' side of some burning issue," Haynes observed in 1907, well before the dramatic increase in the usage of citizen lawmaking during the following decade, "the party machine is equally active, and its activity is more persistent."[69] As this chapter documents, in California and in Colorado, the process of citizen lawmaking has been susceptible to the machinations of party elites. In both states, but to a larger degree in California, party organizations and their statewide candidates have been active players, albeit usually silent, in the initiative process. There is every indication, however, that party involvement in initiative campaigns will continue to become less covert, as was the case in Ohio and Florida in the 2002 general election.

In our portrayal of how political parties in California and Colorado have adapted to the institutional mechanism of direct legislation, we find that these political organizations employ three basic strategies. Parties use citizen lawmaking to mobilize partisan voter turnout, to drive a wedge into the opposing party's coalition, and to raise funds. While the parties' involvement in ballot campaigns is unquestionably driven by an instrumental goal of enacting or thwarting a particular public policy, parties are increasingly viewing the initiative as an educative process to achieve broader electoral goals. This electoral consideration, in turn, has the potential to net large returns: strong evidence shows that California voters follow distinct partisan lines in supporting and opposing ballot propositions across a wide range of policy issues.

Although political parties are certainly less central players than are interest groups in the process of citizen lawmaking, state (and increasingly national) parties are likely to continue to use the initiative process when doing so is to their strategic advantage. Party involvement should only grow in the wake of the McCain-Feingold campaign reform legislation. As the federal parties, no longer permitted to solicit or spend soft money contributions, scurry to dig new canals to divert the seemingly unlimited flow of contributions from wealthy individuals and corporate and union treasuries, parties likely will attempt to channel financial contributions into ballot campaigns in states with competitive candidate elections.[70] Ironically, participation in initiative campaigns has the potential to offset the declining party influence that is expected in the post-soft-money world of campaign finance, a development that runs counter to Progressive Era reformers' antiparty intentions. As Charles Mahtesian astutely observed during the 1990s, "Organized money moves inexorably toward where the action is, and these days, that place is the ballot as often as it is the statehouse."[71] Although the initiative process continues to be used primarily by citizen and interest groups as a means to pressure or circumvent state legislatures, party organizations—while perhaps not terribly fond of the plebiscitary process—clearly have come to appreciate the procedural power of direct democracy.

7 The Educative Possibilities and Limitations of Citizen Lawmaking

Summarizing the "historical legacy" of direct legislation, historian Thomas Goebel grouses that citizen lawmaking "has not lived up to the expectations of its advocates one century ago." On instrumental grounds alone, he contends that the initiative has not bridled corporate interests, which continue to dominate many state legislatures. In his impressive account of the adoption of direct democracy in America, Goebel maintains that in terms of substantive outcomes, citizen lawmaking "has only been yet another tool for business interests to achieve their goals." Though he musters no empirical evidence to bolster his claims, Goebel goes on to indict direct democracy on educative grounds. He contends that the initiative has not produced any positive secondary effects because it has not "contribute[d] in any meaningful way to a revival of democracy in America." According to Goebel, the initiative "has not empowered ordinary citizens, it has not increased political awareness or participation . . . and it has not reduced the power of special interests." He concludes his book on a pessimistic note, writing that "the historical analysis of direct democracy since its inception a century ago makes abundantly clear that the initiative and referendum have never served, and probably never will serve, as the means to strengthen democracy in America, to truly build a government by the people."[1]

Our research brings into stark relief the accuracy of some of these claims. Our book makes no effort to assess the instrumental merits of direct legislation in a normative or empirical sense. We do not attempt to evaluate the substantive public policies that result from direct legislation or to appraise how well citizen lawmaking approximates public opinion or keeps state legislatures in check. Shunning the standard instrumental perspective, which dominates most present-day studies, we have instead focused on the pedagogical impact of citizen lawmaking. What are the secondary, educative effects of direct democracy? Does the process of citizen lawmaking— irrespective of any substantive policy outcomes or preconceived notions regarding its populist foundations—have no measurable positive impact on democratic citizens and political organizations, as Goebel insists, or does direct democracy engender broader expressions of civic participation and democratic life?

In the preceding chapters, we have empirically evaluated citizen lawmaking's educative effects. We have critically examined how the process shapes individuals' attitudes and behaviors as well as how interest groups and political parties have adapted to its institutionalization. Situating our inquiry into direct democracy within the larger historical debate, we assess whether the process of citizen lawmaking operates in accordance with Progressive Era reformers' pedagogical intentions. Above all, the Progressive reformers were educators. One of those reformers, Frederic C. Howe, a social reformer and commissioner of immigration at the Port of New York, touted the "educative influence of referendum elections on measures initiated by the people themselves." Ballot initiatives, Howe told the learned audience at the annual meeting of the Academy of Political Science soon after the 1912 elections, "lead to constant discussion, to a deeper interest in government, and to a psychological conviction that a government is in effect the people themselves. And this is the greatest gain of all. It has been said that the jury is the training school of democracy."[2] Have the optimistic assumptions about direct legislation by Progressives such as Howe been borne out? Are the contemporary educative effects of citizen lawmaking in keeping with Progressive reformers' expectations, or has direct democracy not lived up to its potential, as Goebel would have it?

We find that with respect to voter turnout, civic engagement, and political efficacy, direct democracy does indeed have positive effects on citizens, consistent with democratic norms advanced in the Progressive Era. Based on national survey data, our research indicates that citizens living in states with frequent ballot initiatives are more motivated to vote, are more interested in and better informed about politics, and express more confidence in government responsiveness than do citizens living in noninitiative states. Indeed, we even find that citizen lawmaking has a positive effect on political discussion. While we hesitate to equate this heightened political awareness with some Rousseauian notion of discursive deliberation, we find, like some other scholars, that the initiative process has a significant effect on citizens' attitudes and behaviors. The findings based on the survey data are bolstered by those based on 50-state aggregate data. States with more initiatives on the ballot have higher voter turnout rates over the past quarter century in both midterm and presidential elections. Similarly, we find that the use of ballot initiatives is strongly associated with higher state social capital.

Our positive findings, however, vary with electoral context. Ballot initiatives appear to have the greatest impact in low-information elections such as midterm or noncompetitive presidential contests, when issue campaigns are less likely to compete with media coverage of candidate races. We suggest that initiatives have these positive educative effects because they provide voters with additional political information. Consistent with the research by scholars probing the political psychology of direct democracy contests, we agree that voters can use information shortcuts to participate effectively in the democratic process.[3] In addition, initiative efforts can provide information via emotional media campaigns. The stark contrast of opponent and proponent campaign messages, particularly with high-salience ballot measures, may be an ideal forum for learning about politics and stimulating action.[4] Harold Lasswell argued during the 1930s that issues with a "triple appeal"—those appealing to an individual's passions, rational reason, and morality—will likely lead to action.[5] Not merely the information but also the format in which the information is conveyed often appear to be important.

The beneficial effect of direct participation in governmental decision making on the democratic education of citizens is no mere coincidence. Our data, which are drawn from multiple sources and span numerous decades, reveal a consistent pattern. The educative effects of ballot initiatives on broad levels of political participation, civic engagement, and confidence in government may be as important for American democracy as the initiative's direct effect on public policy. Our analysis of the initiative's effects on individuals bolsters normative claims by theorists who advocate varying forms of participatory democracy, from intimate, face-to-face deliberation to technology-driven digital democracy.[6]

What about the impact of ballot initiatives on interest groups and political parties? Our research reveals that the initiative has distinct educative effects on political organizations, but not always in ways consistent with Progressive Era reformers' expectations. Interest groups and political parties do not sit passively on the sidelines as some of the most important and often most controversial public policy decisions in the states are decided on the ballot. Instead, these political organizations are active and integral players in the game of direct democracy.

On the upside, we confirm other research demonstrating that states with substantial initiative use have more membership (citizen) groups as well as not-for-profit interest groups.[7] We also find that citizens who are more exposed to initiative contests have a greater propensity to contribute money to interest groups (likely to be membership and nonprofit groups), but these citizens are not more likely to give money to political parties or candidates. Together, these findings bolster the contention that initiative elections help to mobilize citizen-led interest groups, in effect balancing the economic interests that dominate many state legislatures. We also find, however, that citizen lawmaking has failed to wholly bridle corporate special interests, which early reformers viewed as the scourge of state legislatures. Contrary to the expectations of Progressive Era advocates, high levels of initiative use may actually lead to the registration of greater numbers of associations (business organizations) than low (or no) use of citizen lawmaking. We also report how many of these associations as well as nonprofit and corporate actors are learning to use the process to fortify their electoral and legislative upper hand in the states. In short, economic interests have responded to ballot initiatives and are attempting to use the process for narrow benefits.[8] Overall, we find that the initiative has positive implications for the diversity and representation of state interest group systems, although some interest groups use the process as a powerful tool for maintaining the balance of interest group power.

In our study of party involvement in ballot campaigns in California and Colorado as well as a few other states, we find that party organizations are becoming inextricably involved in many ballot campaigns. Rather than viewing initiatives instrumentally, as a way to pass or defeat a substantive piece of legislation, party organizations engage in citizen lawmaking for its procedural effects. Parties have learned that ballot measures have a real educative value because they can spur citizens to vote, divide the opposing party's core constituents, and generate contributions to the party. Even though state and local party organizations today are but shells of the political machines of bygone years, citizen lawmaking clearly has proven to be an ineffective instrument for reining in parties. Indeed, direct democracy may strengthen and energize state and local parties, which, ironically, some political scientists argue is a positive development and a corrective to a misguided Progressive Era reform.[9]

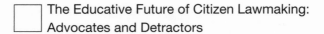 The Educative Future of Citizen Lawmaking:
Advocates and Detractors

While the number and topics of statewide ballot measures will surely continue to ebb and flow in the coming years, the institution of citizen lawmaking is here to stay. Over the past few decades, the popularly of direct voting by electorates has sharply increased. Since 1980 more than 600 statewide direct votes have occurred, as well as thousands more at the city and county levels. In the 1990s, voters considered more than 350 statewide initiatives, the most measures on the ballot in a decade since the Progressive Era.[10] Direct democracy continues to roar along as a growth industry.[11] As journalist Peter Schrag has warned, in his home state of California and elsewhere, the initiative "has not just been integrated into the regular governmental-political system, but has begun to replace it."[12] California's extensive usage of direct democracy may be extreme in the American states, but the process remains alive and well in many other states. Even in states without the initiative, polling has become pervasive, with politicians, political parties, and the media continually conducting surveys to gauge public opinion. The U.S. public has grown accustomed to being consulted on a regular basis.

Nearly a century after its adoption, direct legislation remains celebrated for its instrumental effects, with advocates pointing to the plebiscitary process's substantive policy outcomes. Indeed, ballot initiatives—whether or not they succeed at the polls—make national headlines because they are designed to significantly modify public policy. News stories celebrating bold initiatives—abridging gay rights, ending affirmative action, limiting taxes, or the successful attempt to enshrine the rights of pigs in a state constitution (as was the case in Florida in 2002)—make for good copy. Irrespective of their results, as bizarre or punitive or populist as they may be, citizen lawmaking also makes a compelling story from a democratic standpoint. The process, theoretically at least, is one of the most pristine forms of governance that exists in the states, as power surges directly from the only legitimate fountain of authority—*the people*.[13] Americans remain enamored of the process from an instrumental perspective, generally according it popular approval.

There are, of course, staunch critics of the initiative, the loudest voices coming from the ranks of the elites, including elected officials. Detractors tend to criticize the outcomes of citizen lawmaking, contending among other things that ballot measures often harm minorities, are influenced by vested interests and money, and are written with confusing language, leading to voter ignorance. As constitutional law scholar Harry Scheiber writes,

The record of plebiscitary democracy has evoked from scholarly and lay commentators alike reactions ranging from serious concern to outright disillusionment, and oftentimes sheer despair. There is a singular irony in the content of the recent caveats and complaints: the direct ballot process today is plagued by the very

same ills as the problems that inspired the reformers who originally championed direct democracy during the Populist and then
the Progressive movements of the turn of the century down to the
First World War. The assertions of those reformers that special
interests had perverted the legislative process, and that government had been undermined and the will of the people thwarted,
are echoed today by the critics of direct democracy.[14]

Furthermore, those dubious of the process charge that the ad hoc
policies that result from citizen lawmaking have hamstrung if not
completely debilitated state legislatures' policymaking powers.[15]

Interestingly, what unites most contemporary observers—both
defenders and critics of the initiative—is a primary interest in the
substantive outcomes of citizen lawmaking. While certainly important, this results-oriented view of the process is rather myopic and is
less panoramic than that of many Progressive Era reformers. Most
notably, contemporary portrayals of citizen lawmaking, condemna-
tory and laudatory alike, have neglected to take into account the
educational impact that the initiative process may have on citizens
and political organizations. Rather than assessing the tangible outcomes of citizen lawmaking, our book is an attempt to shift the focus
of scholarly and journalistic inquiry. By continuing the dialogue
begun by the Progressive Era reformers and scholars who first
identified the democratic consequences that might derive from the
initiative process, we have provided a contemporary snapshot of the
educative effects of citizen lawmaking.

Our findings on the educative effects of direct legislation provide
grist for the mills of both proponents and opponents of citizen lawmaking. Advocates of citizen lawmaking will likely be heartened by
our study, finding redemption for the Progressive Era reformers who
sought to bring government under the people's control. If the presence of ballot initiatives enhances voter turnout, civic engagement,
knowledge, and confidence in government, proponents of plebiscitary democracy will likely promote alternative models of participatory governance, including a national referendum and Internet voting.[16] Others will likely tout citizen lawmaking as a means to increase

social capital and reinvigorate the voice of the people. While we intentionally avoid the normative questions of whether ballot initiatives derail representative democracy by weakening legislative institutions, our research suggests that citizen lawmaking may indirectly strengthen American democracy.

Critics of the initiative, too, will likely draw their own conclusions from our study, fixating on our finding that although citizen lawmaking drives voters to the polls, engenders political knowledge, and reinforces civic engagement, it does not correct the existing inequalities in electoral representation—namely, lower levels of participation and civic engagement in the public sphere by the less educated, less partisan, and less affluent. Detractors will note with some contentment that while states with higher initiative use have mobilized citizen interest groups (membership and nonprofit), the process has not substantially altered vested special interests' control of state legislatures. It fact, we present evidence that initiative use leads to greater numbers of economic groups (peak associations) in the states. Critics will surely seize on the fact that political parties—once the bane of Progressive reformers—have learned to use the initiative process to fortify partisan politics. Finally, those who remain skeptical about the deliberative potential of citizen lawmaking will likely argue that the initiative has yet to reawaken a spirit of democracy in America.

New Directions for Research on the Educative Effects of Direct Democracy

Our research does not constitute a comprehensive study of the indirect, educative effects of citizen lawmaking but merely represents a launching point, historically and theoretically grounded in the Progressive Era, for a scholarly and practical discourse on the initiative's procedural dynamics and pedagogical effects. Other secondary effects of citizen lawmaking have not been broached here. Most notably, little is known about how the process (as opposed to the much-discussed outcomes) may tyrannize minorities by dividing citizens along racial, ethnic, religious, and geographic lines during the periods leading up to and following contentious votes on ballot questions.[17] Do citizens living in states with more frequent ballot initiatives, for example, have correspondingly less tolerance for minorities than do citizens in states with no or low initiative usage?[18] Conversely, does the initiative process strengthen and complement representative democracy, creating more "bridging" social capital, in Robert Putnam's words?[19] Scholars have just begun to assess these tricky questions, attempting to flesh out whether the process of citizen lawmaking has any residual effects on individuals' attitudes toward members of various groups.

More research remains to be done in explaining the effects of ballot initiatives on voter turnout. Even though we know that turnout increases with the presence of ballot initiatives, a dearth of scholarly studies examine the linkage between voter turnout and support of or opposition to specific candidates on Election Day.[20] For example, did Latinos in California who had not previously been active voters become mobilized to vote against Governor Pete Wilson when he helped to sponsor a 1994 ballot initiative (Proposition 187) aimed at limiting the rights of illegal immigrants? Similarly, did Florida's African Americans and Hispanics vote in 2002 for Democratic gubernatorial candidate Bill McBride after he came out in support of Amendment 9, an initiative calling for class-size reduction in public schools that was intended to raise questions about Governor Jeb Bush's education record? Researchers have just begun to scratch at the surface of these questions.[21]

Finally, although our study finds that along several measures of civic engagement, citizen lawmaking appears to enhance democratic norms, the question remains to what degree the process of citizen lawmaking can deliver these goods. Political theorist Simone Chambers argues powerfully that unless "carefully designed," ballot measures may "undermine meaningful participation" because the "inflexibility" and "irreversibility" of necessarily majoritarian ballot measures may "not do a good enough job representing the views of 'We the People.'" For Chambers, the initiative affords citizens the right to participate but not necessarily in a meaningful way, since ballot campaigns are often devoid of "dialogic" deliberation.[22] This deliberative concern of democratic theory mimics the concerns that some direct legislation critics voiced a century ago. While recognizing that direct legislation could have an "educative effect on the people," Lord James Bryce, in a revised edition of his classic *American Commonwealth,* warned in 1910 that pure democracy "refers matters needing much elucidation by debate to the determination of those who cannot, on account of their numbers, meet together for discussion, and many of whom may have never thought about the matter."[23] Designing ballot contests to become more dialogic and engaging for an ever-expanding electorate seems to be imperative if the full aspirations of Progressive Era reformers are ever to be realized.

The Past as Prologue

Although this book does not address these complementary educative aspects of citizen lawmaking, our research has implications for the larger unresolved question of the initiative's impact on representative democracy. One of the major political debates in the coming decades will concern the relative merits of direct versus representative democracy. Our findings suggest that the indirect, educative byproducts of direct democracy may better reflect the goals of Progressive reformers than some of the substantive outcomes of the process do. While citizen lawmaking is certainly no panacea for all that ails U.S. civic participation and democratic experience, the initiative has some tangible institutional effects on citizens' attitudes and behaviors as well as on political organizations' activities. Our analyses of several types of empirical data find that the initiative process has beneficial, educative value that measurably shapes the contours of American democratic life, just as Progressive Era reformers had envisioned. With respect to indirect effects on individuals, our analysis supports the Progressive Era contention that citizen lawmaking promotes voter turnout, civic engagement and political knowledge, and confidence in government, but the positive effects may be less dramatic with respect to reining in interest groups' political power and diminishing political parties' presence. Irrespective of the substantive outcomes of ballot measures, then, the process of citizen lawmaking may in some ways help to reduce the democratic deficit in the United States.

Whether the educative value of the process of citizen lawmaking outweighs some of the negative ramifications of the initiative remains a matter of debate. We do not argue that the initiative will cure all that ails representative democracy, though other commentators increasingly take this position. Although representative democracy is the basic structure of all western governments, it is accompanied today by a growing demand for direct popular control of governmental affairs. Some nonprofit organizations are pressing for more discussion of a national forum that would enable citizens to voice their preferences on policy issues, with specific calls for a U.S. national initiative or referendum process. A recent article in the *Economist* contends that "the financial corruption and lobbying by special interests that plague American democracy are harder to stamp out in a representative system than they would be in a system with more direct voter involvement." Financial interests clearly have tried to manipulate many statewide ballot contests, but according to the article, a growing number of people believe that "it is hard to bribe an entire electorate, or even to mislead it for very long, if there is a free flow of information and open discussion."[24] Public opinion polls show that large majorities in Europe as well as in the United States favor national referenda.[25] A 1997 Field Poll found that California voters favor a nationwide initiative by 67 percent, while a 1994 national survey by Americans Talk Issues found that 64 percent of Americans support having national referenda on major issues. Another survey by Rasmussen Research in 1998 found an identical 64 percent in favor of a national initiative.[26] In his study of direct democracy, *Washington Post* columnist David Broder reports that in every American state he visited, the initiative process was viewed as sacrosanct. Although he disagreed with this opinion, Broder predicts that before long, "the converging forces of technology and public opinion [will] coalesce in a political movement for a national initiative—to allow the public to substitute the simplicity of majority rule by referendum for what must seem to many frustrated Americans the arcane, ineffective, out-of-date model of the Constitution."[27]

These sentiments are not new. The call for national initiative and referendum in the United States was articulated by Progressive reformers a century ago. In May 1908, before Teddy Roosevelt and Woodrow Wilson (somewhat reluctantly) touted the virtues of direct democracy on the hustings in 1912, the U.S. Senate deliberated the establishment of a national system of initiative and referendum. Senate Bill 7208 provided "for a modern system whereby the voters of the United States may instruct their National Representatives," and Senate Joint Resolution 94 invited "the cooperation of the States in the establishment of a national initiative and referendum."[28] While neither of those measures made it out of committee to a floor vote, Congress continues periodically to address the merits of a national system of initiative and referendum. The last serious development occurred during the late 1970s and early 1980s. Congressman Richard Gephardt of Missouri proposed a national advisory referendum, contending in 1980 that "when people are given clear choices, the evidence points to increased participation in the democratic process."[29] Alternative designs to expand direct democracy— spurred by the rising expectations of an educated public for whom individual choice is an important value and by the seemingly endless possibilities of information technology—once again challenge the current structure of representative government.

Throughout this book we have held up the historical record as a yardstick, measuring the Progressive Era wisdom against contemporary reality of the educative effects of citizen lawmaking. During that celebrated age of reform, scholars, reformers, legislators, and the general public vigorously discussed the expectations and limitations of citizen lawmaking. By examining empirically some of the normative claims advanced during the Progressive Era, we have reevaluated this enduring debate over the pedagogical implications of the initiative process. Direct democracy is certainly no palliative for America's democratic deficit, but if history be our guide, the educative effects of citizen lawmaking may provide renewed excitement about the possibilities for democratic governance.

Appendix

TABLE A.1. Impact of Ballot Initiatives on Voter Turnout 1972–2000 Presidential Elections

Variables	Usage of the Initiative Process			Quadratic Model of Initiative Use		
	β (PCSE)		p-value	β (PCSE)		p-value
Number of Initiatives on State Ballot$_{i,t}$	.197	(.062)	**.001**	.50 (.141)		**.000**
Number of Initiatives on State Ballot Squared$_{i,t}$				−.026	(.012)	**.023**
Southern State$_{i,t}$	**−5.913**	**(1.03)**	**.000**	**−5.865**	**(1.031)**	**.000**
Senate Election$_{i,t}$	.675	(.658)	.305	.667	(.671)	.320
Gubernatorial Election$_{i,t}$	.131	(.571)	.819	.108	(.567)	.849
Percent High School Graduate or Higher$_{i,t}$	−.024	(.052)	.643	−.028	(.053)	.589
State Racial Diversity$_{i,t}$	**−21.123**	**(2.587)**	**.000**	**−20.673**	**(2.512)**	**.000**
Income Inequality (Gini coefficients)$_{i,t}$	−2.237 (17.732)		.900	−2.481 (17.381)		.886
Registration Requirement (Closing Date)$_{i,t}$	**−.148**	**(.025)**	**.000**	**−.152**	**(.025)**	**.000**
Constant	**67.29**	**(8.959)**	**.000**	**67.485**	**(8.787)**	**.000**
Number of Groups (i)	50			50		
Observations per group	8			8		
R-Squared	.60			.60		
Wald Chi-Square	775.58		**.000**	844.66		**.000**
N	400			400		

Source: For number of initiatives appearing on state ballots; National Conference of State Legislatures (1998, 2000, 2002) and the Initiative and Referenda Institute, Washington, DC (1970–96).

Note: Time series cross-sectional data for the fifty states. Unstandardized regression coefficients with panel corrected standard errors (PCSE) in parentheses. Coefficients in **boldface** are statistically significant at .05 probability or lower using a two-tailed test. The variable i contains the unit to which the observations belong, in this case state number, and controls for variation in turnout rates between the states.

TABLE A.2.   Impact of Ballot Initiatives on Voter Turnout 1970–2002 Midterm Elections

Variables	Usage of the Initiative Process			Quadratic Model of Initiative Use		
	β (PCSE)		p-value	β (PCSE)		p-value
Number of Initiatives on State Ballot$_{i,t}$	.576	(.104)	.000	1.164	(.257)	.000
Number of Initiatives on State Ballot Squared$_{i,t}$				−.058	(.023)	.013
Southern State$_{i,t}$	−6.827	(1.09)	.000	−6.632	(1.128)	.000
Senate Election$_{i,t}$	2.077	(.813)	.011	2.014	(.832)	.016
Gubernatorial Election$_{i,t}$	1.483	(.661)	.025	1.538	(.673)	.022
Percent High School Graduate or Higher$_{i,t}$	.076	(.050)	.128	.070	(.05)	.160
State Racial Diversity$_{i,t}$	−17.595	(2.249)	.000	−16.822	(2.189)	.000
Income Inequality (Gini Coefficients)$_{i,t}$	−65.279	(17.654)	.000	−66.565	(17.577)	.000
Registration Requirement (Closing Date)$_{i,t}$	−.105	(.022)	.000	−.112	(.024)	.000
Constant	66.407	(7.069)	.000	66.957	(7.007)	.000
Number of Groups (i)	50			50		
Observations per group	9			9		
R-Squared	.55			.56		
Wald Chi-Square	430.64		.000	484.56		.000
N	450			450		

Source: For number of initiatives appearing on state ballots, National Conference of State Legislatures (1998, 2000, 2002) and the Initiative and Referenda Institute, Washington, DC (1970–96).

Note: Time series cross-sectional data for the fifty states. Unstandardized regression coefficients with panel corrected standard errors (PCSE) in parentheses. Coefficients in **boldface** are statistically significant at .05 probability or lower using a two-tailed test. The variable i contains the unit to which the observations belong, in this case state number, and controls for variation in turnout rates between the states.

TABLE A.3.　Impact of Ballot Initiatives on the Probability of Voting, 1996, 1998, 2000, Individual-Level Survey Data

Variables	1996 β (SE)	1996 p-value	1998 β (SE)	1998 p-value	2000 β (SE)	2000 p-value
Number of Initiatives on Ballot	**.023 (.014)**	**.099**	**.045 (.020)**	**.028**	−.011 (.021)	.602
State Racial Diversity	**−.885 (.484)**	**.067**	**−1.112 (.468)**	**.017**	**−.871 (.480)**	**.070**
Strong Democrat	.109 (.186)	.558	**.911 (.189)**	**.000**	**.779 (.215)**	**.000**
Strong GOP	−.072 (.205)	.723	**1.632 (.268)**	**.000**	**1.055 (.297)**	**.000**
Independent	−.235 (.233)	.313	.017 (.225)	.939	**−.759 (.208)**	**.000**
Age	**.011 (.004)**	**.006**	**.053 (.004)**	**.000**	**.034 (.004)**	**.000**
Female	.186 (.133)	.163	−.210 (.137)	.125	−.039 (.146)	.788
Hispanic	.303 (.254)	.232	.235 (.244)	.335	−.252 (.276)	.362
African American	.123 (.217)	.568	.116 (.221)	.600	.359 (.246)	.145
Education	.027 (.043)	.532	**.400 (.046)**	**.000**	**.393 (.056)**	**.000**
Income	**.072 (.010)**	**.000**	.001 (.009)	.904	**.084 (.026)**	**.001**
Internet Access	**.591 (.175)**	**.001**	.259 (.158)	.102	**.829 (.171)**	**.000**
Constant	.494 (.359)	.169	**−3.919 (.389)**	**.000**	**−2.811 (.405)**	**.000**
Pseudo R-Square	.0630		.2100		.1941	
LR Chi-Square (df = 12)	**94.77**	**.000**	348.46	**.000**	290.22	**.000**
N	1,376		1,202		1,339	

Source: 1996, 1998, and 2000 American National Election Studies: Postelection Survey, Inter-University Consortium for Social and Political Research, Ann Arbor, MI.

Note: Unstandardized logistic regression coefficients, standard errors in parentheses. Coefficients in **bold** are statistically different from zero at the .1 level using a two-tailed test.

TABLE A.4. Impact of Ballot Initiatives on the Probability of Voting, 1992, Individual-Level Survey Data

1992 Variables	β (SE)	$p > |z|$
Number of Initiatives on Ballot	.202 (.070)	.004
State Racial Diversity	−.751 (.342)	.028
Strong Democrat	.778 (.183)	.000
Strong GOP	.851 (.219)	.000
Independent	−.289 (.197)	.142
Age	.028 (.004)	.000
Female	.090 (.116)	.437
Hispanic	−.490 (.273)	.073
African American	−.070 (.222)	.752
Education	.231 (.029)	.000
Income	.189 (.033)	.000
Political Interest	.496 (.044)	.000
Constant	−6.173 (.519)	.000
Pseudo R–Square	.347	
LR Chi-Square (df = 12)	610.933	.000
N	2371	

Source: 1992 Senate Election Study, Inter-University Consortium for Social and Political Research, Ann Arbor, MI.

Note: Unstandardized logistic regression coefficients, standard errors in parentheses. Coefficients in **bold** are statistically different from zero at the .1 level using a two-tailed test.

TABLE A.5. Impact of Ballot Initiatives on Political Knowledge, Individual-Level Survey Data

Variables	1996 β (SE)	1996 p-value	1998 β (SE)	1998 p-value	2000 β (SE)	2000 p-value
Number of Initiatives on Ballot	.021 (.011)	.066	.006 (.015)	.671	.023 (.015)	.125
Network TV	.051 (.021)	.018	.072 (.020)	.000	.069 (.020)	.001
Newspaper	.071 (.020)	.000	.108 (.019)	.000	.093 (.019)	.000
Internet Election News	−.009 (.209)	.963	1.165 (.188)	.000	.248 (.121)	.040
Strong Democrat	.332 (.145)	.023	−.091 (.145)	.531	.350 (.137)	.011
Strong GOP	.525 (.165)	.002	−.151 (.177)	.394	.475 (.158)	.003
Independent	−.354 (.204)	.083	−.387 (.176)	.028	−.724 (.183)	.000
Age	.005 (.003)	.098	−.004 (.003)	.156	.010 (.003)	.007
Female	−.684 (.109)	.000	−.086 (.105)	.415	−.953 (.105)	.000
Hispanic	−.049 (.206)	.810	−.161 (.186)	.389	−.856 (.222)	.000
African American	−1.277 (.184)	.000	−.267 (.170)	.117	−.714 (.185)	.000
Political Efficacy	.137 (.045)	.003	.016 (.026)	.527	.065 (.023)	.006
Political Interest	.414 (.084)	.000	.256 (.039)	.000	.299 (.041)	.000
Education	.458 (.037)	.000	−.005 (.032)	.861	.406 (.038)	.000
Income	−.081 (.035)	.022	−.013 (.029)	.635	.115 (.045)	.011
Income Squared	.003 (.001)	.020	.003 (.001)	.009	−.003 (.002)	.095
Pseudo R-Square	.1121		.0674		.1479	
LR Chi-Square (df = 17)	474.93	.000	292.47	.000	711.94	.000
N	1207		1184		1321	

Source: 1996, 1998, and 2000 American National Election Studies: Postelection Survey, Inter-University Consortium for Social and Political Research, Ann Arbor, MI.

Note: Unstandardized ordered logistic regression coefficients, standard errors in parentheses. Coefficients in **bold** are statistically different from zero at the .1 level using a two-tailed test.

TABLE A.6.   Impact of Ballot Initiatives on Political Interest, Individual-Level Survey Data

Variables	1996 β (SE)	1996 p-value	1998 β (SE)	1998 p-value	2000 β (SE)	2000 p-value
Number of Initiatives on Ballot	**.018 (.011)**	**.100**	.031 (.016)	.054	.018 (.016)	.277
Network TV	**.205 (.023)**	**.000**	**.144 (.021)**	**.000**	**.193 (.022)**	**.000**
Newspaper	**.075 (.022)**	**.001**	**.151 (.021)**	**.000**	**.045 (.021)**	**.031**
Internet Election News	.232 (.226)	.303	**.526 (.187)**	**.005**	**.677 (.134)**	**.000**
Strong Democrat	**.945 (.157)**	**.000**	.047 (.155)	.759	**.623 (.152)**	**.000**
Strong GOP	**1.327 (.180)**	**.000**	.100 (.185)	.591	**1.081 (.186)**	**.000**
Independent	**−.572 (.223)**	**.010**	−.052 (.192)	.787	**−.445 (.185)**	**.016**
Age	.002 (.004)	.545	.005 (.003)	.150	**.011 (.004)**	**.003**
Female	**−.315 (.116)**	**.007**	.034 (.113)	.766	−.158 (.112)	.160
Hispanic	.139 (.210)	.510	.196 (.185)	.289	**.421 (.223)**	**.058**
African American	**.356 (.196)**	**.068**	**.442 (.184)**	**.016**	**.485 (.192)**	**.011**
Political Efficacy	**.057 (.029)**	**.048**	−.017 (.028)	.550	**−.076 (.026)**	**.004**
Education	**.190 (.039)**	**.000**	**.063 (.035)**	**.072**	**.137 (.041)**	**.001**
Income	.001 (.009)	.890	**.022 (.008)**	**.006**	.031 (.017)	.074
Pseudo R-Square	.1254		.0692		.1265	
LR Chi-Square (df = 15)	**318.70**	**.000**	**173.27**	**.000**	**340.77**	**.000**
N	1216		1197		1333	

Source: 1996, 1998, and 2000 American National Election Studies: Postelection Survey, Inter-University Consortium for Social and Political Research, Ann Arbor, MI.

Note: Unstandardized ordered logistic regression coefficients, standard errors in parentheses. Coefficients in **bold** are statistically different from zero at the .1 level using a two-tailed test.

TABLE A.7. Impact of Ballot Initiatives on Political Discussion, Individual-Level Survey Data

Variables	1996 β (SE)	1996 p-value	1998 β (SE)	1998 p-value	2000 β (SE)	2000 p-value
Number of Initiatives on Ballot	**.009 (.004)**	**.017**	.007 (.005)	.199	−.002 (.004)	.590
Network TV	**.037 (.008)**	**.000**	−.012 (.007)	.089	**.040 (.005)**	**.000**
Newspaper	.012 (.008)	.129	.002 (.007)	.737	**.030 (.005)**	**.000**
Internet Election News	−.042 (.084)	.620	.007 (.064)	.907	**.221 (.031)**	**.000**
Strong Democrat	**.237 (.053)**	**.000**	.019 (.052)	.720	**.131 (.036)**	**.000**
Strong GOP	**.269 (.054)**	**.000**	−.124 (.066)	.060	**.187 (.039)**	**.000**
Independent	−.105 (.102)	.305	**−.146 (.068)**	**.031**	**−.134 (.052)**	**.010**
Age	.001 (.001)	.332	−.004 (.001)	.720	**−.003 (.001)**	**.008**
Female	−.058 (.042)	.164	**.107 (.039)**	**.005**	.009 (.028)	.739
Hispanic	**−.206 (.091)**	**.023**	**−.233 (.070)**	**.001**	.037 (.055)	.500
African American	**−.171 (.079)**	**.029**	.055 (.060)	.353	**−.112 (.051)**	**.028**
Political Efficacy	−.006 (.010)	.582	.008 (.009)	.364	.009 (.006)	.124
Education	**.033 (.014)**	**.018**	.013 (.012)	.257	**.046 (.010)**	**.000**
Income	.000 (.003)	.943	**.010 (.003)**	**.000**	**.019 (.004)**	**.000**
Pseudo R–Square	.0282		.0122		.0630	
LR Chi-Square (df = 15)	**119.37**	**.000**	**53.96**	**.000**	**442.41**	**.000**
N	951		1194		1317	

Source: 1996, 1998, and 2000 American National Election Studies: Postelection Survey, Inter-University Consortium for Social and Political Research, Ann Arbor, MI.

Note: Unstandardized Poisson regression coefficients, standard errors in parentheses. Coefficients in **bold** are statistically different from zero at the .1 level using a two-tailed test.

TABLE A.8.   Impact of Ballot Initiatives on State Social Capital

Variables	State Social Capital Index	
	β (SE)	p-value
Average Number of Initiatives on State Ballots (1970–92)	**.212 (.10)**	.033
State Racial Diversity, 1990	**−1.506 (.60)**	.016
Open Primary	**.386 (.19)**	.044
Median Household Income, 1990	**.000 (.00)**	.005
Public Opinion/Ideology	**−.024 (.01)**	.094
Percentage High School Graduates, 1990	.005 (.02)	.785
Percentage Metropolitan, 1990	**−.014 (.01)**	.013
District-Level Competition	**.018 (.01)**	.026
Constant	**−2.07 (1.21)**	.096
Adj. R-Square	.6321	
F	10.88	.000
N	47	

Source: Dependent variable overall social capital index for the 50 states from Bowling Alone Web site: <www.bowlingalone.com>.

Note: Unstandardized ordinary least squares regression coefficients, standard errors in parentheses. Coefficients in **bold** are statistically different from zero at the .1 level using a two-tailed test. Hawaii, Alaska, and Nebraska excluded because of missing data.

TABLE A.9. Impact of Ballot Initiatives on Attitudes about Government Responsiveness, 1988–98

Variables	External Political Efficacy Index	
	β (SE)	p-value
Number of Initiatives on Ballot	**.061 (.032)**	.05
Divided Government	−.033 (.060)	.58
State Racial Diversity	−.082 (.152)	.59
California Resident	−.152 (.147)	.30
Strong Democrat	.073 (.052)	.16
Strong Republican	**.325 (.059)**	.00
Independent	**−.251 (.065)**	.00
National Economy Worse	**−.114 (.014)**	.00
Age	**−.007 (.001)**	.00
Female	.028 (.038)	.46
African American	**−.183 (.062)**	.00
Asian American	−.292 (.169)	.08
Latino	.176 (.105)	.47
Education	**.252 (.012)**	.00
1990	**−.577 (.062)**	.00
1992	**.326 (.074)**	.00
1994	**−.823 (.063)**	.00
1996	**−.557 (.065)**	.00
1998	**−.443 (.069)**	.00
Pseudo R-Square	.11	
LR Chi-Square (df = 19)	1072.074	.00
N	8783	

Source: Pooled American National Election Study: Postelection Survey, Inter-University Consortium for Social and Political Research, Ann Arbor for 1988–98.

Note: Unstandardized ordered logistic regression coefficients with standard errors in parentheses. Coefficients in **bold** are statistically different from zero at the .1 level using a two-tailed test.

TABLE A.10. Impact of Ballot Initiatives on the Size and Diversity of State Interest Group Populations, 1997

Variables	Total Number of Groups β (SE)	Total Number of Groups p-value	Membership (Individuals) β (SE)	Membership (Individuals) p-value	Associational (Economic Peak Organizations) β (SE)	Associational (Economic Peak Organizations) p-value	Institutional (No Individual Members) β (SE)	Institutional (No Individual Members) p-value	Not-for-Profit β (SE)	Not-for-Profit p > |z|	For-Profit β (SE)	For-Profit p > |z|
Number of Initiatives on Ballot, 1990–96	**4.80** (3.11)	.131	**1.43** (.58)	.02	**1.24** (.60)	.05	2.21 (2.40)	.36	**2.70** (1.04)	.01	2.09 (2.40)	.39
Gross State Product, 1997 (in $ millions)	**.00** (.00)	.00	**.00** (.00)	.00	**.00** (.00)	.00	**.00** (.00)	.00	**.00** (.00)	.00	**.00** (.00)	.00
Squared Gross State Product, 1997 (in $ millions)	**–.00** (.00)	.01	–.00 (.00)	.31	**–.00** (.00)	.02	**–.00** (.00)	.01	–.00 (.00)	.92	**–.00** (.00)	.00
Government Expenditures, 1997 (as % of GSP)	–1220.63 (1229.09)	.326	–233.85 (227.28)	.33	–77.7 (237.05)	.74	–1029.05 (943.25)	.28	–293.76 (410.82)	.48	–903.81 (943.77)	.34
Divided Government, 1996	–33.11 (60.20)	.58	9.74 (11.13)	.39	8.43 (11.58)	.47	–56.69 (46.20)	.23	5.43 (20.12)	.79	–33.36 (46.22)	.47
State Ideology/Public Opinion, 1997	–251.256 (271.11)	.36	–53.74 (50.13)	.39	–28.36 (52.29)	.59	–169.84 (208.06)	.23	–53.59 (90.61)	.56	–194.22 (208.17)	.36
Constant	**377.78** (185.26)	.05	**90.57** (34.26)	.01	**71.89** (35.37)	.05	231.14 (142.18)	.11	**104.52** (61.92)	.10	267.29 (142.26)	.07
N	50		50		50		50		50		50	
F	31.879	.00	21.02	.00	31.37	.00	23.73	.00	22.91	.00	27.93	.00
Adjusted R^2	.791		.710		.788		.736		.728		.767	

Source: David Lowery, <www.unc.edu/depts/polisci/Lowery/index.html>; Jennifer Wolak, Adam Newmark, Todd McNoldy, David Lowery, and Virginia Gray, "Much of Politics Is Still Local: Multi-State Lobbying in State Interest Communities," *Legislative Studies Quarterly* 27 (2000): 527–55; *State Politics and Policy Data Resource,* <http://www.unl.edu/SPPQ/datasets.html>; Initiative and Referendum Institute, <http://www.i&rinstitute.org>; Gerald Wright, "Zip File of the CBS/*New York Times* National Polls, Ideology, and Party Identification, 1977–1998," <http://php.indiana.edu/~wright1/>.

Note: Unstandardized ordinary least squares regression coefficients, standard errors in parentheses. Coefficients in **bold** are statistically different from zero at the .1 level using a two-tailed test.

TABLE A.11.   Impact of Ballot Initiatives on Individual Contributions to Interest Groups

Variables	1996 β (SE)	1996 $p > \lvert z \rvert$	1998 β (SE)	1998 $p > \lvert z \rvert$	2000 β (SE)	2000 $p > \lvert z \rvert$
Number of Initiatives on Ballot	.010 (.026)	.676	**.107 (.038)**	**.006**	−.075 (.058)	.197
State Racial Diversity	−.251 (.938)	.789	**−1.953 (1.137)**	**.086**	−1.361 (.925)	.141
Strong Democrat	.057 (.398)	.886	−.025 (.445)	.954	−.309 (.420)	.461
Strong GOP	**1.064 (.361)**	**.003**	−.709 (.763)	.353	−.386 (.414)	.352
Independent	**.902 (.499)**	**.071**	.161 (.524)	.759	−1.440 (1.030)	.162
Age	.011 (.008)	.191	.003 (.010)	.776	**.020 (.009)**	**.043**
Female	−.121 (.275)	.660	−.018 (.331)	.955	**−.701 (.297)**	**.018**
Hispanic	−.546 (.754)	.469	**.993 (.472)**	**.035**	−1.024 (1.037)	.324
African American	**−1.750 (1.039)**	**.092**	.607 (.485)	.210	.176 (.565)	.755
Union Member	**1.287 (.314)**	**.000**	.599 (.415)	.149	**.779 (.384)**	**.043**
Education	**.387 (.089)**	**.000**	.078 (.107)	.467	**.272 (.106)**	**.011**
Income	**−.039 (.022)**	**.073**	**.114 (.034)**	**.001**	.016 (.038)	.659
Internet Access	**.687 (.300)**	**.022**	−.067 (.384)	.860	**.791 (.432)**	**.067**
Liberal Ideology	**.592 (.331)**	**.074**	**1.003 (.396)**	**.011**	−.209 (.368)	.569
Moderate Ideology	−.749 (.757)	.332	.151 (.512)	.767	**−.913 (.422)**	**.031**
Constant	**−5.300 (.817)**	**.000**	**−5.971 (1.088)**	**.000**	**−4.834 (.890)**	**.000**
Pseudo R-Square	.1374		.1320		.1154	
LR Chi-Square (15)	**68.99**	**.000**	47.45	**.000**	52.16	**.000**
N	1,170		1,137		1,258	

Source: 1996, 1998, and 2000 American National Election Studies: Postelection Survey, Inter-University Consortium for Social and Political Research, Ann Arbor, MI.

Note: Unstandardized logistic regression coefficients, standard errors in parentheses. Coefficients in **bold** are statistically different from zero at the .1 level using a two-tailed test.

TABLE A.12. Impact of Political Party on the Vote for California Ballot Initiatives, 1998 June Primary, County-Level Data

Variables	Prop. 223: Spending Limits on Administration in Public Schools		Prop. 224: State-Funded Design and Engineering Services		Prop. 225: Proposed U.S. Constitutional Amendment to Limit Congressional Terms		Prop. 226: Limiting Political Contributions by Unions without Permission from Employees		Prop. 227: Ending Bilingual Education in Public Schools	
	β (SE)	p-value	β (SE)	p-value	β (SE)	p-value	β (SE)	p-value	β (SE)	p-value
Constant	**33.443** (9.843)	.001	**49.985** (8.950)	.000	**38.733** (5.889)	.000	**19.981** (5.320)	.000	**42.353** (8.380)	.000
Percentage Registered Republican	**.202** (.099)	.048	.063 (.090)	.489	**.490** (.060)	.000	**.723** (.054)	.000	**.748** (.085)	.000
Unemployment Rate, 1998	–.174 (.170)	.310	.116 (.154)	.454	**.317** (.101)	.003	**.181** (.092)	.053	**.306** (.144)	.039
Racial Diversity	**10.319** (5.791)	.080	–8.402 (5.266)	.117	**–6.756** (3.465)	.056	–2.380 (3.130)	.451	**–16.186** (4.930)	.002
White Ethnic Diversity	.016 (.306)	.958	**–.624** (.279)	.029	–.095 (.183)	.608	.085 (.166)	.610	–.117 (.261)	.656
F	1.897	.125	4.246	.005	40.646	.000	73.793	.000	48.767	.000
Adjusted R^2	.06		.19		.74		.84		.77	
N	58		58		58		58		58	

Source: Data from U.S. Census Bureau, <www.census.gov>, and California Secretary of State, <www.ss.ca.gov/elections/elections_elections.htm>.
Note: Unstandardized regression coefficients, standard error in parentheses. Coefficients in **bold** are statistically different from zero at the .1 level using a two-tailed test. County-level data.

TABLE A.13. Impact of Political Party on the Vote for California Ballot Initiatives, 1998 November General Election, County-Level Data

Variables	Prop. 4: Ban Use of Specified Traps and Animal Poisons		Prop. 5: Tribal-State Gaming Compact/Tribal Casinos		Prop. 6: Prohibition on Slaughter of Horses and Sale of Horsemeat		Prop. 7: Air Quality Improvement Tax Credits & Environmental Protection	
	β (SE)	p-value	β (SE)	p-value	β (SE)	p-value	β (SE)	p-value
Constant	84.164	.000	80.203	.000	59.313	.000	61.190	.000
	(11.398)		(11.791)		(9.968)		(9.710)	
Percentage Registered Republican	−.514	.000	−.338	.006	−.007	.943	−.418	.000
	(.115)		(.119)		(101)		(.098)	
Unemployment Rate, 1998	−1.292	.527	−.517	.014	−.753	.000	−.831	.000
	(.196)		(.203)		(.172)		(.167)	
Racial Diversity	9.699	.000	14.670	.039	16.321	.007	14.201	.016
	(6.706)		(6.937)		(5.865)		(5.713)	
White Ethnic Diversity	−.463	.938	−.836	.027	−.348	.267	−.411	.180
	(.355)		(.367)		(.310)		(.302)	
F	29.084	.000	13.724	.000	11.526	.000	25.327	.000
Adjusted R^2	.66		.47		.43		.63	
N	58		58		58		58	

(continues)

TABLE A.13.—*Continued*

Variables	Prop. 8: Permanent Class Size Reduction Public School		Prop. 9: Electric Utilities Assessment; Bonds		Prop. 10: State and County Early Childhood Development Programs; Tobacco Surtax		Prop. 11: Local Sales and Use Taxes; Revenue Sharing	
	β (SE)	*p*-value	β (SE)	*p*-value	β (SE)	*p*-value	β (SE)	*p*-value
Constant	**33.189**	.000	**47.806**	.000	**68.998**	.000	**63.340**	.000
	(6.665)		(7.699)		(9.994)		(8.037)	
Percentage Registered Republican	.074	.279	**-.440**	.000	**-.512**	.000	**-.238**	.005
	(.067)		(.078)		(.101)		(.081)	
Unemployment Rate, 1998	.055	.637	-.219	.104	**-.986**	.000	**-.841**	.000
	(.115)		(.133)		(.172)		(.138)	
Racial Diversity	**9.014**	.025	-7.244	.116	**14.675**	.016	7.508	.118
	(3.921)		(4.529)		(5.880)		(4.728)	
White Ethnic Diversity	-.264	.209	.077	.748	-.169	.589	-.071	.777
	(.207)		(.240)		(.311)		(.250)	
F	6.340	.000	13.423	.000	33.175	.000	22.546	.000
Adjusted R^2	.27		.47		.69		.60	
N	58		58		58		58	

Source: Data from U.S. Census Bureau, <www.census.gov>, and California Secretary of State, <www.ss.ca.gov/elections/elections_elections.htm>.

Note: Unstandardized regression coefficients, standard error in parentheses. Coefficients in **bold** are statistically different from zero at the .1 level using a two-tailed test. County-level data.

TABLE A.14. Impact of Political Party on the Vote for California Ballot Initiatives, Individual-Level Survey Data

	California 1994 Election			California 1996 Election		
Variables	Prop. 187: Illegal Immigration β (SE)	Prop. 186: Health Care β (SE)	Vote for Governor Wilson (R) β (SE)	Prop. 209: Affirmative Action β (SE)	Prop. 215: Medical Marijuana β (SE)	Vote for President Clinton (D) β (SE)
Democratic Partisanship	−1.18 (.11)	1.11 (.12)	−2.77 (.12)	−1.36 (.10)	1.00 (.11)	2.65 (.12)
African American	−.33 (.20)	.10 (.20)	−1.5 (.25)	−1.49 (.21)	.16 (.22)	1.44 (.25)
Latino	−1.32 (.20)	.21 (.19)	−1.28 (.20)	−.87 (.15)	−.17 (.16)	.61 (.17)
Asian American	−.43 (.28)	.41 (.29)	−.90 (.29)	−.62 (.23)	−.88 (.25)	.19 (.25)
Education	−.36 (.06)	.21 (.06)	−.41 (.06)	−.16 (.05)	.17 (.05)	.10 (.05)
Income	.03 (.04)	−.22 (.05)	.11 (.05)	.14 (.04)	−.05 (.04)	−.21 (.04)
Age	.02 (.04)	.02 (.04)	.13 (.04)	.10 (.03)	−.19 (.03)	−.001 (.04)
Male	.27 (.11)	.006 (.12)	.42 (.12)	.17 (.09)	.04 (.11)	−.16 (.11)
Personal Finances Worse	.13 (.04)	−.02 (.04)	.09 (.04)	.14 (.03)	−.07 (.03)	−.31 (.04)
Constant	1.32 (.31)	−1.31 (.32)	1.65 (.33)	.08 (.26)	.62 (.29)	.27 (.29)
LR Chi-Square	263.173	142.145	993.731	455.11	153.68	973.022
% Cases Correctly Predicted	68.23	68.99	80.94	70.18	66.46	79.30
N	1,577	1,548	2,067	2,079	1,580	2,169

Source: Data from Voter News Service exit polls of California voters conducted after the 1994 and 1996 November elections.

Note: Unstandardized logit regression coefficients, standard errors in parentheses. Coefficients in **bold** are statistically different from zero at the .1 level using a two-tailed test.

Notes

PREFACE

1. Robert Putnam, *Bowling Alone: The Collapse and Revival of American Community* (New York: Simon and Schuster, 2000).

2. There is some variation among the states with respect to how initiatives may be used to adopt statutes or constitutional amendments. As of 2002, citizens in 18 states could use initiatives to make changes to state constitutions (16 via direct initiatives and 2 via indirect initiatives), and citizens in 22 states could use initiatives to make changes to state statutes (13 via direct initiatives, 5 via indirect initiatives, and 4 via either direct or indirect initiatives) ("Statewide Initiative and Referendum," *The Book of the States,* vol. 33 [Lexington, KY: Council of State Governments, 2001], 233, table 5.14).

3. David Schmidt, *Citizen Lawmakers: The Ballot Initiative Revolution* (Philadelphia: Temple University Press, 1989), 25–26; "Ducking the Initiative," *Wall Street Journal,* September 6, 2000; Jeff Jacoby, "A Jewel in the Crown of American Self-Government," *Boston Globe,* June 7, 2001.

4. Charles Mahtesian, "Grassroots Charade," *Governing,* November 1998, 38–42; Peter Schrag, *Paradise Lost: California's Experience, America's Future* (New York: New Press, 1998), 195; Lydia Chavez, *The Color Bind: California's Battle to End Affirmative Action* (Berkeley: University of California Press, 1998), 244–45; David Broder, *Democracy Derailed: Initiative Campaigns and the Power of Money* (New York: Harcourt Brace, 2000), 1; Richard Ellis, *Democratic Delusions: The Initiative Process in America* (Lawrence: University Press of Kansas, 2002), 203.

5. M. Dane Waters, "Trends in State Initiatives and Referenda," in *The Book of the States,* vol. 34 (Lexington, KY: Council of State Governments, 2002), 239–42; M. Dane Waters, ed., *The Battle over Citizen Lawmaking* (Durham, NC: Carolina Academic Press, 2001).

6. Caroline J. Tolbert, "Direct Democracy and Institutional Realignment in the American States," *Political Science Quarterly* 118 (2003): 467–89; Caroline J. Tolbert, "Public Policy and Direct Democracy in the Twentieth Century: The More Things Change, the More They Stay the Same," in M. Dane Waters, ed., *The Battle over Citizen Lawmaking* (Durham, NC: Carolina Academic Press, 2001), 52.

7. For example, New York governor George Pataki called for the adoption of the initiative in his 2002 State of the State address. That year, a national conference,

The Democracy Symposium, led by a former U.S. senator from Alaska, Mike Gravel, was convened to promote the spread of the initiative at all levels of American government. See Donald Wolfensberger, *Congress and the People: Deliberative Democracy on Trial* (Washington, DC: Woodrow Wilson Center Press, 2000).

8. Article V, Colorado State Constitution, at <www.sos.state.co.us/pubs /elections/2001_const.pdf>, July 10, 2002.

9. William B. Munro, ed., *The Initiative, Referendum, and Recall* (New York: Appleton, 1912), 20.

10. Elisabeth Gerber, "Legislative Response to the Threat of Popular Initiatives," *American Journal of Political Science* 40 (1996): 99–128; Shaun Bowler, Todd Donovan, and Caroline J. Tolbert, eds., *Citizens as Legislators: Direct Democracy in the United States* (Columbus: Ohio State University Press, 1998); Edward Lascher, Michael Hagen, and Steven Rochlin, "Gun behind the Door? Ballot Initiatives, State Policies, and Public Opinion," *Journal of Politics* 58 (1996): 760–75; John Camobreco, "Preferences, Fiscal Policies, and the Initiative Process," *Journal of Politics* 60 (1998): 819–29; Daniel A. Smith, "Homeward *Bound?* Micro-Level Legislative Responsiveness to Ballot Initiatives," *State Politics and Policy Quarterly* 1 (2001): 50–61; Daniel A. Smith, "Overturning Term Limits: The Legislature's Own Private Idaho?" *PS: Political Science and Politics* 36 (2003): 215–20.

11. Munro, *Initiative, Referendum, and Recall*, 20–21.

12. Paul Reinsch, "The Initiative and Referendum," *Proceedings of the Academy of Political Science in the City of New York* 3 (1912): 158.

13. See, for example, James March and Johan Olsen, *Rediscovering Institutions: The Organizational Basis of Politics* (New York: Free Press, 1989); Sven Steinmo, Kathleen Thelen, and Frank Longstreth, eds., *Structuring Politics: Historical Institutionalism in Comparative Analysis* (New York: Cambridge University Press, 1992); John Allswang, *The Initiative and Referendum in California, 1898–1998* (Stanford: Stanford University Press, 2000).

14. Kenneth Miller, "Constraining Populism: The Real Challenge of Initiative Reform," *Santa Clara Law Review* 41 (2001): 1037–84; Anne Campbell, "In the Eye of the Beholder: The Single Subject Rule for Ballot Initiatives," in M. Dane Waters, ed., *The Battle over Citizen Lawmaking* (Durham, NC: Carolina Academic Press, 2001); Elisabeth Gerber, Arthur Lupia, Mathew D. McCubbins, and D. Roderick Kiewiet, *Stealing the Initiative: How State Government Responds to Direct Democracy* (Upper Saddle River, NJ: Prentice Hall, 2001); D. A. Smith, "Homeward *Bound?*"; D. A. Smith, "Overturning Term Limits."

CHAPTER 1

1. Quoted in George Hammell, "Direct Legislation," *Twentieth Century Magazine* 21 (1911): 284.

2. Woodrow Wilson, *The State: Elements of Historical and Practical Politics*, rev. ed. (Boston: Heath, 1898), 311. On numerous occasions, Wilson belied his subsequent populist tastes. In *Constitutional Government in the United States*, published

in 1908, Wilson writes, "A government must have organs; it cannot act inorganically, by masses. It must have a law-making body; it can no more make law through its voters than it can make law through its newspapers." Earlier in the text, he explicitly dismissed the initiative and referendum, reasoning "that we sometimes allow ourselves to assume that the 'initiative' and the 'referendum,' now so much talked of and so imperfectly understood, are a more through means of getting at public opinion that the process of our representative assemblies" (*Constitutional Government in the United States* [New York: Columbia University Press, 1908], 191, 104). Speaking on March 9, 1909, to the Civic League of St. Louis, Wilson (then president of Princeton University) stated unequivocally, "You know we have heard a great deal recently about the government of the country by the people of the country, and I must say that it seems to me we have been talking a great deal of nonsense. A government can be democratic only in the sense that it is a government restrained, controlled by public opinion. It can never be a government conducted by public opinion. What I mean to say is this: that POPULAR INITIATIVE IS AN INCONCEIVABLE THING!" (quoted in James Boyle, *The Initiative and Referendum: Its Folly, Fallacies, and Failure*, 3d ed. [Columbus, OH: Smythe, 1912], 66–67).

3. Richard Hofstadter, *The Age of Reform* (New York: Vintage, 1955), 206, 262. In 1912, historian Charles Beard observed that critics of direct democracy often compared the mechanisms in practice with "the theory of representative government, which is more or less unconsciously assumed to be its practice by those who have set themselves against the new system. . . . When considering, therefore, a system of initiative and referendum," Beard noted, "it is the *practice* of representative government as it now prevails in the United States, rather than its *theory*, which should be the basis of making contrasts" ("Introductory Note," in Charles Beard and Birl Shultz, eds., *Documents on the State-Wide Initiative, Referendum, and Recall* [New York: Macmillan, 1912], 32–33).

4. For the evolution of Wilson's views on the initiative, referendum, and recall, see Woodrow Wilson, *The Papers of Woodrow Wilson*, ed. Arthur Link (Princeton: Princeton University Press, 1977), esp. vols. 22–24.

5. Quoted in George Hammell, "News of Fundamental Democratic and Economic Advance: Direct Legislation," *Twentieth Century Magazine* 23 (1911): 471.

6. Quoted in Hammell, "Direct Legislation," 21:284.

7. Lewis Johnson, "Direct Legislation as an Ally of Representative Government," in William B. Munro, ed., *The Initiative, Referendum, and Recall* (New York: Appleton, 1912), 142.

8. Quoted in Hammell, "News," 23:471.

9. Woodrow Wilson, "The Issues of Reform," in William B. Munro, ed., *The Initiative, Referendum, and Recall* (New York: Appleton, 1912), 87–88.

10. See, for example, Simeon Baldwin, *The Relation of Education to Citizenship* (New Haven: Yale University Press, 1912); John Dewey, *The Public and Its Problems* (New York: Holt, 1927).

11. James Bryce, *The American Commonwealth*, rev. ed. (1893; New York: Macmillan, 1910), 1:475. Bryce was no Pollyanna concerning the initiative, writing that "it might be expected to lower the authority and sense of responsibility in the

legislature; and it refers matters needing much elucidation by debate to the determination of those who cannot, on account of their numbers, meet together for discussion, and many of whom may have never thought about the matter." He also worried about the "wisdom of arrangements that leave so much to the vote of a multitude which may act hastily, excited by the prospect of some benefit to be obtained, some grievance to be removed, through a sweeping and perhaps insufficiently debated change in the law," because "the safeguards provided by the rules restraining legislative action cannot always be relied upon" (474, 479).

12. William S. U'Ren, "Remarks on Mr. Herbert Croly's Paper on 'State Political Reorganization,'" *Proceedings of the American Political Science Association* 8 (1911): 139.

13. Though he was elected to the U.S. Senate on the Republican ticket in 1906, Bourne had previously been affiliated with both the Democratic and the Populist Parties. A Harvard-trained lawyer, Bourne later became the president of the National Republican Progressive League. See Leonard Schlup, "Republican Insurgent: Jonathan Bourne and the Politics of Progressivism, 1908–1912," *Oregon Historical Quarterly* 87 (fall 1986): 229–44; Allen H. Eaton, *The Oregon System: The Story of Direct Legislation in Oregon* (Chicago: McClurg, 1912), 95–97.

14. Jonathan Bourne Jr., "The Practical Conservation of Popular Sovereignty," *Twentieth Century Magazine* 14 (1910): 132.

15. Delos F. Wilcox, *Government by All the People; or, The Initiative, the Referendum, and the Recall as Instruments of Democracy* (New York: Macmillan, 1912), 88.

16. Theodore Roosevelt, "Nationalism and Popular Rule," *The Outlook,* January 21, 1911, reprinted in Munro, ed., *Initiative, Referendum, and Recall,* 64–65. Roosevelt, stumping for the presidency on the Progressive Bull Moose ticket in 1912, declared in his "Charter of Democracy" speech in Ohio that, "I believe in the Initiative and Referendum, which should be used not to destroy representative government, but to correct it whenever it becomes misrepresentative" (quoted in Schmidt, *Citizen Lawmakers,* 9). However, Roosevelt cautioned that the initiative "is a device and nothing more, is a means and not an end. The end is good government, obtained through genuine popular rule." For a discussion of one of Roosevelt's earliest pronouncements in favor of direct legislation, see Daniel A. Smith and Joseph Lubinski, "Direct Democracy during the Progressive Era: A Crack in the Populist Veneer?" *Journal of Policy History* 14 (2002): 354–55.

17. Charles Zueblin, "The Training of the Citizen," *Chautauquan* (October 1903): 161–68, quoted in Kevin Mattson, *Creating a Democratic Public: The Struggle for Urban Participatory Democracy during the Progressive Era* (University Park: Pennsylvania State University Press, 1998), 25.

18. William B. Munro, *The Government of the United States: National, State, and Local,* 3d ed. (New York: Macmillan, 1931), 577.

19. See Gerber, "Legislative Response"; John Matsusaka, "Fiscal Effects of the Voter Initiative: Evidence from the Last 30 Years," *Journal of Political Economy* 103 (1995): 587–623; Caroline J. Tolbert, "Changing Rules for State Legislatures: Direct Democracy and Governance Policies," in Shaun Bowler, Todd Donovan,

and Caroline J. Tolbert, eds., *Citizens as Legislators* (Columbus: Ohio State University Press, 1998). In her oft-cited study on legislative response to initiatives, Gerber offers a formal spatial model theorizing that interest groups can affect state legislatures' policy decisions by threatening to place initiatives on the ballot. Using logistic regression to analyze the adoption of antiabortion parental consent laws in the states, she finds that legislation passed in states that permit the initiative more closely reflects the median voter's preference than do laws passed in states that do not allow direct legislation. Because interest groups in states with the initiative process can "challenge" legislation in an "ex post" fashion, legislators in those states, "must always be aware of the possibility of future initiative proposals." According to Gerber, interest groups threatening to alter public policy via the initiative compel legislators to become more responsive to voter demands. She finds the indirect threat posed by an initiative is especially significant in states where the process of qualifying a measure on the ballot is relatively easy and inexpensive.

20. See Lascher, Hagen, and Rochlin, "Gun behind the Door?"; Camobreco, "Preferences, Fiscal Policies, and the Initiative Process"; Michael Hagen, Edward Lascher, and John Camobreco, "Response to Matsusaka: Estimating the Effect of Ballot Initiatives on Policy Responsiveness," *Journal of Politics* 63 (2001): 1257–63. Lascher, Hagen, and Rochlin find that public opinion affects the adoption of state policies in six of the eight policy areas (consumer policy, criminal justice policy, education expenses, ERA, Medicaid, and tax progressivity), but in none of the areas "does the presence of the initiative process significantly enhance the connection between opinion and policy." In the two other policy areas they analyze, gambling and AFDC, the effect of the initiative process is significant, but in the wrong direction. For a critique of the methodology used by Lascher, Hagen, and Rochlin, see John Matsusaka, "Problems with a Methodology Used to Evaluate the Voter Initiative," *Journal of Politics* 63 (2001): 1250–56.

21. There are strong micro-level determents of legislative behavior when it comes to responding to ballot initiatives. At times it may be rational for legislators in initiative states to support a countermajoritarian bill if it is consistent with the preferences of constituents in the legislators' specific districts rather than with the statewide popular vote. See D. A. Smith, "Homeward *Bound?*"; D. A. Smith, "Overturning Term Limits."

22. See Clinton Rossiter and James Lare, eds., *The Essential Lippmann: A Political Philosophy for Liberal Democracy* (New York: Random House, 1963).

23. George Haynes, "'People's Rule' in Oregon, 1910," *Political Science Quarterly* 26 (1911): 61. For a lengthy discussion of ballot language of antitax ballot initiatives and the faux populists behind the measures, see Daniel A. Smith, *Tax Crusaders and the Politics of Direct Democracy* (New York: Routledge, 1998), 157–67.

24. Mary Parker Follett, *The New State: Group Organization and the Solution of Popular Government* (New York: Longmans, Green, 1918), 177.

25. Walter Weyl, *The New Democracy* (New York: Macmillan, 1912), 307.

26. Beard, "Introductory Note," in Beard and Shultz, *Documents*, 24.

27. Populist James W. Sullivan, by some accounts the father of direct democracy in America, did celebrate how the initiative could extend the "sphere" of every citizen. But Sullivan's primary aim was still instrumental. According to the historian Steven Piott, Sullivan's logic was as follows: "Participation would enhance interest in the political economy, this interest would generate education, and education would facilitate decisions designed to promote the public welfare." In general, Populists touted the instrumental changes that could be realized though the adoption of the initiative and referendum, not the educative effects (*Giving Voters a Voice: The Origins of the Initiative and Referendum in America* [Columbia: University of Missouri Press, 2003], 252).

28. J. W. Garner, "Primary vs. Representative Government," *Proceedings of the American Political Science Association* 4 (1907): 168.

29. Bryce, *American Commonwealth,* 1:474.

30. Weyl, *New Democracy,* 310.

31. Munro, *Initiative, Referendum, and Recall,* 22.

32. Edwin Cottrell, "Twenty Five Years of Direct Legislation in California," *Public Opinion Quarterly* (1939): 45.

33. Proponents of citizen lawmaking celebrated the fact that little ballot drop-off occurred in early Oregon direct legislation elections (see George Haynes, "The Education of Voters," *Political Science Quarterly* 22 [1907]: 494; Haynes, "'People's Rule' in Oregon"). In 1910, however, none of the nine ballot measures that passed in Oregon (four constitutional amendments and five statutes) received more than half the votes cast for governor (see Eaton, *Oregon System,* 161).

34. Mattson, *Creating a Democratic Public,* 8. While he alludes to direct (or "pure") democracy in his discussion of the "process of public discussion and collective education" during the Progressive Era, Mattson focuses on the institutionalization of social centers and public forums and on the city-beautiful movement that briefly flourished during the period.

35. Herbert Croly, *Progressive Democracy* (New York: Macmillan, 1914), 145.

36. Croly, *Progressive Democracy,* 268–70. Two years earlier, Croly was not as generous in his assessment of direct democracy, calling it "political heresy": "The system of direct government is expected to have its period of efflorescence, like Know-Nothingism, Grangerism and Populism and then gradually sink into utter and deserved oblivion" ("State Political Reorganization," *Proceedings of the American Political Science Association* 8 [1911]: 122).

37. Munro, *Government,* 576.

38. Garner, "Primary vs. Representative Government," 167.

39. Quoted in Mattson, *Creating a Democratic Public,* 25; Zueblin, "Training."

40. Reinsch, "Initiative and Referendum," 158.

41. George Judson King, "How Oregon 'Stood Pat,'" *Twentieth Century Magazine* 21 (1911): 119.

42. Haynes, "'People's Rule' in Oregon," 62.

43. Bourne, "Practical Conservation," 132. To assist voters, the state of Oregon published a 202-page "pamphlet" with pro and con arguments on each of the 32 questions. Bourne's sentiments also were reflected in a public statement circulated in Oregon following the 1910 general election:

The vote on measures has been generally intelligent, and the system is of great educational value. The official pamphlet is carefully studied by a great many of the voters. . . . Many of the undersigned who have been members of the legislature believe that the percentage of voters who carefully read every one of the thirty-two measures submitted at the recent election is fully as high as the percentage of members of the legislature who read every one of the five hundred to eight hundred bills they are called upon to vote for or against in the legislature. In what are called the slum districts and precincts the vote on measures is commonly a comparatively small percentage of the vote for officers. No measure containing a "joker" has yet been approved by the people.

While providing no empirical evidence, the statement went on to claim, "The people are giving more and more attention to the measures submitted. Both the teachers and the pupils in the public schools are taking an ever-increasing interest in public questions, and in studying the science of government." The statement was signed by dozens of supporters of the Oregon system, including Jonathan Bourne Jr. and George E. Chamberlain, U.S. senators (Oregon); P. L. Campbell, president of the University of Oregon and U.S. senator; Will Daly, president of the Oregon State Federation of Labor; Thomas B. Kay, Oregon state treasurer; and Will R. King, Thomas A. McBride, and W. T. Slater, justices of the Oregon Supreme Court. Statement of support quoted by Katherine B. Mills, "Direct Legislation," *Twentieth Century Magazine* 18 (1911): 557.

44. Munro, *Initiative, Referendum, and Recall,* 21; Garner, "Primary vs. Representative Government," 167–68.

45. Johnson, "Direct Legislation," 149.

46. Wilcox, *Government,* 109.

47. Bourne, "Practical Conservation," 132.

48. William MacLeod Raine, "The Rebellion against Privilege in Colorado," *Twentieth Century Magazine* 14 (1910): 100. Evans and his Republican sycophants in the legislature strongly opposed the direct democracy reforms proposed by Colorado governor John Shafroth during the 1909 legislative session (see D. A. Smith and Lubinski, "Direct Democracy," 353–54).

49. See Allswang, *Initiative and Referendum,* 8–18. As legal historian Harry Scheiber rightly notes, "The judgment [of direct democracy] will also depend, ineluctably, on one's view of the concrete substantive results of the direct ballot—results represented by the merits of the legislation and constitutional innovations that are enacted" ("Foreword: The Direct Ballot and State Constitutionalism," *Rutgers Law Journal* 28 [1997]: 794).

50. Hofstadter, *Age of Reform,* 257.

51. Samuel McCall, "Representative as against Direct Legislation," in William B. Munro, ed., *The Initiative, Referendum, and Recall* (New York: Appleton, 1912), 180.

52. Haynes, "Education of Voters," 486.

53. Haynes, "'People's Rule' in Oregon," 46–47. Haynes concluded, however, that "it would have been difficult for any Oregon voter to have remained totally

ignorant of the principal points involved in the more important measures on which he was to vote."

54. McCall, "Representative as against Direct Legislation," 179.

55. Haynes, "Education of Voters," 485.

56. The research of Burton Hendrick, quoted in George Hammell, "Direct Legislation," *Twentieth Century Magazine* 24 (1911): 571. In contrast, in a survey of polling results in Cincinnati, Charles O. Gardner found that "the non-voter is to be found in rich and well-to-do sections almost as frequently as in districts where ignorance and vice reign supreme" ("Problems of Percentages in Direct Government," *American Political Science Review* 10 [1916]: 506).

57. Robert Cushman, "Recent Experience with the Initiative and Referendum," *American Political Science Review* 10 (1916): 538.

58. Haynes, "'People's Rule' in Oregon," 60. Professor Ellis P. Oberholtzer of the University of Pennsylvania claimed that in Oregon that year, "confusion" surely "must have possessed the minds of 99 out of every 100 voters of the State because of the great number and conflicting variety of the submitted measures" (*The Referendum in America [Together with Some Chapters on the Initiative and the Recall]*, rev. ed. [New York: Scribner's, 1911], 405).

59. A. Lawrence Lowell, "The Referendum in the United States," in William B. Munro, ed., *The Initiative, Referendum, and Recall* (New York: Appleton, 1912), 130.

60. Croly, *Progressive Democracy*, 306. As Hofstadter wrote a generation later, "Confronted by an array of technical questions, often phrased in legal language, the voters shrank from the responsibilities the new system attempted to put upon them. Small and highly organized groups with plenty of funds and skillful publicity could make use of these devices, but such were not the results the proponents of initiative and referendum sought; nor was the additional derationalization of politics that came with the propaganda campaigns demanded by referendums" (*Age of Reform*, 268).

61. Garner, "Primary vs. Representative Government," 168.

62. Eaton, *Oregon System.*

63. Beard, "Introductory Note," in Beard and Shultz, *Documents;* James Barnett, *The Operation of the Initiative, Referendum, and Recall in Oregon* (New York: Macmillan, 1915); George Haynes, "People's Rule on Trial," *Political Science Quarterly* 28 (1913): 18–33; A. Lawrence Lowell, *Public Opinion and Popular Government* (New York: Longmans, Green, 1913); Arnold Hall, *Popular Government* (New York: Macmillan, 1921).

64. See F. W. Coker, "Safeguarding the Petition in the Initiative and Referendum," *American Political Science Review* 10 (1916): 540–45; W. A. Schnader, "Proper Safeguards for the Initiative and Referendum Petition," *American Political Science Review* 10 (1916): 515–31; D. A. Smith and Lubinski, "Direct Democracy," 365–66.

65. See Shaun Bowler and Todd Donovan, *Demanding Choices: Opinion, Voting, and Direct Democracy* (Ann Arbor: University of Michigan Press, 1998), 15; David McCuan, Shaun Bowler, Todd Donovan, and Ken Fernandez, "California's Political Warriors: Campaign Professionals and the Initiative Process," in Shaun Bowler, Todd Donovan, and Caroline J. Tolbert, eds., *Citizens as Legislators: Direct*

Democracy in the United States (Columbus: Ohio State University Press, 1998), 55–79; Thomas Goebel, *A Government by the People: Direct Democracy in America, 1890–1940* (Chapel Hill: University of North Carolina Press, 2002), 159–63.

66. Wilcox contended, "A special private interest is always in the minority in a large community and can be beaten every time it calls for a count of noses," though he admitted, "there is some danger of the people's being wearied by much importunity, and letting a minority have its way in a moment of apathy." Despite his qualms, Wilcox was confident that the initiative would allow citizens to draft and pass new laws in the general interest. His book offers a classic defense for "the *a priori* reasons for believing that the new political instruments will be more effective in establishing popular self-government" (*Government*, vii, 102–3, 112–13).

67. Cushman, "Recent Experience," 538–39.

68. Haynes, "Education of Voters," 486. Haynes concluded, "On the whole, considering the immense complexity of the task which was set before them, it must be acknowledged that the Oregon voters stood the test remarkably well." However, he admitted, "The writer is not a convert to the idea that the increased use of the initiative and referendum in America is desirable" (496).

69. Oberholtzer, *Referendum in America*, 503.

70. Follett, *New State*, 177.

71. In 1894, the New Jersey state assembly narrowly defeated an amendment, drafted by the Direct Legislation League of New Jersey, that would have added the mechanisms of direct democracy to the state constitution (Piott, *Giving Voters a Voice*, 9).

72. Frederick Stimson, "Certain Retrogressive Policies of the Progressive Party," *Proceedings of the American Political Science Association* 9 (1912): 149.

73. See Gardner, "Problems," 512; S. Gale Lowrie, "New Forms of the Initiative and Referendum," *American Political Science Review* 5 (1911): 566.

74. Munro, *Initiative, Referendum, and Recall*, 1.

75. Lowrie, "New Forms," 566.

76. John Works, "The Political Regeneration of California," *Twentieth Century Magazine* 23 (1911): 394.

77. Garner, "Primary vs. Representative Government," 174.

78. Arthur Link and Richard McCormick, *Progressivism* (Arlington Heights, IL: Harlan Davidson, 1983).

79. Wilcox, *Government*, 106. Indeed, chapter 9 of Wilcox's jeremiad is titled, "First Argument in Favor of the Initiative: That It Would Utilize the Individual in Politics."

80. See Bruce Cain and Kenneth Miller, "The Populist Legacy: Initiatives and the Undermining of Representative Government," in Larry Sabato, Bruce Larson, and Howard Ernst, eds., *Dangerous Democracy? The Battle over Ballot Initiatives in America* (Lanham, MD: Rowman and Littlefield, 2002); but see also D. A. Smith, *Tax Crusaders*, chap. 3.

81. Hofstadter, *Age of Reform*, 259.

82. William Allen White, *The Old Order Changeth: A View of American Democracy* (New York: Macmillan, 1910), 34–39.

83. Hofstadter, *Age of Reform*, 257.

84. Hofstadter lambasted the "ambiguous character" of Progressivism: "My criticism of the Progressivism of [1890–1917] is . . . that [reformers] set impossible standards, that they were victimized, in brief, by a form of moral absolutism" (*Age of Reform*, 16–18).

85. Hofstadter, *Age of Reform*, 261.

86. The Populist Party was forged out of agrarian frustrations and anxieties at the dawn of the industrial era. By the presidential election of 1892, the party added to its platform a provision "commending" a set of direct democracy reforms; by 1896, the party officially endorsed the initiative and referendum (Piott, *Giving Voters a Voice*, 253). The party also advocated the free coinage of gold and silver, public ownership of railroads, a graduated federal income tax, the direct election of U.S. senators, and a more equitable distribution of wealth. For a brief summary of the "dueling legacies" of the Populists and Progressives, see Cain and Miller, "Populist Legacy," 34–38.

87. While U'Ren was elected chairman of Oregon's Populist Party in 1894, he was "never a completely committed Populist." See Goebel, *Government*, 80–81; Schmidt, *Citizen Lawmakers*, 261–63; Piott, *Giving Voters a Voice*, 253–55.

88. Goebel, *Government*, 31–32.

89. James W. Sullivan, *Direct Legislation by the Citizenship through the Initiative and Referendum* (New York: True Nationalist, 1893). Nathan Cree also published a treatise on direct democracy, *Direct Legislation by the People* (Chicago: McClurg, 1892).

90. Speaking at a 1910 conference of single-tax advocates, U'Ren stated, "I went just as crazy over the single tax idea as any one else ever did. I knew I wanted single tax, and that was about all I did know. . . . I learned what the initiative and referendum is [*sic*], and then I saw the way to single tax. So I quit talking single tax, not because I was any the less in favor of it but because I saw that the first job was to get the initiative and referendum, so that the people, independently of the legislature, may get what they want rather than take what the legislature will let them have. . . . All the work we have done for direct legislation has been done with the single tax in view, but we have not talked single tax because that was not the question before the house" (quoted in Barnett, *Operation*, 4–5). Oregonian zealots for the single tax, led by the Oregon Tax Reform Association, failed in four consecutive biennial elections beginning in 1908 to convince the electorate to adopt various proposals (James Gilbert, "Single-Tax Movement in Oregon," *Political Science Quarterly* 6 [1916]: 25). See also David Schuman, "The Origins of State Constitutional Direct Democracy: William Simon U'Ren and the Oregon System," *Temple Law Review* 67 (1994): 947–63. On U'Ren's sentiments toward legislative governance, see U'Ren, "Remarks," 138.

91. Winston Crouch, "The Constitutional Initiative in Operation," *American Political Science Review* 33 (1939): 634. See also Tom Stitton, *John Randolph Haynes: California Progressive* (Stanford, CA: Stanford University Press, 1992); Goebel, *Government*, 85–90.

92. With the notable exception of Oregon, where the initiative was adopted in 1902 and was first deployed in 1904, the popular enthusiasm for direct democracy reforms across the rest of the country remained scattered until the late 1900s. For

example, in South Dakota and Utah, where voters adopted the initiative in 1898 and 1900, it was not utilized until 1908 and 1958, respectively. Piott, *Giving Voters a Voice*, provides the most extensive documentation of the adoption of direct democracy reforms in the American states during the Progressive Era.

93. Quoted in George Hammell, "News of Fundamental Democratic and Economic Advance: Direct Legislation," *Twentieth Century Magazine* 24 (1911): 183.

94. See H. H. B. Meyer, *Select List of References on Initiative, Referendum, and Recall* (Washington, DC: Library of Congress, 1911).

95. Voters in South Dakota and Ohio adopted the initiative (and referendum) by three-to-two margins (Schmidt, *Citizen Lawmakers*, 16–18).

96. John Shafroth, "Imperative Need of Direct Legislation," *Twentieth Century Magazine* 24 (1911): 519. For Shafroth's role in spearheading direct legislation in Colorado, see D. A. Smith and Lubinski, "Direct Democracy," 353–54.

97. Schmidt, *Citizen Lawmakers*, 16–18. Voters in Minnesota defeated yet another amendment trying to establish the initiative in 1916.

98. For discussions of direct democracy's urban bias, see Daniel A. Smith, "Representation and the Spatial Dimension of Direct Democracy," paper presented at American Political Science Association Conference, Boston, August 29–September 1, 2002; Daniel A. Smith, "Representation and the Urban Bias of Direct Democracy," paper presented at the Western Political Science Association Conference, Long Beach, CA, March 21–24, 2002.

99. See Charles Kettleborough, "Initiative and Referendum," *American Political Science Review* 8 (1914): 251; Frank Bates, "Constitutional Amendments and Referred Acts, November Election 1914," *American Political Science Review* 9 (1915): 103; George Haynes, "How Massachusetts Adopted the Initiative and Referendum," *Political Science Quarterly* 34 (1919): 469.

100. Goebel, *Government*, 69–71. In the South, Wilson and the national leaders of the Democratic Party expressly opposed the spread of the initiative, fearing that it would threaten white supremacy and empower "ignorant" voters (Goebel, *Government*, 127–29).

101. Oberholtzer, *Referendum in America*, 391; Thomas Goebel, "'A Case of Democratic Contagion': Direct Democracy in the American West, 1890–1920," *Pacific Historical Review* 66 (1997): 213–30; Steven Piott, "The Origins of the Initiative and Referendum in America," *Hayes Historical Journal* 11 (1992): 5–17; Charles Price, "The Initiative: A Comparative State Analysis and Reassessment of a Western Phenomenon," *Western Political Quarterly* 28 (1975): 243–62.

102. Schmidt, *Citizen Lawmakers*, 115; Caroline J. Tolbert, "Rethinking Lowi's Constituent Policy," *Environment and Planning C: Government and Policy* 20 (2002): 75–93.

103. Caroline J. Tolbert, "Direct Democracy and Institutional Realignment in the American States," *Political Science Quarterly* 118 (2003): 467–89.

104. See Tolbert, "Direct Democracy"; Schmidt, *Citizen Lawmakers*, 15–20; Goebel, *Government*; Allswang, *Initiative and Referendum*; Ellis, *Democratic Delusions;* D. A. Smith and Lubinski, "Direct Democracy."

105. David Broder, "Ballot Initiatives Subvert Election Process," *Denver Post*, May 14, 2000.

106. Ellis, *Democratic Delusions*, 177.

107. See D. A. Smith and Lubinski, "Direct Democracy," 362.

108. Bates, "Constitutional Amendments," 104–6.

109. Ellis, *Democratic Delusions*, 190.

110. Goebel, *Government*, 198.

111. Mattson, *Creating a Democratic Public*, 114.

112. Munro, *Government*, 579.

113. William Howard Taft, *Popular Government: Its Essence, Its Permanence, and Its Perils* (New Haven: Yale University Press, 1913), 54; "Anti-Democracy in California," *New York Times*, October 18, 1911. Progressive Era criticisms of the initiative were even more extensive than what has been offered here. In the course of his book, Wilcox debunks the criticisms that citizen lawmaking would "destroy constitutional stability," "foster tyranny of the majority," "tend to the subversion of judicial authority," "result in unscientific legislation," "lead to radical legislation," and "be used by special interests" (*Government*, ix).

114. Munro, *Initiative, Referendum, and Recall*, 22.

CHAPTER 2

1. See Samuel McSeveney, "The Fourth Party System and Progressive Politics," in L. Sandy Maisel and William Shade, eds., *Parties and Politics in American History* (New York: Garland, 1994); Walter Dean Burnham, ed., *The Current Crisis in American Politics* (New York: Norton, 1982); Joel Silbey, *The American Political Nation, 1838–1893* (Stanford, CA: Stanford University Press, 1991); Paul Kleppner, *Continuity and Change in Electoral Politics, 1893–1928* (Westport, CT: Greenwood, 1987); J. Morgan Kousser, *The Shaping of Southern Politics: Suffrage Restriction and the Establishment of the One-Party South, 1880–1910* (New Haven: Yale University Press, 1974); Mark Kornbluh, *Why America Stopped Voting: The Decline of Participatory Democracy and the Emergence of Modern American Politics* (New York: New York University Press, 2000).

2. Wilcox, *Government*, 107.

3. See, for example, Sullivan, *Direct Legislation;* Cree, *Direct Legislation;* Haynes, "'People's Rule' in Oregon"; Beard, "Introductory Note," in Beard and Shultz, *Documents;* Barnett, *Operation;* Gardner, "Problems."

4. Theda Skocpol and Morris Fiorina, eds., *Civic Engagement in American Democracy* (Washington, DC: Brookings Institution Press, 1999); Putnam, *Bowling Alone.*

5. G. B. Powell, "American Voter Turnout in Comparative Perspective," *American Political Science Review* 80 (1986): 17–43; Thomas Patterson, *The Vanishing Voter: Public Involvement in an Age of Uncertainty* (New York: Knopf, 2002); Matthew Crenson and Benjamin Ginsberg, *Downsizing Democracy: How America Sidelined Its Citizens and Privatized Its Public* (Baltimore: Johns Hopkins University Press, 2002); Frances Fox Piven and Richard Cloward, *Why Americans Still Don't Vote: And Why Politicians Want It That Way* (Boston: Beacon, 2000).

6. Pippa Norris, *Digital Divide: Civic Engagement, Information Poverty, and the Internet Worldwide* (New York: Cambridge University Press, 2001); Karen Moss-

berger, Caroline J. Tolbert, and Mary Stansbury, *Virtual Inequality: Beyond the Digital Divide* (Washington, DC: Georgetown University Press, 2003).

7. In the late 1990s, for example, Marc Strassman unsuccessfully tried to place an initiative on the 2000 California ballot that would have required the secretary of state to implement Internet voting and voter registration (Paul Van Slambrouck, "In California, Taking the Initiative," *Christian Science Monitor,* November 13, 1998).

8. D. A. Smith, *Tax Crusaders,* 53. In the June 1978 primary, the drop-off for the total number of voters who came to the polls but did not vote for a gubernatorial candidate was 9 percent, whereas the drop-off for Proposition 13 was only 3 percent (David Magleby, *Direct Legislation: Voting on Ballot Propositions in the United States* [Baltimore: Johns Hopkins University Press, 1984], 90–93).

9. In 1993, Norquist predicted that initiatives limiting legislative terms and cutting taxes and government spending, as well as anticrime, victims' rights, and parental rights ballot measures, would bring fiscal and "social conservative Republican voters to the polls" in 1994 and 1996 (Grover G. Norquist, "Prelude to a Landslide: How Grass-Roots Populism Could Help Republicans in 1996," *Policy Review* 66 [1993]: 30).

10. B. Guy Peters, *The Future of Governing: Four Emerging Models* (Lawrence: University Press of Kansas, 1996); Matthew Mendelsohn and Andrew Parkin, eds., *Referendum Democracy: Citizens, Elites, and Deliberation in Referendum Campaigns* (New York: Palgrave, 2001).

11. See Peters, *Future of Governing;* Schmidt, *Citizen Lawmakers.*

12. Broder, *Democracy Derailed;* Schrag, *Paradise Lost.*

13. Peters, *Future of Governing;* David Osborne and Ted Gaebler, *Reinventing Government: How the Entrepreneurial Spirit Is Transforming the Public Sector* (Reading, MA: Addison-Wesley, 1992).

14. See James Fishkin, *Democracy and Deliberation* (New Haven: Yale University Press, 1993); James Fishkin, *The Voice of the People* (New Haven: Yale University Press, 1995); M. Morell, "Citizens' Evaluations of Participatory Democratic Procedures: Normative Theory Meets Empirical Science," *Political Research Quarterly* 52 (1999): 293–322; Carole Pateman, *Participation and Democratic Theory* (New York: Cambridge University Press, 1970); John Dryzek, *Discursive Democracy: Politics, Policy, and Political Science* (Cambridge: Cambridge University Press, 1990); John Dryzek, *Deliberative Democracy and Beyond: Liberals, Critics, and Contestations* (Oxford: Oxford University Press, 2000); Benjamin Barber, *Strong Democracy* (Princeton: Princeton University Press, 1984); Jon Elster, ed., *Deliberative Democracy* (Cambridge: Cambridge University Press, 1998); P. Norris, *Digital Divide;* Mossberger, Tolbert, and Stansbury, *Virtual Inequality;* Peters, *Future of Governing.*

15. Barber, *Strong Democracy,* 235–36.

16. Quoted in Magleby, *Direct Legislation,* 77.

17. "Making Democracy More Interesting," *New York Times,* November 27, 1978; "Turnout Could Hinge on Initiatives," *Congress Daily,* October 6, 1998.

18. Schmidt, *Citizen Lawmakers,* 27; Thomas Cronin, *Direct Democracy: The Politics of Initiative, Referendum, and Recall* (Cambridge: Harvard University Press, 1989).

19. Schrag, *Paradise Lost;* Ellis, *Democratic Delusions.*

20. David Everson, "The Effects of Initiatives on Voter Turnout: A Comparative State Analysis," *Western Political Quarterly* 34 (1981): 415–25.

21. Magleby, *Direct Legislation*, 96–98.

22. Caroline J. Tolbert, Daniel Lowenstein, and Todd Donovan, "Election Law and Rules for Using Initiatives," in Shaun Bowler, Todd Donovan, and Caroline J. Tolbert, eds., *Citizens as Legislators: Direct Democracy in the United States* (Columbus: Ohio State University Press, 1998).

23. Cronin, *Direct Democracy;* Magleby, *Direct Legislation;* Schmidt, *Citizen Lawmakers;* Price, "The Initiative."

24. Burnham, *Current;* Frances Fox Piven and Richard Cloward, *Why Americans Don't Vote* (New York: Pantheon, 1988); Steven Rosenstone and John Mark Hansen, *Mobilization, Participation, and Democracy in America* (New York: Macmillan, 1993); Robert Jackson, Robert Brown, and Gerald Wright, "Registration, Turnout, and the Electoral Representativeness of U.S. State Electorates," *American Politics Quarterly* 26 (1998): 259–87; Angus Campbell, Philip Converse, Warren Miller, and Donald Stokes, *The American Voter* (Chicago: University of Chicago Press, 1960).

25. See the Initiative and Referendum Institute's Web site, <www .iandrinstitute.org>, for a listing of citizen initiatives and legislative referenda appearing on state election ballots in various years. See also Price, "The Initiative"; Tolbert, "Direct Democracy"; Daniel Elazar, *American Federalism: A View from the States,* 3d ed. (New York: Harper and Row, 1984).

26. The data are from the Initiative and Referendum Institute's Web site, <www.iandrinstitute.org>, which constitutes the most comprehensive source of information on direct democracy elections in the United States, and the National Conference of State Legislatures.

27. Mark Smith, "The Contingent Effects of Ballot Initiatives and Candidate Races on Turnout," *American Journal of Political Science* 45 (2001): 700–706. Smith measures the saliency of initiative legislative referenda contests by front-page news coverage, which recognizes that not all measures should have the same mobilizing effects. While we treat all initiatives as equal, our measure can be used more easily across time and place. See Caroline J. Tolbert, John Grummel, and Daniel A. Smith, "The Effects of Ballot Initiatives on Voter Turnout in the American States," *American Politics Research* 29 (2001): 625–48.

28. A dummy variable for gubernatorial races is coded one if the state had a gubernatorial race and zero if otherwise. An identical coding scheme is used for U.S. Senate races.

29. Raymond Wolfinger and Steven Rosenstone, *Who Votes?* (New Haven: Yale University Press, 1980).

30. Raw data are from the biannual *Book of the States* for 1970–98.

31. Wolfinger and Rosenstone, *Who Votes?*

32. U.S. census, 1970–2000. Many advocates of direct democracy were duly concerned that less educated voters would not vote on initiatives on the ballot, leading to an "automatic disenfranchisement of the unfit—those of least intelligence and public spirit voluntarily refraining, as a rule, from voting upon the measures sub-

mitted" (Frank Parsons, *Direct Legislation; or, The Veto Power in the Hands of the People* (Philadelphia: Taylor, 1900), quoted in Goebel, *Government,* 59–60.

33. Laura Langer, "Measuring Income Distribution across Space and Time in the American States," *Social Science Quarterly* 80 (1999): 55–67.

34. V. O. Key, *Southern Politics in State and Nation* (New York: Knopf, 1949); Rodney Hero, *Faces of Inequality: Social Diversity in American Politics* (New York: Oxford University Press, 1998); Rodney Hero and Caroline J. Tolbert, "A Racial/Ethnic Diversity Interpretation of Politics and Policy in the States of the U.S." *American Journal of Political Science* 40 (1996): 851–71.

35. Kim Hill and Jan Leighley, "Racial Diversity, Voter Turnout, and Mobilizing Institutions in the United States," *American Politics Quarterly* 27 (1999): 275–95.

36. Hero and Tolbert, "Racial/Ethnic Diversity Interpretation." The index is a measure of a state's racial/ethnic population. The index was computed with the following formula: minority diversity = 1 [(proportion Latino)^2 + (proportion African American)^2 + (proportion non-Hispanic white)^2 + (proportion Asian)^2].

37. M. Smith, "Contingent Effects." Using a chow test based on ordinary least squares (OLS) regression models for presidential and midterm elections, we found that the two models were statistically different and should be estimated separately: F (15, 669), H0 = 2.87 F =3.30, p = .01 (reject null).

38. This research faces a common ecological inference problem with which some readers are probably familiar—that is, we use geographically aggregated data at the state level to make inferences about individual-level behavior. While our primary interest is in understanding general voting patterns across states, because of this condition, there is the potential for misleading inferences about individual-level voting decisions. The second part of the chapter uses individual survey data to overcome this problem. See Caroline J. Tolbert, Ramona S. McNeal, and Daniel A. Smith, "Enhancing Civic Engagement," *State Politics and Policy* 3 (2003): 23–41.

39. Magleby, *Direct Legislation,* chap. 5.

40. We calculate predicted state turnout rates, holding constant socioeconomic and electoral factors and varying the number of initiatives appearing on state ballots using the display command in STATA. Estimated probabilities based on coefficients reported in table A.1, column 2, using 50-state data. For presidential elections, it is assumed that Senate and gubernatorial races appear on the ballot and that it is a nonsouthern state. The following variables were set at their mean: high school graduation rate, racial diversity, Gini coefficient, voter registration, and number of initiatives squared.

41. Robert Jackson, "The Mobilization of U.S. State Electorates in the 1998 and 1990 Elections," *Journal of Politics* 59 (1997): 520–37; Rosenstone and Hansen, *Mobilization, Participation, and Democracy.*

42. See, for example, Fishkin, *Democracy and Deliberation;* Barber, *Strong Democracy.*

43. We use STATA software to calculate predicted state turnout rates, holding constant socioeconomic and electoral factors and varying the number of initiatives appearing on state ballots. Estimated probabilities based on coefficients reported in table A.2, column 2, using 50-state data. For midterm elections, it is assumed that

there are Senate and gubernatorial races on the ballot and that it is a nonsouthern state. The following variables were set at their mean: high school graduation rate, racial diversity, Gini coefficient, the number of initiatives squared, and voter registration.

44. Bowler and Donovan, *Demanding Choices*.

45. We do not show the analysis because of space constraints.

46. Chavez, *Color Bind;* D. A. Smith, *Tax Crusaders;* Schrag, *Paradise Lost*.

47. Angus Campbell et al., *American Voter;* Wolfinger and Rosenstone, *Who Votes?*

48. Caroline J. Tolbert and Ramona S. McNeal, "Unraveling the Effects of the Internet on Political Participation," *Political Research Quarterly* 56 (2003): 175–85.

49. King, Tomz, and Wittenberg, "Making the Most of Statistical Analysis."

50. Robert Huckfeldt and John Sprague, "Choice, Social-Structure, and Political Information—The Informational Coercion of Minorities," *American Journal of Political Science* 32 (1988): 467–82.

51. See Daniel A. Smith and Caroline J. Tolbert, "The Initiative to Party: Partisanship and Ballot Initiatives in California," *Party Politics* 7 (2001): 739–57.

CHAPTER 3

1. See, for example, Haynes, "'People's Rule' in Oregon"; Zueblin, "Training"; Munro, *Initiative, Referendum, and Recall;* Gardner, "Problems"; Weyl, *New Democracy;* Croly, *Progressive Democracy*.

2. Jonathan Bourne Jr., "A Defense of Direct Legislation," in William B. Munro, ed., *The Initiative, Referendum, and Recall* (New York: Appleton, 1912), 203.

3. Putnam, *Bowling Alone*, 35.

4. Sidney Verba, Kay Schlozman, and Henry Brady, *Voice and Equality: Civic Voluntarism in American Politics* (Cambridge: Harvard University Press, 1995); Michael Delli Carpini and Scott Keeter, *What Americans Know about Politics and Why It Matters* (New Haven: Yale University Press, 1996); Michael Delli Carpini and Scott Keeter, "Measuring Political Knowledge: Putting First Things First," *American Journal of Political Science* 37 (1993): 1179–1206.

5. See Putnam, *Bowling Alone*, 36; Delli Carpini and Keeter, *What Americans Know about Politics*.

6. Barber, *Strong Democracy;* Pateman, *Participation and Democratic Theory*. See also James Wenzel, Todd Donovan, and Shaun Bowler, "Direct Democracy and Minorities: Changing Attitudes about Minorities Targeted by Initiatives," in Shaun Bowler, Todd Donovan, and Caroline J. Tolbert, eds., *Citizens as Legislators: Direct Democracy in the United States* (Columbus: Ohio State University Press, 1998), 228–48; David Butler and Austin Ranney, eds., *Referendums around the World: The Growing Use of Direct Democracy* (Washington, DC: AEI Press, 1994).

7. Bruce Ackerman, *We the People: Foundations* (Cambridge: Harvard University Press, 1993), 287. But see Simone Chambers's rebuttal of this line of argument in "Constitutional Referendums and Democratic Deliberation," in Matthew Mendelsohn and Andrew Parkin, eds., *Referendum Democracy: Citizens, Elites, and Deliberation in Referendum Campaigns* (New York: Palgrave, 2001).

8. See, among others, John Hibbing and Elizabeth Theiss-Morse, "Process Preferences and American Politics: What the People Want Government to Be," *American Political Science Review* 95 (2001): 145–53; Mark Smith, "Ballot Initiatives and the Democratic Citizen," *Journal of Politics* 64 (2002): 892–903; Matthew Mendelsohn and Fred Cutler, "The Effect of Referenda on Democratic Citizens: Information, Politicization, Efficacy, and Tolerance," *British Journal of Political Science* 30 (2000): 669–98; Matthias Benz and Alois Stutzer, "Are Voters Better Informed When They Have a Larger Say in Politics?" *Public Choice* (forthcoming).

9. Putnam, *Bowling Alone,* 163.

10. D. A. Smith, *Tax Crusaders;* David Magleby and Kelly Patterson, "Consultants and Direct Democracy," *PS: Political Science and Politics* 31 (1998): 160–69; Stephen C. Craig, Amie Kreppel, and James G. Kane, "Public Opinion and Direct Democracy: A Grassroots Perspective," in Matthew Mendelsohn and Andrew Parkin, eds., *Referendum Democracy: Citizens, Elites, and Deliberation in Referendum Campaigns* (New York: Palgrave, 2001).

11. Putnam, *Bowling Alone,* 164. Simone Chambers, "Constitutional Referendums and Democratic Deliberation," offers an insightful theoretical discussion of how direct democracy may undermine meaningful participation.

12. Broder, *Democracy Derailed;* Schrag, *Paradise Lost;* D. A. Smith, *Tax Crusaders;* Ellis, *Democratic Delusions.*

13. For exceptions, see M. Smith, "Ballot Initiatives"; Mendelsohn and Cutler, "Effect of Referenda"; Benz and Stutzer, "Are Voters Better Informed When They Have a Larger Say in Politics?"

14. Glenn Leshner and Michael McKean, "Using TV News for Political Information during an Off-Year Election: Effects on Political Knowledge and Cynicism," *Journal of Mass Communications Quarterly* 74 (1997): 69–83; D. H. Weaver, "What Voters Learn from Media," *Annual of the AAPSS* 546 (1996): 34–47; D. H. Weaver and D. Drew, "Voter Learning in the 1990 Off-Year Election: Did the Media Matter?" *Journalism Quarterly* 70 (1993): 356–68; S. Chaffee and J. McLeon, "Individual vs. Social Predictors of Information-Seeking," *Journalism Quarterly* 50 (1973): 95–120; S. Chaffee and S. F. Kanihan, "Learning about Politics from the Media," *Political Communication* 14 (1997): 421–30.

15. Arthur Lupia, "Shortcuts versus Encyclopedias: Information and Voting Behavior in California Insurance Reform Elections," *American Political Science Review* 88 (1994): 63–76; Bowler and Donovan, *Demanding Choices.*

16. On the negative effects of the media on political knowledge, see R. W. McChesney, *Rich Media, Poor Democracy: Communication Politics in Dubious Times* (Urbana: University of Illinois Press, 1999); James Fallows, *Breaking the News: How the Media Undermine American Democracy* (New York: Pantheon, 1996); but see J. McLeod and D. McDonald, "Beyond Simple Exposure: Media Orientations and Their Impact on the Political Process," *Communication Research* 12 (1985): 3–34. On agenda setting and positive media effects, see M. E. McCombs and D. L. Shaw, "The Agenda-Setting Function of Mass Media," *Public Opinion Quarterly* 36 (1972): 176–87; S. Iyengar and D. R. Kinder, *News That Matters: Agenda-Setting and Priming in a Television Age* (Chicago: University of Chicago Press, 1987); D. H. Weaver, D. A. Graber, M. E. McCombs, and C. H. Eyal, *Media Agenda-Setting in a Presiden-*

tial Election: Issues, Images, and Interest (New York: Praeger, 1981). On how voters acquire information with regard to candidate traits and issue positions, see Weaver et al., *Media Agenda-Setting;* Chaffee and McLeon, "Individual vs. Social Predictors of Information-Seeking"; Weaver and Drew, "Voter Learning in the 1990 Off-Year Election."

17. On the effects of the media on those with low political knowledge, see Philip Converse, "Information Flow and the Stability of Partisan Attitudes," in A. Campbell, ed., *Elections and the Political Order* (New York: Wiley, 1966); G. Comstock, "The Impact of Television on American Institutions," *Journal of Communication* 18 (1978): 12–28. On the media effects of those with higher political knowledge, see Christopher Atkin, "Instrumental Utilities and Information Seeking," in P. Clark, ed., *New Models for Mass Communication Research* (Beverly Hills, CA: Sage, 1973); F. Chew, "The Relationship of Information Needs to Issue Relevance and Media Use," *Journalism Quarterly* 71 (1994): 676–88; Jon A. Krosnick and Laura A. Brannon, "The Impact of the Gulf War on the Ingredients of Presidential Evaluations: Multidimensional Effects of Political Involvement," *American Political Science Review* 87 (1993): 963–75.

18. Angus Campbell et al., *American Voter;* Delli Carpini and Keeter, "Measuring Political Knowledge"; John Zaller, *The Nature and Origins of Mass Opinion* (Cambridge: Cambridge University Press, 1992).

19. Norman Nie and Kristi Andersen, "Mass Belief System Revisited: Political Change and Attitude Structure," *Journal of Politics* 36 (1974): 541–91; Norman Nie, Sidney Verba, and John Petrocik, *The Changing American Voter* (Cambridge: Harvard University Press, 1979).

20. Robert Luskin, "Explaining Political Sophistication," *Political Behavior* 12 (1990): 331–61.

21. Jane Mansbridge, *Beyond Adversary Democracy* (Chicago: University of Chicago Press, 1983); Barber, *Strong Democracy;* Pateman, *Participation and Democratic Theory.*

22. McCuan et al., "California's Political Warriors." See also Todd Donovan, Shaun Bowler, David McCuan, and Ken Fernandez, "Contending Players and Strategies: Opposition Advantages in Initiative Elections," in Shaun Bowler, Todd Donovan, and Caroline J. Tolbert, eds., *Citizens as Legislators: Direct Democracy in the United States* (Columbus: Ohio State University Press, 1998).

23. Quoted in McCuan et al., "California's Political Warriors," 67. See also the rich discussion of information cues in Elisabeth Gerber, *The Populist Paradox: Interest Group Influence and the Promise of Direct Legislation* (Princeton: Princeton University Press, 1999); Lupia, "Shortcuts versus Encyclopedias"; Bowler and Donovan, *Demanding Choices.*

24. M. Smith, "Ballot Initiatives."

25. Benz and Stutzer, "Are Voters Better Informed When They Have a Larger Say in Politics?"

26. In addition to measuring the number of initiatives on the ballot in the current election, we also estimated our models with the average annual number of initiatives appearing on state election ballots from 1970 to 1992 (Tolbert, Lowenstein,

and Donovan, "Election Law") as a broader measure of the historical use of the initiative process. The statistical significance and substantive interpretations of empirical models were the same as those reported in the appendix. The correlation between the number of initiatives on the ballot in 1996, 1998, and 2000 and the average annual variable is extremely high (Pearson $r = .90$ to $.96$), showing consistent use of the process by citizens over time.

27. See Shaun Bowler and Todd Donovan, "Democracy, Institutions, and Attitudes about Citizen Influence on Government," *British Journal of Political Science* 32 (2002): 371–90, for a similar measurement of partisanship. When partisanship is measured by the seven-point ordinal index rather than a series of dummy variables, the substantive findings of the analysis are unchanged.

28. P. Norris, *Digital Divide;* Mossberger, Tolbert and Stansbury, *Virtual Inequality;* Tolbert and McNeal, "Unraveling"; Bruce Bimber, "Information and Political Engagement in America: The Search for Effects of Information Technology at the Individual Level," *Political Research Quarterly* 54 (2001): 53–67.

29. M. Smith, "Ballot Initiatives"; Mendelsohn and Cutler, "Effect of Referenda"; Benz and Stutzer, "Are Voters Better Informed When They Have a Larger Say in Politics?"

30. For an earlier treatment, see D. A. Smith and Tolbert, "Initiative to Party."

31. Chavez, *Color Bind.*

32. See Daniel A. Smith, "Special Interests and Direct Democracy: An Historical Glance," in M. Dane Waters, ed., *The Battle over Citizen Lawmaking* (Durham, NC: Carolina Academic Press, 2001).

33. The number of initiatives dropped considerably between 1996 and 2000. There were 69 statewide initiatives on the ballots in 18 states in 2000, compared with 93 initiatives on the ballots of 20 states in 1996 (data from Initiative and Referendum Institute, "I and R Usage," at <www.iandrinstitute.org>, January 4, 2002).

34. Mendelsohn and Cutler, "Effect of Referenda."

35. Putnam, *Bowling Alone,* 21.

36. We obtained data for Putnam's social capital index from Putnam's Web site, <www.bowlingalone.com>, July 7, 2002. Putnam's social-capital index is really a primordial stew that includes numerous individual and aggregate level measures of civic engagement. His index includes the following 14 variables: (1) "I spend a lot of time visiting friends." (2) Agree that "Most people can be trusted." (3) Agree that "Most people are honest." (4) Attendance at any public meeting on town or school affairs in last year (percent). (5) Number of civic and social organizations per 1,000 population. (6) Average number of club meetings attended in last year. (7) Average number of group memberships. (8) Average number of times volunteered in last year. (9) Average number of times entertained at home in last year. (10) Average number of times worked on community project in last year. (11) Number of nonprofit (501[c]3) organizations per 1,000 population. (12) Served as officer of some club or organization in last year (percent). (13) Served on committee of some local organization in last year (percent). (14) Turnout in presidential elections, 1988 and 1992.

37. Putnam, *Bowling Alone,* 291.

38. See Tolbert, Lowenstein, and Donovan, "Election Law."

39. Hero, *Faces of Inequality;* Hero and Tolbert, "Racial/Ethnic Diversity Interpretation."

40. Competition index developed by Tom Holbrook and Elizabeth VanDunk, "Electoral Competition in the American States," *American Political Science Review* 87 (1993): 955–62.

41. Ideology index developed by Robert Erikson, Gerald Wright, and John McIver, *Statehouse Democracy* (New York: Cambridge University Press, 1993).

42. See Hill and Leighley, "Racial Diversity, Voter Turnout, and Mobilizing Institutions," for similar control variables. Data from 1990 U.S. census.

CHAPTER 4

1. See John Hibbing and Elizabeth Theiss-Morse, *Congress as Public Enemy: Public Attitudes toward Political Institutions* (Cambridge: Cambridge University Press, 1995); John Hibbing and Elizabeth Theiss-Morse, eds., *What Is It about Government That Americans Dislike?* (Cambridge: Cambridge University Press, 2001); Joseph Nye, Philip Zelikow, and David King, eds., *Why People Don't Trust Government* (Cambridge: Harvard University Press, 1997).

2. Based on Harris polls, cited in Putnam, *Bowling Alone,* 46–48. See also Todd Donovan and Shawn Bowler, *Reforming the Republic* (Upper Saddle River, NJ: Prentice Hall, 2004).

3. Mark Baldassare, *California in the New Millennium: The Changing Social and Political Landscape* (Berkeley: University of California Press, 2000), 12. See also Stephen C. Craig, ed., *Broken Contract? Changing Relationships between Americans and Their Government* (Boulder, CO: Westview, 1996).

4. Osborne and Gaebler, *Reinventing Government;* Barber, *Strong Democracy;* Bowler, Donovan, and Tolbert, *Citizens as Legislators;* Peters, *Future of Governing;* Ian Budge, *The New Challenge of Direct Democracy* (Cambridge, MA: Polity, 1996); Fishkin, *Democracy and Deliberation;* Elster, *Deliberative Democracy;* Dryzek, *Deliberative Democracy.*

5. Munro, *Initiative, Referendum, and Recall,* 21.

6. Johnson, "Direct Legislation," 149.

7. Jonathan Bourne Jr., "Functions of the Initiative, Referendum, and Recall," in *Annals of the American Academy of Political and Social Science* (Philadelphia: Hummel, 1912), 3:43. See also Schlup, "Republican Insurgent"; Scheiber, "Foreword."

8. See, for example, George Haynes, "Massachusetts Public Opinion Bills," *Proceedings of the American Political Science Association* 4 (1907): 152–63; Gardner, "Problems."

9. "Initiatives bask in the 'mythic idea' of popular sovereignty and in the bedrock principle of consent of the governed" (Richard Collins, "Part II: New Directions in Direct Democracy: How Democratic Are Initiatives?" *University of Colorado Law Review* 72 [2001]: 995).

10. Marc J. Hetherington, "The Political Relevance of Political Trust," *American Political Science Review* 92 (1998): 791–808; Marc J. Hetherington, "The Effects of Political Trust on the Presidential Vote, 1968–96," *American Political Science Review* 93 (1999): 311–26; Paul Abramson, *Political Attitudes in America: Formation and Change* (San Francisco: Freeman, 1993); Pippa Norris, *Critical Citizens: Global Support for Democratic Governance* (Oxford: Oxford University Press, 1999); Jack Citrin, "Who's the Boss? Direct Democracy and the Popular Control of Government," in Craig, ed., *Broken Contract?*; Paul Abramson, John Aldrich, and David Rohde, *Change and Continuity in the 1996 Elections* (Washington, DC: CQ Press, 1998).

11. Donovan and Bowler, *Reforming the Republic;* C. Anderson and C. Guilory, "Political Institutions and Satisfaction with Democracy: A Cross-National Analysis of Consensus and Majoritarian Systems," *American Political Science Review* 91 (1997): 66–81; Stacy B. Gordon and Gary Segura, "Cross-National Variation in the Political Sophistication of Individuals: Capability or Choice?" *Journal of Politics* 59 (1997): 126–47; Huckfeldt and Sprague, "Choice, Social-Structure, and Political Information."

12. James March and Johan Olsen, "The New Institutionalism: Organizational Factors in Political Life," *American Political Science Review* 78 (1984): 734–49; March and Olsen, *Rediscovering Institutions;* Steinmo, Thelen, and Longstreth, *Structuring Politics;* Sven Steinmo, "Political Institutions and Tax Policy in the United States, Sweden, and Britain," *World Politics* 41 (1989): 500–534; B. Guy Peters, *Institutional Theory in Political Science: The New Institutionalism* (London: Pinter, 1999).

13. Matsusaka, "Fiscal Effects"; Gerber, *Populist Paradox;* Gerber, "Legislative Response"; Elisabeth Gerber and Simon Hug, "Minority Rights and Direct Legislation: Theory, Method, and Evidence," in Matthew Mendelsohn and Andrew Parkin, eds., *Referendum Democracy: Citizens, Elites, and Deliberation in Referendum Campaigns* (New York: Palgrave, 2001). But see Lascher, Hagen, and Rochlin, "Gun behind the Door?"; Camobreco, "Preferences, Fiscal Policies, and the Initiative Process." See also the recent debate on this question: Matsusaka, "Problems"; Hagen, Lascher, and Camobreco, "Response to Matsusaka." For micro-level studies of legislator response to ballot initiatives, see D. A. Smith, "Overturning Term Limits"; D. A. Smith, "Homeward *Bound?*"

14. Barber, *Strong Democracy;* Pateman, *Participation and Democratic Theory;* Morell, "Citizens' Evaluations."

15. Barber, *Strong Democracy,* Pateman, *Participation and Democratic Theory;* Mansbridge, *Beyond Adversary Democracy.*

16. Putnam, *Bowling Alone.*

17. Hibbing and Theiss-Morse, "Process Preferences and American Politics."

18. Anthony Downs, *An Economic Theory of Democracy* (New York: Harper and Row, 1957); James Enlow and Melvin Hinich, *The Spatial Theory of Voting* (Cambridge: Cambridge University Press, 1984).

19. Jack Citrin, "Comment: The Political Relevance of Trust in Government," *American Political Science Review* 68 (1974): 973.

20. Hibbing and Theiss-Morse, "Process Preferences and American Politics."

21. M. Stephen Weatherford, "Measuring Political Legitimacy," *American Political Science Review* 86 (1992): 149.

22. David Kimball and Samuel Patterson, "Living up to Expectations: Public Attitudes toward Congress," *Journal of Politics* 59 (1997): 701–28.

23. John Hibbing and Elizabeth Theiss-Morse, "The Media's Role in Public Negativity toward Congress: Distinguishing Emotional Reactions and Cognitive Evaluations," *American Journal of Political Science* 42 (1998): 475–98.

24. Hibbing and Theiss-Morse, "Process Preferences and American Politics."

25. Hibbing and Theiss-Morse, "Process Preferences and American Politics."

26. Citrin, "Who's the Boss?"

27. Martin Gilens, James Glasser, and Tali Mendelberg, "Having a Say: Political Efficacy in the Context of Direct Democracy," paper presented at the annual meeting of the American Political Science Association, San Francisco, September 2001.

28. Arguing that "not all propositions are created equal," Gilens, Glasser, and Mendelberg find, however, that citizens residing in states with "salient" ballot propositions report increased external and internal political efficacy.

29. Bowler and Donovan, "Democracy, Institutions, and Attitudes." Rodney Hero and Caroline Tolbert build on the work of Bowler and Donovan by analyzing similar survey questions over an extended period of time. "Minority Voices and Citizen Attitudes about Government Responsiveness in the American States: Do Social and Institutional Context Matter?" *British Journal of Political Science* 34 (2004): 109–21.

30. Schrag, *Paradise Lost*; Broder, *Democracy Derailed*.

31. Baldassare, *California in the New Millennium*.

32. Tolbert, "Changing Rules"; Schrag, *Paradise Lost*; Broder, *Democracy Derailed*; Alan Rosenthal, *The Decline of Representative Democracy: Process, Participation, and Power in State Legislatures* (Washington, DC: CQ Press, 1998).

33. Zoltan Hajnal, Elisabeth Gerber, and H. Louch, "Minorities and Direct Legislation: Evidence from California Ballot Proposition Elections," *Journal of Politics* 64 (2002): 154–77; Bruno S. Frey and Lorenz Goette, "Does the Popular Vote Destroy Civil Rights?" *American Journal of Political Science* 42 (1998): 1343–48; Caroline J. Tolbert and Rodney Hero, "Dealing with Diversity: Racial/Ethnic Context and Social Policy Change," *Political Research Quarterly* 54 (2001): 571–604.

34. Baldassare, *California in the New Millennium*, 3.

35. Wenzel, Donovan, and Bowler, "Direct Democracy and Minorities," 228–48.

36. D. A. Smith, *Tax Crusaders*; Craig, Kreppel, and Kane, "Public Opinion and Direct Democracy"; Daniel A. Smith and Robert J. Herrington, "The Process of Direct Democracy: Colorado's 1996 Parental Rights Amendment," *Social Science Journal* 37 (2000): 179–94.

37. David Magleby, *Direct Legislation: Voting on Ballot Propositions in the United States* (Baltimore: Johns Hopkins University Press, 1984); D. A. Smith, *Tax Crusaders*; Broder, *Democracy Derailed*.

38. McCuan et al., "California's Political Warriors"; David Magleby, "Direct

Legislation in the American States," in David Butler and Austin Ranney, eds., *Referendums around the World: The Growing Use of Direct Democracy* (Washington, DC: AEI Press, 1994); D. A. Smith and Lubinski, "Direct Democracy"; Allswang, *Initiative and Referendum*.

39. McCuan et al., "California's Political Warriors," 100; Donovan et al., "Contending Players and Strategies."

40. The discussion of the variables and data is drawn from Hero and Tolbert, "Minority Voices and Citizen Attitudes."

41. Tolbert, Lowenstein, and Donovan, "Election Law."

42. Each nationwide face-to-face survey was conducted by the Inter-University Consortium for Social and Political Research, Ann Arbor, Michigan.

43. Bowler and Donovan, "Democracy, Institutions, and Attitudes."

44. Richard Niemi, Stephen Craig, and F. Mattei, "Measuring Internal Political Efficacy in the 1988 National Election Study," *American Political Science Review* 85 (1991): 1407–13.

45. See Bowler and Donovan, "Democracy, Institutions, and Attitudes," for similar measurement of the dependent variable. See Tolbert, Lowenstein, and Donovan, "Election Law," for the index of initiative use. There are numerous ways to measure state variation in usage of direct democracy institutions. Bowler and Donovan, "Democracy, Institutions, and Attitudes," use the total number of initiatives that have appeared on state election ballots since the inception of the process to measure cumulative exposure to direct democracy mechanisms. Since voters today were not part of the electorate in the early 1900s, the measure used in this research is deemed more appropriate. It also takes into account the frequency of initiative use in states that recently adopted the process, such as Florida. There is a high correlation among the various measures of usage of the initiative process, suggesting that the substantive findings of the analysis would not change with a different operationalization. The correlation between the total number of initiatives appearing on state election ballots since the adoption of the process and the number of initiatives appearing on state election ballots during 1970–92 is .92. The total number of initiatives appearing on state election ballots over time correlates with average annual use of the process in the last two decades at .81. Average annual usage of the process from 1970 to 1992 correlates with average annual usage of the process since adoption at .97.

46. Hill and Leighley, "Racial Diversity, Voter Turnout, and Mobilizing Institutions."

47. Following Hero and Tolbert, "Racial/Ethnic Diversity Interpretation," an index of state minority diversity was created from 1996 Current Population Survey data and 1980 and 1990 U.S. census data of the percentage Latino, African American, white, and Asian American in each state.

48. Bowler and Donovan, "Democracy, Institutions, and Attitudes."

49. Michael Lewis-Beck and Tom Rice, *Forecasting Elections* (Washington, DC: CQ Press, 1992).

50. See Bowler and Donovan, "Democracy, Institutions, and Attitudes," for similar operationalization of partisanship.

51. Bowler and Donovan, "Democracy, Institutions, and Attitudes," used OLS

regression rather than ordered logistic regression, but the two statistical techniques result in comparable findings.

52. R. O. de la Garza et al., *Latino Voices: Mexican, Puerto Rican, and Cuban Perspectives on American Politics* (Boulder, CO: Westview, 1992); Baldassare, *California in the New Millennium*.

53. Baldassare, *California in the New Millennium*.

54. Hajnal, Gerber, and Louch, "Minorities and Direct Legislation."

55. See Mendelsohn and Parkin, *Referendum Democracy*.

56. Bowler and Donovan, "Democracy, Institutions, and Attitudes."

CHAPTER 5

1. See John Chambers, *The Tyranny of Change: America in the Progressive Era, 1890–1920* (New York: St. Martin's, 1992); John Cooper, *Pivotal Decades: The United States, 1900–1920* (New York: Norton, 1990); Link and McCormick, *Progressivism;* Lewis Gould, *Reform and Regulation: American Politics from Roosevelt to Wilson* (Prospect Heights, IL: Waveland, 1996); Gabriel Kolko, *The Triumph of Conservatism: A Reinterpretation of American History, 1900–1916* (Chicago: Quadrangle, 1963); Martin Shefter, *Political Parties and the State: The American Historical Experience* (Princeton: Princeton University Press, 1994).

2. Sullivan, *Direct Legislation,* 91.

3. Reinsch, "Initiative and Referendum," 157.

4. Frank Norris, *The Octopus: A Story of California* (New York: Doubleday, Page, 1901).

5. Hiram Johnson, "Inaugural Address," 1911, at <www.governor.ca.gov/govsite/govsgallery/h/biography/governor_23.html >, January 7, 2003.

6. Cushman, "Recent Experience," 538–39.

7. Broder, *Democracy Derailed;* Ellis, *Democratic Delusions,* 109.

8. Goebel, *Government,* 185–99.

9. See Daniel Lowenstein, "A Patternless Mosaic: Campaign Finance and the First Amendment after Austin," *Capital University Law Review* 21 (1992): 381–427; Daniel Lowenstein, "Campaign Spending and Ballot Propositions: Recent Experience, Public Choice Theory, and the First Amendment," *UCLA Law Review* 29 (1982): 505–641; John Shockley, "Money in Politics: Judicial Roadblocks to Campaign Finance Reform," *Hastings Constitutional Law Quarterly* 10 (1983): 679–92; John Shockley, "Direct Democracy, Campaign Finance, and the Courts: Can Corruption, Undue Influence, and Declining Voter Confidence Be Found?" *University of Miami Law Review* 39 (1985): 377–428; Magleby, *Direct Legislation;* Betty Zisk, *Money, Media, and the Grass Roots: State Ballot Issues and the Electoral Process* (Newbury Park, CA: Sage, 1987); D. A. Smith, *Tax Crusaders;* D. A. Smith and Herrington, "Process of Direct Democracy."

10. See Shaun Bowler and Todd Donovan, "Do Voters Have a Cue? Television Advertisements as a Source of Information in Citizen-Initiated Referendum Campaigns," *European Journal of Political Research* 41 (2002): 777–93; Gerber, *Populist Paradox;* Elisabeth Gerber and Arthur Lupia, "Voter Competence in Direct Legisla-

tion Elections," in Stephen L. Elkin and Karol Edward Soltan, eds., *Citizen Competence and Democratic Institutions* (University Park: Pennsylvania State University Press, 1999); Elizabeth Garrett and Elisabeth Gerber, "Money in the Initiative and Referendum Process: Evidence of Its Effects and Prospects for Reform," in M. Dane Waters, ed., *The Battle over Citizen Lawmaking* (Durham, NC: Carolina Academic Press, 2001). More generally, see Bradley Smith, *Unfree Speech: The Folly of Campaign Finance Reform* (Princeton: Princeton University Press, 2001).

11. Initiative and Referendum Institute, "Revised Overview of Statewide Initiatives, Popular Referendum, and Legislative Referendum on the 1998 Election Ballot," at <www.iandrinstitute.org>, September 7, 2002. Figures for ballot measure spending are slightly understated because they do not include independent expenditures or expenditures made by educational committees. See Daniel A. Smith, "Campaign Financing of Ballot Initiatives in the American States," in Larry Sabato, Bruce Larson, and Howard Ernst, eds., *Dangerous Democracy? The Battle over Ballot Initiatives in America* (Lanham, MD: Rowman and Littlefield, 2001), 77–78.

12. M. Dane Waters, "Initiative and Referendum Institute's November 2002 General Election Pre-Election Report," at <www.iandrinstitute.org>, August 10, 2002; Ballot Initiative Strategy Center Foundation, "Money and Ballot Measures in the 2002 Election," at <www.ballotfunding.org>, January 7, 2003.

13. The amount spent for and against the measure—which included $63.2 million by Indian tribes supporting the measure and $25.4 million by casino operators and organized labor opposing it—easily broke the previous spending record of $55.9 million set in 1988 on an auto insurance measure. The San Manuel Tribe alone spent $25.5 million promoting the measure. In addition, electric companies spent $38.1 million to defeat Proposition 9, a measure that would have deregulated the electric utility industry, and tobacco companies drained $29.7 million (including more than $20 million from Philip Morris) from their corporate coffers in a failed bid to defeat Proposition 10, which raised taxes on cigarettes by 50 cents a pack to pay for early childhood education and health programs. See Dan Morain, "Wealth Buys Access to State Politics," *Los Angeles Times,* April 18, 1999; Dan Morain, "Governor Race Set Spending Record," *Los Angeles Times,* February 4, 1999.

14. Gerber, *Populist Paradox*, 2; California Commission on Campaign Financing, *Democracy by Initiative* (Los Angeles: Center for Responsive Government, 1992), 263–64.

15. During the run-up to the November 1996 election, the committee received a total of $549,795 in contributions. Only 39 of the 2,842 contributions the committee received were for $1,000 or more, yet they accounted for 85 percent of the total amount, or $469,033. Two companies, U.S. Sugar and Flo-Sun Sugar, along with the Sugar Cane Growers Association, contributed $339,947, or 62 percent of the total (Daniel A. Smith, "Unmasking the Tax Crusaders," *State Government News* 41 [March 1998]: 18–21).

16. Burt Hubbard, "Ballot Measure Funds Set Record," *Rocky Mountain News,* December 4, 1998; Floyd Ciruli, "Direct Democracy: Colorado's New Growth Industry," at <www.ciruli.com/variable1–96.html>, December 30, 1998.

17. Erin Billings, "Big Bucks Couldn't Sway State Voters," *Missoula (Montana) Missoulian,* December 6, 1998; Carey Goldberg, "2 States Consider Boldly Revamp-

ing Campaign Finance," *New York Times,* October 19, 1998; Washington Public Disclosure Commission, "1998 Ballot Measures—Contribution and Expenditure Totals," 1999, at <www.pdc.wa.gov/>, November 30, 2002; Henry Cordes, "Initiative 414 Spending Set Record," *Omaha (Nebraska) World-Herald,* January 7, 1999.

18. Ballot Initiative Strategy Center Foundation, "Buying Laws at the Ballot" (2000), at <www.ballotfunding.org>, December 13, 2002.

19. Ballot Initiative Strategy Center Foundation, "Buying Laws at the Ballot." The influence of big money—whether from special interests or from well-heeled citizens—tends to be the greatest during the prequalification phase of the initiative process (Elizabeth Garrett, "Money, Agenda Setting, and Direct Democracy," *Texas Law Review* 77 [1999]: 1845–90). To qualify measures for the ballot by obtaining a sufficient number of signatures on petitions, a growing number of ballot issue sponsors rely solely on contributions from a handful of individuals (Daniel A. Smith, "The Millionaire's Club: Why Leave Ballot Initiatives to the Rich?" *Denver Post,* August 18, 2002).

20. For a discussion of interest groups' surreptitious activities in ballot campaigns and a brief discussion of whether interest groups may be prohibited from engaging in issue ads that name federal candidates prior to an election, see Elizabeth Garrett and Daniel A. Smith, "Veiled Political Actors: The Real Threat to Campaign Disclosure Statutes," Working Paper, USC/Caltech Center for the Study of Law and Politics, <http://lawweb.usc.edu/cslp/pages/papers.html>, February 1, 2004.

21. For overviews of the role special interests have played in direct democracy contests, see D. A. Smith, "Campaign Financing"; D. A. Smith, "Special Interests and Direct Democracy."

22. Wilcox, *Government,* 103.

23. Beard, "Introductory Note," in Beard and Shultz, *Documents,* 49.

24. For discussions of the controversial votes on the fishing initiatives, see Cushman, "Recent Experience"; Eaton, *Oregon System;* Bowler and Donovan, *Demanding Choices,* 118–28.

25. Ellis, *Democratic Delusions,* 185.

26. D. A. Smith and Lubinski, "Direct Democracy"; City Club of Denver, *Direct Legislation in Colorado* (Denver: Eames, 1927).

27. For details of professionalized ballot campaigns in California, see Stanley Kelley, *Professional Public Relations and Political Power* (Baltimore: Johns Hopkins University Press, 1956), 39–66; McCuan et al., "California's Political Warriors"; V. O. Key, "Publicity of Campaign Expenditures on Issues in California," *American Political Science Review* 4 (1936): 713–23; Cottrell, "Twenty Five Years"; Winston Crouch, *The Initiative and Referendum in California* (Los Angeles: Haynes Foundation, 1950); Robert Pritchell, "The Influence of Professional Campaign Management Firms in Partisan Elections in California," *Western Political Quarterly* 11 (1958): 278–300; Goebel, *Government,* chaps. 7–8; Allswang, *Initiative and Referendum,* chaps. 1–2; Paula Baker, "Campaigns and Potato Chips; or, Some Causes and Consequences of Political Spending," *Journal of Policy History* 14 (2002): 4–29.

28. John Owens and Larry Wade find that in California, initiative expenditures have not increased appreciably since the 1930s. In fact, they find that spending on

ballot measures, in constant dollars, has dropped over the years: "Between 1924 and 1962 per capita costs in 1972 dollars averaged $.10 per election," they show, "while for the period 1964–84 they averaged $.08" ("Campaign Spending on California Ballot Propositions, 1924–1984: Trends and Voting Effects," *Western Political Quarterly* 39 [1986]: 679–80).

29. Virginia Gray and David Lowery, *The Population Ecology of Interest Representation: Lobbying Communities in the American States* (Ann Arbor: University of Michigan Press, 1996).

30. See Fredrick Boehmke, "The Effect of Direct Democracy on the Size and Diversity of State Interest Group Populations," *Journal of Politics* 64 (2002): 828. In partitioning interest groups into two categories, citizen and economic, Boehmke classifies Gray and Lowery's interest group subpopulations of "government" and "social" as "citizen" groups, the same nomenclature Gerber uses. Gerber finds that contrary to popular conception, "citizen" rather than "economic" groups are the true beneficiaries in direct democracy elections, as economic groups are severely constrained in their ability to use ballot initiatives to the detriment of broader interests. Gerber operationalizes her model by specifying whether issue committees obtain a majority of their funding from "economic interests" or "citizen interests." Her binary typology collapses discrete actors under the two broad classifications. Under her category of "citizen interests," she combines individuals, citizen groups, and labor unions. Individual contributors who give small amounts to issue campaigns are classified the same as millionaires. Labor unions are classified as citizen groups as well, as their members, according to Gerber, "are not official representatives of their employer but autonomous individuals who pay their own dues." While this may be technically true in right-to-work states (but not in closed-shop states), others understand unions as rational actors whose members have narrow economic interests and who become members (voluntarily or through coercion) to enhance their professional or occupational status (Gerber, *Populist Paradox,* 69–71, 111–16, 139–41). Our findings, however, that initiatives encourage citizen interests is consistent with Gerber's research.

31. Virginia Gray and David Lowery, "The Institutionalization of State Communities of Organized Interests," *Political Research Quarterly* 54 (2001): 265–84; Virginia Gray and David Lowery, "The Stability and Expression of Density Dependence in State Communities of Organized Interest," *American Politics Research* 29 (2001): 374–91.

32. Gray and Lowery's interest group subcategories for 1975, 1980, and 1990 differ from those for 1997. For the 1990 data, they partition interest groups into 10 categories. With the 1997 data, they offer 26 categories (which they call guilds) as well as an unknown category and use the terms *for profit* and *not for profit* in a similar manner as Boehmke's citizen and economic interest groups. See Gray and Lowery, *Population Ecology;* Jennifer Wolak, Adam Newmark, Todd McNoldy, David Lowery, and Virginia Gray, "Much of Politics Is Still Local: Multi-State Lobbying in State Interest Communities," *Legislative Studies Quarterly* 27 (2002): 527–55.

33. Considering the high financial barriers to running an initiative campaign, constraints should be placed on the assumptions of Boehmke's model. Boehmke

assumes that in initiative states, if an interest group is rebuffed by the legislature, "the group can appeal directly to voters by proposing an initiative in the hope that voters will support adopting the policy," assuming that interest groups in initiative states have more "leverage" over the legislature because of the "threat of proposing an initiative" ("Effect of Direct Democracy," 829). For the prohibitive costs of running an initiative campaign, see Elizabeth Garrett, "Perspective on Direct Democracy: Who Directs Direct Democracy?" *University of Chicago Law School Roundtable* 4 (1997): 17–36; Garrett, "Money, Agenda Setting, and Direct Democracy."

34. According to Gray and Lowery, between 1990 and 1997 there was little growth in the number of membership organizations and a decline in the number of associations registered to lobby in the states. In contrast, the institutional sector grew by nearly 9 percent (Gray and Lowery, "Institutionalization of State Communities"; Gray and Lowery, "Stability and Expression of Density Dependence").

35. In a draft of his article, Boehmke used a measure of historical usage (the number of initiatives on a state's ballot over the previous five years) but found that it was not a significant predictor of the size or diversity of a state's interest group population. (Fredrick Boehmke, "The Effect of Direct Democracy on the Size and Diversity of State Interest Group Populations," paper presented at the annual meeting of the Midwest Political Science Association, April 2001).

36. Our measure of initiative use for 1990–96 tallies the number of statewide initiatives on the ballot over the seven-year period, which includes general, primary, special, and odd-year elections. Because we use interest group data from only one year and do not use pooled data as Boehmke does, we omit his "indicator" variables for each year in his multiyear sample. See Boehmke, "Effect of Direct Democracy," 830.

37. Figures from Initiative and Referendum Institute, at <www.iandrinstitute.org>, July 10, 2002.

38. Erikson, Wright, and McIver, *Statehouse Democracy.* A state's 1997 real GSP and its square are measured in millions of dollars. State government expenditures as a percentage of GSP are also in millions of dollars. Divided government is a dichotomous variable, coded one if a state had divided government in 1996 and zero otherwise. State political ideology is measured by taking the difference between the percentages of state liberal identifiers and conservative identifiers in 1997. See the work of William Mitchell and Michael Munger, "Economic Models of Interest Groups: An Introductory Survey," *American Journal of Political Science* 35 (1991): 512–46; Dennis Mueller, *The Political Economy of Growth* (New Haven: Yale University Press, 1983); Gray and Lowery, *Population Ecology.*

39. It is possible that there is a simultaneity problem, as states with more interest groups could have more initiatives on the ballot, the reverse of what we (and Boehmke) hypothesize. There is a weak correlation between the total size of state interest group populations in 1997 and initiative use between 1990 and 1996 ($r = .254$, $p = .075$, two-tailed, $n = 50$). Previous research on this topic, however, finds that this hypothesized inverse relationship is weak; see Susan Banducci, "Direct Legislation: When Is It Used and When Does It Pass?" in Shaun Bowler, Todd Donovan, and Caroline J. Tolbert, eds., *Citizens as Legislators: Direct Democracy in the United States* (Columbus: Ohio State University Press, 1998), 116.

40. David Truman, *The Governmental Process: Political Interests and Public Opinion* (New York: Knopf, 1951), 508–14.

41. See Goebel, *Government,* chap. 4.

42. Voluntary contributions, of course, are critical to the survival of many interest groups, especially citizen or not-for-profit organizations. Contributing money to political campaigns (both candidate and issue) is an important form of political participation. Pluralist scholars and their critics have long argued that this form of citizen participation is necessary to ensure that diverse voices are heard in the political process. See Truman, *Governmental Process;* E. E. Schattschneider, *The Semisovereign People* (New York: Holt, Rinehart, and Winston, 1960); Kay Schlozman, "What Accent the Heavenly Chorus? Political Equality and the American Pressure System," *Journal of Politics* 46 (1984): 1006–32; Kay Schlozman and John Tierney, *Organized Interests and American Democracy* (New York: Harper and Row, 1986).

43. In addition to measuring the number of initiatives appearing on the ballot in the current election, we also used the average annual number of initiatives appearing on state election ballots from 1970 to 1992 as a broader measure of the historical use of the initiative process. The statistical significance and substantive interpretations of the nine empirical models were unchanged. The correlation between the number of initiatives on ballot in 1996, 1998, and 2000 and the average annual variable is extremely high (Pearson $r = .90$ to .96).

44. Lewis-Beck and Rice, *Forecasting Elections;* Wolfinger and Rosenstone, *Who Votes?* Magleby, *Direct Legislation.*

45. See Bowler and Donovan, "Democracy, Institutions, and Attitudes." When partisanship is measured by the seven-point ordinal index rather than a series of dichotomous variables, the analysis's substantive findings remain unchanged.

46. Budge, *New Challenge of Direct Democracy.*

47. Hill and Leighley, "Racial Diversity, Voter Turnout, and Mobilizing Institutions."

48. See chapter 2 for measurement of the state racial diversity index using 1996 Current Population Survey data and 2000 U.S. census data.

49. Additional analysis not shown as a result of space constraints. See Caroline J. Tolbert, Ramona McNeal, and Daniel A. Smith, "Enhancing Civic Engagement: The Effect of Direct Democracy on Political Participation and Knowledge," *State Politics and Policy Quarterly* 3 (2003): 23–41.

50. See Daniel A. Smith, "Howard Jarvis' Legacy? An Assessment of Antitax Initiatives in the American States," *State Tax Notes* 22 (2001): 753–64.

51. Galen Nelson, "Fighting Regressive Tax Measures," at <www.ballot.org/resources/galentaxes.html>, September 10, 2002.

52. John Jacobs, "Unmasking 226's 'Paycheck Protection' Masquerade," *Sacramento Bee,* May 28, 1998.

53. Nelson, "Fighting Regressive Tax Measures."

54. Ed Quillen, "Which Basin Should Colorado Destroy to Aid Developers?" *Denver Post,* May 4, 1999.

55. Beth Silver, "Big Washington Business Mulls Ballot Initiatives," *Tacoma (Washington) News Tribune,* January 5, 2001.

56. Waters, *Battle.*

57. Garrett and Smith, "Veiled Political Actors."

58. Ellis, *Democratic Delusions,* 109.

CHAPTER 6

1. Munro, *Initiative, Referendum, and Recall,* 17.

2. Shafroth, "Imperative Need," 516.

3. See Hermann Lieb, *The Initiative and Referendum* (Chicago: Lieb, 1902), 49.

4. Weyl, *New Democracy,* 298. For a Progressive Era defense of the functionality of parties and their importance in the articulation of public opinion, see Lowell, *Public Opinion and Popular Government.*

5. Quoted in Cronin, *Direct Democracy,* 46–48.

6. Quoted in Barnett, *Operation,* 185.

7. Quoted in Barnett, *Operation,* 186. Barnett contended that the direct primary ("a child of direct legislation") was more responsible than the mechanisms of direct democracy for the "practical annihilation of party organization" in Oregon.

8. Oberholtzer, *Referendum in America,* 392–93. More generally, however, Oberholtzer thought that the initiative process (especially as practiced in Oregon), while perhaps displacing the traditional bosses, created and perpetuated a new machine that dominated governmental policies. Dubious that party machines would be a thing of the past, Oberholtzer concluded that in Oregon, "instead of the old 'machine' [initiative proponents] have established their own—the Grange—the Federation of Labor—the People's Power League. For the old bosses they have brought themselves forward as new bosses." By displacing the traditional party machine, the backers of the Oregon system perpetuated "devices by which clubs of farmers, fishermen, orchardmen and graziers, flattered and cajoled by a few leaders, can control the policy of the government, both local and State" (*Referendum in America,* 502).

9. Cronin, *Direct Democracy,* 56.

10. McCuan et al., "California's Political Warriors," 60.

11. Magleby, *Direct Legislation,* 189, 174.

12. See, for example, Thomas Christin and Simon Hug, "Referendums and Citizen Support for European Integration," *Comparative Political Studies* 35 (2002): 586–617.

13. Ian Budge, "Political Parties in Direct Democracy," in Matthew Mendelsohn and Andrew Parkin, eds., *Referendum Democracy: Citizens, Elites, and Deliberation in Referendum Campaigns* (New York: Palgrave, 2002), 67–87; Budge, *New Challenge of Direct Democracy;* Richard Hasen, "Parties Take the Initiative (and Vice Versa)," *Columbia Law Review* 100 (2000): 731–52; D. A. Smith and Tolbert, "Initiative to Party."

14. See Mattson, *Creating a Democratic Public,* chap. 5, for a nuanced discussion of Follett's work. Though admittedly Pollyannaish in his interpretation of com-

munity-based institutions during the Progressive Era, Mattson argues that the consumer culture and the mass media that emerged during the post–World War I era displaced the incipient democratic institutions (such as adult education, social centers, and the forum movement) that emerged during the 1910s.

15. Quoted in Lieb, *Initiative and Referendum,* 165.

16. Follett, *New State,* 178.

17. Donovan et al., "Contending Players and Strategies," 94. For a criticism of this and other typologies for classifying initiatives, see D. A. Smith and Herrington, "Process of Direct Democracy."

18. Donovan et al., "Contending Players and Strategies," 83–89.

19. By mid-October, 25 contributors who gave a combined $65,250 to Taft's campaign also had contributed $170,300 to the No on 1 campaign (Ballot Initiative Strategy Center Foundation, "Ohio: State Update, Ballot Funding Highlights," November 1, 2002, at <www.ballotfunding.org/oh.html>, December 20, 2002).

20. Taft, *Popular Government,* 54.

21. Schrag, *Paradise Lost,* 226.

22. Schrag, *Paradise Lost,* 225–31; Chavez, *Color Bind,* 37.

23. California Secretary of State, "Late Contributions and Independent Expenditures," 1998 Primary Election, at <www.ss.ca.gov/prd/bmprimary98>.

24. Magleby and Patterson, "Consultants and Direct Democracy," 160–62.

25. D. A. Smith, *Tax Crusaders.*

26. Howard Gelt, interview by Daniel A. Smith, Denver, November 30, 1998.

27. D. A. Smith, *Tax Crusaders,* 153.

28. California Republican Party official, telephone interview by Daniel A. Smith, December 1, 1998.

29. California Democratic Party official, telephone interview by Daniel A. Smith, December 8, 1998.

30. Phil Perington, telephone interview by Daniel A. Smith, December 8, 1998.

31. Steve Curtis, telephone interview by Daniel A. Smith, December 1, 1998.

32. California Secretary of State, "Late Contributions and Independent Expenditures." The state Republican Party also made an in-kind contribution of $3,300 to the issue committee opposing Proposition 224.

33. California Republican Party official, telephone interview by Smith.

34. California Secretary of State, "Late Contributions and Independent Expenditures."

35. Ricky Young, "DNC Donation to State Issues Criticized," *Denver Post,* December 11, 1998.

36. With tongue firmly planted in cheek, Meek said that Gore "got us at least about four or five votes. . . . As you know, in this state that's good for at least two" (Tim Reynolds, "Gore Calls Voters in Support of Florida Class-Size Initiative," Associated Press, September 17, 2002).

37. Michael Peltier, "Bush's Biggest Foe May Be Education Initiative," *Naples (Florida) News,* June 17, 2002; "Class-Size Reality: New Figures Expose Political Distortions," *Bradenton (Florida) Herald,* December 18, 2002.

38. Chavez, *Color Bind,* 252.

39. Schrag, *Paradise Lost,* 226.
40. California Secretary of State, "Yes on Prop. 209," 1996, at <www.ss.ca.gov /prd/bmc96/prop209.htm>; Chavez, *Color Bind,* 252.
41. Don Bain, telephone interview by Daniel A. Smith, November 2, 1998; Curtis, telephone interview by Smith; Gelt, interview by Smith; Perington, telephone interview by Smith.
42. Bain, telephone interview by Smith.
43. Thomas Cronin and Robert Loevy, *Colorado Politics and Government* (Lincoln: University of Nebraska Press, 1993).
44. D. A. Smith, *Tax Crusaders;* D. A. Smith, "Howard Jarvis' Legacy?" Carl Levin, "Incomplete Hearings from the Senate Campaign Finance Investigation," *Congressional Record,* 105th Cong., 1st sess., November 10, 1997.
45. California Republican Party official, telephone interview by Smith.
46. California Republican Party official, telephone interview by Smith. In this sense, the parties have adopted positions on a range of ballot measures that could be categorized as "entrepreneurial/populist" and "interest-group" (Donovan et al., "Contending Players and Strategies," 84).
47. California Democratic Party official, telephone interview by Smith.
48. California Secretary of State, "Late Contributions and Independent Expenditures."
49. Daniel A. Smith. "Strings Attached: Outside Money in Colorado's Seventh Congressional District," in David Magleby and Quin Monson, eds., *The Last Hurrah? Soft Money and Issue Advocacy in the 2002 Congressional Elections* (Washington, DC: Brookings Institution Press, 2004), 202.
50. Bowler and Donovan, *Demanding Choices,* 3.
51. Magleby, *Direct Legislation,* 176.
52. Elisabeth Gerber and Arthur Lupia, "Campaign Competition and Policy Responsiveness in Direct Political Behavior," *Political Behavior* 17 (1995): 290.
53. Jack Citrin, Beth Reingold, Evelyn Walters, and Donald P. Green, "The 'Official English' Movement and the Symbolic Politics of Language in the United States," *Western Political Quarterly* 43 (1990): 546.
54. Bowler and Donovan, *Demanding Choices;* Shaun Bowler and Todd Donovan, "Economic Conditions and Voting on Ballot Propositions," *American Politics Quarterly* 22 (1994): 27–40.
55. Arthur Lupia, "Shortcuts versus Encyclopedias"; Bowler and Donovan, *Demanding Choices.* For a review of this literature, see Garrett and Smith, "Veiled Political Actors."
56. Bowler and Donovan, *Demanding Choices,* 140.
57. Tolbert, Lowenstein, and Donovan, "Election Law."
58. Chavez, *Color Bind;* Schrag, *Paradise Lost.*
59. A primary weakness of using aggregate-level data is that California counties are extremely unequal in size, ranging in population from 1,118 residents in Alpine County to approximately 9.3 million in Los Angeles County, with a mean county population of 558,329 (1990). If party were more related to initiative voting in the less populated counties than in Los Angeles and San Francisco, this could skew the results. The use of survey data in addition to the aggregate data lessens this problem.
60. Bowler and Donovan, "Economic Conditions."

61. Key, *Southern Politics in State and Nation;* Hero, *Faces of Inequality;* Hero and Tolbert, "Racial/Ethnic Diversity Interpretation"; Caroline J. Tolbert and Rodney Hero, "Race/Ethnicity and Direct Democracy: An Analysis of California's Illegal Immigration Initiative," *Journal of Politics* 58 (1996): 806–18.

62. Hero and Tolbert, "Racial/Ethnic Diversity Interpretation," for the construction of the state racial diversity index, using the percentage of Latino, African American, white, and Asian in each of California's 58 counties. The index is a measure of a county's racial/ethnic population. The index of county white ethnic diversity was created by adding the percentage Greek, Hungarian, Italian, Polish, Portuguese, Russian, and Irish reported in the 1990 census. Ethnic affiliation is a self-reported category. There was significant variation in the index of white ethnic diversity across California counties.

63. We also examined county-level voting on the 10 initiatives appearing on the 1994 California general election ballot. Party affiliation (percent registered Republicans) was a statistically significant predictor of variations in the county level vote for 8 of the 10 initiatives, even after controlling for unemployment rates and level of racial/ethnic diversity. Political party affiliation was associated with the county level vote for 80 percent of the initiatives on the 1994 California ballot.

64. D. A. Smith, "Representation and the Urban Bias."

65. For an in-depth study of the Colorado Parental Rights Amendment initiative, see D. A. Smith and Herrington, "Process of Direct Democracy."

66. While party affiliation reported in surveys is highly suggestive of actual partisanship, measurement error is always a possibility. Future research exploring the relationship between the strength of party affiliation and initiative voting could increase the validity of the results.

67. See Michael Alvarez and Tara Butterfield, "The Resurgence of Nativism in California? The Case of Proposition 187 and Illegal Immigration," *Social Science Quarterly* 81 (2000): 167–79.

68. Follett, *New State,* 178.

69. Haynes, "Education of Voters," 486. Political scientist S. Gale Lowrie also recognized the possible negative consequences of party involvement in the initiative process: "Political history is replete with examples of institutions, democratic in their origin, which with the decline of popular interest become ready tools in the hands of the avaricious. The effective initiative must be one where the people are given an opportunity of putting in the form of law principles well understood and desired, but which furnishes little room for the politician and boss whose control of elective machinery is strong enough to secure the stamp of popular approval upon plans designed to further personal rather than public interests" ("New Forms," 572).

70. Galen Nelson, "A Bullet through the Ballot: On Killing Election Reform," <www.tompaine.com/feature.cfm/ID/7162>, February 4, 2003.

71. Mahtesian, "Grassroots Charade," 42.

CHAPTER 7

1. Goebel, *Government,* 198–99.

2. Frederic C. Howe, "The Constitution and Public Opinion," *Proceedings of the Academy of Political Science in the City of New York* 5 (1915): 18.

3. Lupia, "Shortcuts versus Encyclopedias"; Bowler and Donovan, *Demanding Choices*. See also Herbert Simon, "A Behavioral Model of Rational Choice," *Quarterly Journal of Economics* 69 (1955): 99–118.

4. M. Smith, "Ballot Initiatives."

5. Harold Lasswell, "The Triple-Appeal Principle: A Contribution of Psychoanalysis to Political and Social Science," *American Journal of Sociology* 37 (1932): 523–38.

6. Fishkin, *Democracy and Deliberation;* Fishkin, *Voice of the People;* P. Norris, *Digital Divide.*

7. Boehmke, "Effect of Direct Democracy."

8. Although economic interests have difficulty in persuading voters to adopt policy proposals, big money is important in defeating initiative propositions placed on the ballot by citizen groups (Gerber, *Populist Paradox;* D. A. Smith, "Campaign Financing").

9. As intermediary institutions, political parties play critical roles in educating citizens and turning out the vote, and parties' involvement in campaigns may be preferable to that of special interests. See, for example, Sidney Milkis, *Political Parties and Constitutional Development: Remaking American Democracy* (Baltimore: Johns Hopkins University Press, 1999); John Green and Paul Herrnson, eds., *Responsible Partisanship? The Evolution of American Political Parties since 1950* (Lawrence: University Press of Kansas, 2002).

10. The volume of initiatives on state ballots has contracted slightly since 1996, when a record 93 initiatives appeared on state ballots. In 2002, voters considered 49 initiatives during the general election, a 30 percent drop from 2000. Defenders of citizen lawmaking blamed the decline on state legislatures' and courts' overzealous regulation of the process. See Waters, *Battle.*

11. David Postman, "Initiative Movement Is Down but Not Out," *Seattle Times,* September 23, 2002; Liza Porteus, "Liberals Take Offensive on Ballot Issues," *FoxNews.com,* August 8, 2002.

12. Peter Schrag, "Take the Initiative, Please," *American Prospect,* October 1, 1996.

13. For a critical analysis of how "populist entrepreneurs" have exploited the initiative's populist rhetoric, see D. A. Smith, *Tax Crusaders.*

14. Scheiber, "Foreword," 789.

15. Timothy Egan, "They Give, but They Also Take: Voters Muddle States' Finances," *New York Times,* March 2, 2002; Ellis, *Democratic Delusions;* Broder, *Democracy Derailed;* Rosenthal, *Decline of Representative Democracy;* Schrag, *Paradise Lost;* National Conference of State Legislatures, *Initiative and Referendum in the Twenty-first Century: Final Report and Recommendations of the NCSL I&R Task Force* (Denver: National Conference of State Legislatures, 2002).

16. Wolfensberger, *Congress and the People.* See also the proceedings from the February 16, 2002, *Democracy Symposium* sponsored by the Democracy Foundation, which called for "a federal statute that establishes procedures through which citizens can legislate, using the ballot initiative and an administrative agency, the Electoral Trust, to implement those procedures in every government jurisdiction of the United States," at <www.democracysymposium.org>.

17. Derrick Bell, "The Referendum: Democracy's Barrier to Racial Equality," *Washington Law Review* 54 (1977): 1–29; Hans Linde, "On Reconstructing 'Republican Government,'" *Oklahoma City University Law Review* 19 (1994): 193–211; Julian Eule, "Representative Government: The People's Choice," *Chicago-Kent Law Review* 67 (1991): 777–90; Barbara Gamble, "Putting Civil Rights to a Popular Vote," *American Journal of Political Science* 41 (1997): 245–69; D. A. Smith, "Overturning Term Limits."

18. Wenzel, Donovan, and Bowler, "Direct Democracy and Minorities," 228–48; Caroline J. Tolbert and John Grummel, "White Voter Support for California's Proposition 209," *State Politics and Policy Quarterly* 3 (2003): 183–202.

19. Putnam, *Bowling Alone;* see also Hibbing and Theiss-Morse, "Process Preferences and American Politics"; Craig, Kreppel, and Kane, "Public Opinion and Direct Democracy."

20. Todd Donovan and Daniel A. Smith, "Turning on and Turning out: Assessing the Indirect Effects of Ballot Measures," paper presented at the Fourth Annual Conference on State Politics and Policy, Akron, Ohio, April 30–May 2, 2004.

21. For one of the earliest and most thorough studies of who participates in initiative campaigns and whether the process is representative or systematically excludes those citizens with less financial, educational, and organizational resources, see Magleby, *Direct Legislation,* chaps. 5–6.

22. Chambers, "Constitutional Referendums and Democratic Deliberation," 232. Chambers acknowledges that the mechanisms of direct democracy "can potentially serve as catalysts for a higher level of engagement and participation and this is a good thing" (240).

23. Bryce, *American Commonwealth,* 1:474.

24. "Power to the People: A Pervasive Web Will Increase Demands for Direct Democracy," *The Economist,* January 25, 2003, 17–23.

25. Mendelsohn and Parkin, *Referendum Democracy;* Mads Qvortrup, *A Comparative Study of Referendums: Government by the People* (Manchester: Manchester University Press, 2002).

26. Polls cited in Broder, *Democracy Derailed,* 229.

27. Broder, *Democracy Derailed,* 242. Interestingly, Dane Waters, the president of the Initiative and Referendum Institute, a nonprofit organization whose mission among other things is to defend "the initiative process and the right of citizens to reform their government," is on record as opposing a national initiative and referendum (Broder, *Democracy Derailed,* 240).

28. U.S. Senate Bill 7208, 60th Cong., 1st sess., May 22, 1908; U.S. Senate Joint Resolution 94, 60th Cong., 1st sess., May 22, 1908. See also U.S. Senate, "Memorial of Initiative and Referendum League of America Relative to a National Initiative and Referendum," 60th Cong., 1st sess., Document 516, May 25, 1908.

29. Cronin, *Direct Democracy,* 177. Interestingly, Cronin discusses neither the 1908 Senate bill nor the Senate joint resolution in his history of the drive for a U.S. national initiative and referendum.

References

Abramson, Paul. *Political Attitudes in America: Formation and Change.* San Francisco: Freeman, 1993.

Abramson, Paul, John Aldrich, and David Rohde. *Change and Continuity in the 1996 Elections.* Washington, DC: CQ Press, 1998.

Ackerman, Bruce. *We the People: Foundations.* Cambridge: Harvard University Press, 1993.

Allswang, John. *The Initiative and Referendum in California, 1898–1998.* Stanford, CA: Stanford University Press, 2000.

Alvarez, Michael, and Tara Butterfield. "The Resurgence of Nativism in California? The Case of Proposition 187 and Illegal Immigration." *Social Science Quarterly* 81 (2000): 167–79.

Anderson, C., and C. Guilory. "Political Institutions and Satisfaction with Democracy: A Cross-National Analysis of Consensus and Majoritarian Systems." *American Political Science Review* 91 (1997): 66–81.

Atkin, Christopher. "Instrumental Utilities and Information Seeking." In P. Clark, ed., *New Models for Mass Communication Research.* Beverly Hills, CA: Sage, 1973.

Baker, Paula. "Campaigns and Potato Chips; or, Some Causes and Consequences of Political Spending." *Journal of Policy History* 14 (2002): 4–29.

Baldassare, Mark. *California in the New Millennium: The Changing Social and Political Landscape.* Berkeley: University of California Press, 2000.

Baldwin, Simeon. *The Relation of Education to Citizenship.* New Haven: Yale University Press, 1912.

Ballot Initiative Strategy Center. "Buying Laws at the Ballot" (2000). At www.ballotfunding.org, December 13, 2002.

Ballot Initiative Strategy Center. "Money and Ballot Measures in the 2002 Election." At www.ballotfunding.org, January 7, 2003.

Ballot Initiative Strategy Center. "Ohio: State Update, Ballot Funding Highlights." November 1, 2002. At www.ballotfunding.org/oh.html, December 20, 2002.

Banducci, Susan. "Direct Legislation: When Is It Used and When Does It Pass?" In Shaun Bowler, Todd Donovan, and Caroline J. Tolbert, eds., *Citizens as Legislators: Direct Democracy in the United States.* Columbus: Ohio State University Press, 1998.

Barber, Benjamin. *Strong Democracy.* Princeton: Princeton University Press, 1984.

Barnett, James. *The Operation of the Initiative, Referendum, and Recall in Oregon.* New York: Macmillan, 1915.

Bates, Frank. "Constitutional Amendments and Referred Acts, November Election 1914." *American Political Science Review* 9 (1915): 101–7.

Beard, Charles, and Birl Shultz, eds. *Documents on the State-Wide Initiative, Referendum, and Recall.* New York: Macmillan, 1912.

Bell, Derrick. "The Referendum: Democracy's Barrier to Racial Equality." *Washington Law Review* 54 (1977): 1–29.

Benz, Matthias, and Alois Stutzer. "Are Voters Better Informed When They Have a Larger Say in Politics?" *Public Choice* 119 (2004): 31–59.

Bimber, Bruce. "Information and Political Engagement in America: The Search for Effects of Information Technology at the Individual Level." *Political Research Quarterly* 54 (2001): 53–67.

Boehmke, Fredrick. "The Effect of Direct Democracy on the Size and Diversity of State Interest Group Populations." *Journal of Politics* 64 (2002): 827–44.

Bourne, Jonathan, Jr. "A Defense of Direct Legislation." In William B. Munro, ed., *The Initiative, Referendum, and Recall.* New York: Appleton, 1912.

Bourne, Jonathan, Jr. "Functions of the Initiative, Referendum, and Recall." In *Annals of the American Academy of Political and Social Science,* vol. 3. Philadelphia: Hummel, 1912.

Bourne, Jonathan, Jr. "The Practical Conservation of Popular Sovereignty." *Twentieth Century Magazine* 14 (1910): 132–34.

Bowler, Shaun, and Todd Donovan. *Demanding Choices: Opinion, Voting, and Direct Democracy.* Ann Arbor: University of Michigan Press, 1998.

Bowler, Shaun, and Todd Donovan. "Democracy, Institutions, and Attitudes about Citizen Influence on Government." *British Journal of Political Science* 32 (2002): 371–90.

Bowler, Shaun, and Todd Donovan. "Do Voters Have a Cue? Television Advertisements as a Source of Information in Citizen-Initiated Referendum Campaigns." *European Journal of Political Research* 41 (2002): 777–93

Bowler, Shaun, and Todd Donovan. "Economic Conditions and Voting on Ballot Propositions." *American Politics Quarterly* 22 (1994): 27–40.

Bowler, Shaun, Todd Donovan, and Caroline J. Tolbert, eds. *Citizens as Legislators: Direct Democracy in the United States.* Columbus: Ohio State University Press, 1998.

Boyle, James. *The Initiative and Referendum: Its Folly, Fallacies, and Failure.* 3d ed. Columbus, OH: Smythe, 1912.

Broder, David. *Democracy Derailed: Initiative Campaigns and the Power of Money.* New York: Harcourt Brace, 2000.

Bryce, James. *The American Commonwealth.* Vol. 1. Rev. ed. 1893; New York: Macmillan, 1910.

Budge, Ian. *The New Challenge of Direct Democracy.* Cambridge, MA: Polity, 1996.

Budge, Ian. "Political Parties in Direct Democracy." In Matthew Mendelsohn and Andrew Parkin, eds., *Referendum Democracy: Citizens, Elites, and Deliberation in Referendum Campaigns.* New York: Palgrave, 2002.

Burnham, Walter Dean, ed. *The Current Crisis in American Politics.* New York: Norton, 1982.

Butler, David, and Austin Ranney, eds. *Referendums around the World: The Growing Use of Direct Democracy.* Washington, DC: AEI Press, 1994.

Cain, Bruce, and Kenneth Miller. "The Populist Legacy: Initiatives and the Undermining of Representative Government." In Larry Sabato, Bruce Larson, and Howard Ernst, eds., *Dangerous Democracy? The Battle over Ballot Initiatives in America.* Lanham, MD: Rowman and Littlefield, 2002.

California Commission on Campaign Financing. *Democracy by Initiative.* Los Angeles: Center for Responsive Government, 1992.

California Secretary of State. "Late Contributions and Independent Expenditures." 1998 Primary Election. At www.ss.ca.gov/prd/bmprimary98.

California Secretary of State. "Yes on Prop. 209." 1996. At www.ss.ca.gov/prd /bmc96/prop209.htm.

Camobreco, John. "Preferences, Fiscal Policies, and the Initiative Process." *Journal of Politics* 60 (1998): 819–29.

Campbell, Angus, Philip Converse, Warren Miller and Donald Stokes. *The American Voter.* Chicago: University of Chicago Press, 1960.

Campbell, Anne. "In the Eye of the Beholder: The Single Subject Rule for Ballot Initiatives." In M. Dane Waters, ed., *The Battle over Citizen Lawmaking.* Durham, NC: Carolina Academic Press, 2001.

Chaffee, S., and S. F. Kanihan. "Learning about Politics from the Media." *Political Communication* 14 (1997): 421–30.

Chaffee, S., and J. McLeon. "Individual vs. Social Predictors of Information-Seeking." *Journalism Quarterly* 50 (1973): 95–120.

Chambers, John. *The Tyranny of Change: America in the Progressive Era, 1890–1920.* New York: St. Martin's, 1992.

Chambers, Simone. "Constitutional Referendums and Democratic Deliberation." In Matthew Mendelsohn and Andrew Parkin, eds., *Referendum Democracy: Citizens, Elites, and Deliberation in Referendum Campaigns.* New York: Palgrave, 2001.

Chavez, Lydia. *The Color Bind: California's Battle to End Affirmative Action.* Berkeley: University of California Press, 1998.

Chew, F. "The Relationship of Information Needs to Issue Relevance and Media Use." *Journalism Quarterly* 71 (1994): 676–88.

Christin, Thomas, and Simon Hug. "Referendums and Citizen Support for European Integration." *Comparative Political Studies* 35 (2002): 586–617.

Ciruli, Floyd. "Direct Democracy: Colorado's New Growth Industry." At www .ciruli.com/variable1–96.html, December 30, 1998.

Citrin, Jack. "Comment: The Political Relevance of Trust in Government." *American Political Science Review* 68 (1974): 973–88.

Citrin, Jack. "Who's the Boss? Direct Democracy and the Popular Control of Government." In Stephen C. Craig, ed., *Broken Contract? Changing Relationships between Americans and Their Government.* Boulder, CO: Westview, 1996.

Citrin, Jack, Beth Reingold, Evelyn Walters, and Donald P. Green. "The 'Official

English' Movement and the Symbolic Politics of Language in the United States." *Western Political Quarterly* 43 (1990): 535–59.

City Club of Denver. *Direct Legislation in Colorado.* Denver: Eames, 1927.

Coker, F. W. "Safeguarding the Petition in the Initiative and Referendum." *American Political Science Review* 10 (1916): 540–45.

Collins, Richard. "Part II: New Directions in Direct Democracy: How Democratic Are Initiatives?" *University of Colorado Law Review* 72 (2001): 983–1003.

Comstock, G. "The Impact of Television on American Institutions." *Journal of Communication* 18 (1978): 12–28.

Converse, Philip. "Information Flow and the Stability of Partisan Attitudes." In A. Campbell, ed., *Elections and the Political Order.* New York: Wiley, 1966.

Cooper, John. *Pivotal Decades: The United States, 1900–1920.* New York: Norton, 1990.

Cottrell, Edwin. "Twenty Five Years of Direct Legislation in California." *Public Opinion Quarterly* (1939): 30–45.

Craig, Stephen C., ed. *Broken Contract? Changing Relationships between Americans and Their Government.* Boulder, CO: Westview, 1996.

Craig, Stephen C., Amie Kreppel, and James G. Kane. "Public Opinion and Support for Direct Democracy: A Grassroots Perspective." In Matthew Mendelsohn and Andrew Parkin, eds., *Referendum Democracy: Citizens, Elites, and Deliberation in Referendum Campaigns.* New York: Palgrave, 2001.

Cree, Nathan. *Direct Legislation by the People.* Chicago: McClurg, 1892.

Crenson, Matthew, and Benjamin Ginsberg. *Downsizing Democracy: How America Sidelined Its Citizens and Privatized Its Public.* Baltimore: Johns Hopkins University Press, 2002.

Croly, Herbert. *Progressive Democracy.* New York: Macmillan, 1914.

Croly, Herbert. "State Political Reorganization." *Proceedings of the American Political Science Association* 8 (1911): 122–35.

Cronin, Thomas. *Direct Democracy: The Politics of Initiative, Referendum, and Recall.* Cambridge: Harvard University Press, 1989.

Cronin, Thomas, and Robert Loevy. *Colorado Politics and Government.* Lincoln: University of Nebraska Press, 1993.

Crouch, Winston. "The Constitutional Initiative in Operation." *American Political Science Review* 33 (1939): 634–45.

Crouch, Winston. *The Initiative and Referendum in California.* Los Angeles: Haynes Foundation, 1950.

Cushman, Robert. "Recent Experience with the Initiative and Referendum." *American Political Science Review* 10 (1916): 532–39.

de la Garza, R., L. DeSipio, F. C. Garcia, J. Garcia, and A. Falcon. *Latino Voices: Mexican, Puerto Rican, and Cuban Perspectives on American Politics.* Boulder, CO: Westview, 1992.

Delli Carpini, Michael, and Scott Keeter. "Measuring Political Knowledge: Putting First Things First." *American Journal of Political Science* 37 (1993): 1179–1206.

Delli Carpini, Michael, and Scott Keeter. *What Americans Know about Politics and Why It Matters.* New Haven: Yale University Press, 1996.

Dewey, John. *The Public and Its Problems.* New York: Holt, 1927.

Donovan, Todd, Shaun Bowler, David McCuan, and Ken Fernandez. "Contending Players and Strategies: Opposition Advantages in Initiative Elections." In Shaun Bowler, Todd Donovan, and Caroline J. Tolbert, eds., *Citizens as Legislators: Direct Democracy in the United States.* Columbus: Ohio State University Press, 1998.

Donovan, Todd, and Daniel A. Smith. "Turning on and Turning out: Assessing the Indirect Effects of Ballot Measures on Voter Participation." Paper presented at the Fourth Annual Conference on State Politics and Policy, Akron, Ohio, April 30–May 2, 2004.

Downs, Anthony. *An Economic Theory of Democracy.* New York: Harper and Row, 1957.

Dryzek, John. *Deliberative Democracy and Beyond: Liberals, Critics, and Contestations.* Oxford: Oxford University Press, 2000.

Dryzek, John. *Discursive Democracy: Politics, Policy, and Political Science.* Cambridge: Cambridge University Press, 1990.

Eaton, Allen H. *The Oregon System: The Story of Direct Legislation in Oregon.* Chicago: McClurg, 1912.

Elazar, Daniel. *American Federalism: A View from the States.* 3d ed. New York: Harper and Row, 1984.

Ellis, Richard. *Democratic Delusions: The Initiative Process in America.* Lawrence: University Press of Kansas, 2002.

Elster, Jon, ed. *Deliberative Democracy.* Cambridge: Cambridge University Press, 1998.

Enlow, James, and Melvin Hinich. *The Spatial Theory of Voting.* Cambridge: Cambridge University Press, 1984.

Erikson, Robert, Gerald Wright, and John McIver. *Statehouse Democracy.* New York: Cambridge University Press, 1993.

Eule, Julian. "Representative Government: The People's Choice." *Chicago-Kent Law Review* 67 (1991): 777–90.

Everson, David. "The Effects of Initiatives on Voter Turnout: A Comparative State Analysis." *Western Political Quarterly* 34 (1981): 415–25.

Fallows, James. *Breaking the News: How the Media Undermine American Democracy.* New York: Pantheon, 1996.

Fishkin, James. *Democracy and Deliberation.* New Haven: Yale University Press, 1993.

Fishkin, James. *The Voice of the People.* New Haven: Yale University Press, 1995.

Follett, Mary Parker. *The New State: Group Organization and the Solution of Popular Government.* New York: Longmans, Green, 1918.

Frey, Bruno, and L. Goette. "Does the Popular Vote Destroy Civil Rights?" *American Journal of Political Science* 42 (1998): 1343–48.

Gamble, Barbara. "Putting Civil Rights to a Popular Vote." *American Journal of Political Science* 41 (1997): 245–69.

Gardner, Charles O. "Problems of Percentages in Direct Government." *American Political Science Review* 10 (1916): 500–514.

Garner, J. W. "Primary vs. Representative Government." *Proceedings of the American Political Science Association* 4 (1907): 164–74.

Garrett, Elizabeth. "Money, Agenda Setting, and Direct Democracy." *Texas Law Review* 77 (1999): 1845–90.

Garrett, Elizabeth. "Perspective on Direct Democracy: Who Directs Direct Democracy?" *University of Chicago Law School Roundtable* 4 (1997): 17–36.

Garrett, Elizabeth, and Elisabeth Gerber. "Money in the Initiative and Referendum Process: Evidence of Its Effects and Prospects for Reform." In M. Dane Waters, ed., *The Battle over Citizen Lawmaking.* Durham, NC: Carolina Academic Press, 2001.

Garrett, Elizabeth, and Daniel A. Smith. "Veiled Political Actors: The Real Threat to Campaign Disclosure Statutes." Working Paper, USC/Caltech Center for the Study of Law and Politics. http://lawweb.usc.edu/cslp/pages/papers.html, February 1, 2004.

Gerber, Elisabeth. "Legislative Response to the Threat of Popular Initiatives." *American Journal of Political Science* 40 (1996): 99–128.

Gerber, Elisabeth. *The Populist Paradox: Interest Group Influence and the Promise of Direct Legislation.* Princeton: Princeton University Press, 1999.

Gerber, Elisabeth, and Simon Hug. "Minority Rights and Direct Legislation: Theory, Method, and Evidence." In Matthew Mendelsohn and Andrew Parkin, eds., *Referendum Democracy: Citizens, Elites, and Deliberation in Referendum Campaigns.* New York: Palgrave, 2001.

Gerber, Elisabeth, and Arthur Lupia. "Campaign Competition and Policy Responsiveness in Direct Political Behavior." *Political Behavior* 17 (1995): 287–306.

Gerber, Elisabeth, and Arthur Lupia. "Voter Competence in Direct Legislation Elections." In Stephen L. Elkin and Karol Edward Soltan, eds., *Citizen Competence and Democratic Institutions.* University Park: Pennsylvania State University Press, 1999.

Gerber, Elisabeth, Arthur Lupia, Mathew D. McCubbins, and D. Roderick Kiewiet. *Stealing the Initiative: How State Government Responds to Direct Democracy.* Upper Saddle River, NJ: Prentice Hall, 2001.

Gilbert, James. "Single-Tax Movement in Oregon." *Political Science Quarterly* 6 (1916): 25–52.

Gilens, Martin, James Glasser, and Tali Mendelberg. "Having a Say: Political Efficacy in the Context of Direct Democracy." Paper presented at the annual meeting of the American Political Science Association, San Francisco, September 2001.

Goebel, Thomas. "'A Case of Democratic Contagion': Direct Democracy in the American West, 1890–1920." *Pacific Historical Review* 66 (1997): 213–30.

Goebel, Thomas. *A Government by the People: Direct Democracy in America, 1890–1940.* Chapel Hill: University of North Carolina Press, 2002.

Gordon, Stacy B., and Gary Segura. "Cross-National Variation in the Political Sophistication of Individuals: Capability or Choice?" *Journal of Politics* 59 (1997): 126–47.

Gould, Lewis. *Reform and Regulation: American Politics from Roosevelt to Wilson.* Prospect Heights, IL: Waveland, 1996.

Gray, Virginia, and David Lowery. "The Institutionalization of State Communities of Organized Interests." *Political Research Quarterly* 54 (2001): 265–84.

Gray, Virginia, and David Lowery. *The Population Ecology of Interest Representation: Lobbying Communities in the American States.* Ann Arbor: University of Michigan Press, 1996.

Gray, Virginia, and David Lowery. "The Stability and Expression of Density Dependence in State Communities of Organized Interest." *American Politics Research* 29 (2001): 374–91.

Green, John, and Paul Herrnson, eds. *Responsible Partisanship? The Evolution of American Political Parties since 1950.* Lawrence: University Press of Kansas, 2002.

Hagen, Michael, Edward Lascher, and John Camobreco. "Response to Matsusaka: Estimating the Effect of Ballot Initiatives on Policy Responsiveness." *Journal of Politics* 63 (2001): 1257–63.

Hajnal, Zoltan, Elisabeth Gerber, and H. Louch. "Minorities and Direct Legislation: Evidence from California Ballot Proposition Elections." *Journal of Politics* 64 (2002): 154–77.

Hall, Arnold. *Popular Government.* New York: Macmillan, 1921.

Hammell, George. "Direct Legislation." *Twentieth Century Magazine* 21 (1911): 282–84.

Hammell, George. "Direct Legislation." *Twentieth Century Magazine* 24 (1911): 570–72.

Hammell, George. "News of Fundamental Democratic and Economic Advance: Direct Legislation." *Twentieth Century Magazine* 23 (1911): 471–74.

Hammell, George. "News of Fundamental Democratic and Economic Advance: Direct Legislation." *Twentieth Century Magazine* 24 (1911): 180–83.

Hasen, Richard. "Parties Take the Initiative (and Vice Versa)." *Columbia Law Review* 100 (2000): 731–52.

Haynes, George. "The Education of Voters." *Political Science Quarterly* 22 (1907): 484–97.

Haynes, George. "How Massachusetts Adopted the Initiative and Referendum." *Political Science Quarterly* 34 (1919): 454–75.

Haynes, George. "Massachusetts Public Opinion Bills." *Proceedings of the American Political Science Association* 4 (1907): 152–63.

Haynes, George. "'People's Rule' in Oregon, 1910." *Political Science Quarterly* 26 (1911): 32–62.

Haynes, George. "People's Rule on Trial." *Political Science Quarterly* 28 (1913): 18–33.

Hero, Rodney. *Faces of Inequality: Social Diversity in American Politics.* New York: Oxford University Press, 1998.

Hero, Rodney E., and Caroline J. Tolbert. "Minority Voices and Citizen Attitudes about Government Responsiveness in the American States: Do Social and Institutional Context Matter?" *British Journal of Political Science* 34 (2004): 109–21.

Hero, Rodney, and Caroline J. Tolbert. "A Racial/Ethnic Diversity Interpretation of Politics and Policy in the States of the U.S." *American Journal of Political Science* 40 (1996): 851–71.

Hetherington, Marc J. "The Effect of Political Trust on the Presidential Vote, 1968–96." *American Political Science Review* 93 (1999): 311–26.

Hetherington, Marc J. "The Political Relevance of Political Trust." *American Political Science Review* 92 (1998): 791–808.

Hibbing, John, and Elizabeth Theiss-Morse. *Congress as Public Enemy: Public Attitudes toward Political Institutions.* Cambridge: Cambridge University Press, 1995.

Hibbing, John, and Elizabeth Theiss-Morse. "The Media's Role in Public Negativity toward Congress: Distinguishing Emotional Reactions and Cognitive Evaluations." *American Journal of Political Science* 42 (1998): 475–98.

Hibbing, John, and Elizabeth Theiss-Morse. "Process Preferences and American Politics: What the People Want Government to Be." *American Political Science Review* 95 (2001): 145–53.

Hibbing, John, and Elizabeth Theiss-Morse, eds. *What Is It about Government That Americans Dislike?* Cambridge: Cambridge University Press, 2001.

Hill, Kim, and Jan Leighley. "Racial Diversity, Voter Turnout, and Mobilizing Institutions in the United States." *American Politics Quarterly* 27 (1999): 275–95.

Hofstadter, Richard. *The Age of Reform.* New York: Vintage, 1955.

Holbrook, Tom, and Elizabeth VanDunk. "Electoral Competition in the American States." *American Political Science Review* 87 (1993): 955–62.

Howe, Frederic C. "The Constitution and Public Opinion." *Proceedings of the Academy of Political Science in the City of New York* 5 (1915): 7–19.

Huckfeldt, Robert, and John Sprague. "Choice, Social-Structure, and Political Information—The Informational Coercion of Minorities." *American Journal of Political Science* 32 (1988): 467–82.

Initiative and Referendum Institute. "I and R Usage." At www.iandrinstitute.org, January 4, 2002.

Initiative and Referendum Institute. "Revised Overview of Statewide Initiatives, Popular Referendum, and Legislative Referendum on the 1998 Election Ballot." At www.iandrinstitute.org, September 7, 2002.

Iyengar, S., and D. R. Kinder. *News That Matters: Agenda-Setting and Priming in a Television Age.* Chicago: University of Chicago Press, 1987.

Jackson, Robert. "The Mobilization of U.S. State Electorates in the 1998 and 1990 Elections." *Journal of Politics* 59 (1997): 520–37.

Jackson, Robert, Robert Brown, and Gerald Wright. "Registration, Turnout, and the Electoral Representativeness of U.S. State Electorates." *American Politics Quarterly* 26 (1998): 259–87.

Johnson, Lewis. "Direct Legislation as an Ally of Representative Government." In William B. Munro, ed., *The Initiative, Referendum, and Recall.* New York: Appleton, 1912.

Kelley, Stanley. *Professional Public Relations and Political Power.* Baltimore: Johns Hopkins University Press, 1956.

Kettleborough, Charles. "Initiative and Referendum." *American Political Science Review* 8 (1914): 251–57.

Key, V. O. "Publicity of Campaign Expenditures on Issues in California." *American Political Science Review* 4 (1936): 713–23.

Key, V. O. *Southern Politics in State and Nation*. New York: Knopf, 1949.

Kimball, David, and Samuel Patterson. "Living up to Expectations: Public Attitudes toward Congress." *Journal of Politics* 59 (1997): 701–28.

King, Gary, Michael Tomz, and Jason Wittenberg. "Making the Most of Statistical Analysis: Improving Interpretation and Presentation." *American Journal of Political Science* 44 (2000): 347–61.

King, George Judson. "How Oregon 'Stood Pat.'" *Twentieth Century Magazine* 21 (1911): 114–20.

Kleppner, Paul. *Continuity and Change in Electoral Politics, 1893–1928*. Westport, CT: Greenwood, 1987.

Kolko, Gabriel. *The Triumph of Conservatism: A Reinterpretation of American History, 1900–1916*. Chicago: Quadrangle, 1963.

Kornbluh, Mark. *Why America Stopped Voting: The Decline of Participatory Democracy and the Emergence of Modern American Politics*. New York: New York University Press, 2000.

Kousser, J. Morgan. *The Shaping of Southern Politics: Suffrage Restriction and the Establishment of the One-Party South, 1880–1910*. New Haven: Yale University Press, 1974.

Krosnick, Jon A., and Laura A. Brannon. "The Impact of the Gulf War on the Ingredients of Presidential Evaluations: Multidimensional Effects of Political Involvement." *American Political Science Review* 87 (1993): 963–75.

Langer, Laura. "Measuring Income Distribution across Space and Time in the American States." *Social Science Quarterly* 80 (1999): 55–67.

Lascher, Edward, Michael Hagen, and Steven Rochlin. "Gun behind the Door? Ballot Initiatives, State Policies, and Public Opinion." *Journal of Politics* 58 (1996): 760–75.

Lasswell, Harold. "The Triple-Appeal Principle: A Contribution of Psychoanalysis to Political and Social Science." *American Journal of Sociology* 37 (1932): 523–38.

Leshner, Glenn, and Michael McKean. "Using TV News for Political Information during an Off-Year Election: Effects on Political Knowledge and Cynicism." *Journal of Mass Communications Quarterly* 74 (1997): 69–83.

Lewis-Beck, Michael, and Tom Rice. *Forecasting Elections*. Washington, DC: CQ Press, 1992.

Lieb, Hermann. *The Initiative and Referendum*. Chicago: Lieb, 1902.

Linde, Hans. "On Reconstructing 'Republican Government.'" *Oklahoma City University Law Review* 19 (1994): 193–211.

Link, Arthur, and Richard McCormick. *Progressivism*. Arlington Heights, IL: Harlan Davidson, 1983.

Lowell, A. Lawrence. *Public Opinion and Popular Government*. New York: Longmans, Green, 1913.

Lowell, A. Lawrence. "The Referendum in the United States." In William B. Munro, ed., *The Initiative, Referendum, and Recall*. New York: Appleton, 1912.

Lowenstein, Daniel. "Campaign Spending and Ballot Propositions: Recent Experience, Public Choice Theory, and the First Amendment." *UCLA Law Review* 29 (1982): 505–641.

Lowenstein, Daniel. "A Patternless Mosaic: Campaign Finance and the First Amendment after Austin." *Capital University Law Review* 21 (1992): 381–427.

Lowrie, S. Gale. "New Forms of the Initiative and Referendum." *American Political Science Review* 5 (1911): 566–72.

Lupia, Arthur. "Shortcuts versus Encyclopedias: Information and Voting Behavior in California Insurance Reform Elections." *American Political Science Review* 88 (1994): 63–76.

Luskin, Robert. "Explaining Political Sophistication." *Political Behavior* 12 (1990): 331–61.

Magleby, David. *Direct Legislation: Voting on Ballot Propositions in the United States.* Baltimore: Johns Hopkins University Press, 1984.

Magleby, David. "Direct Legislation in the American States." In David Butler and Austin Ranney, eds., *Referendums around the World: The Growing Use of Direct Democracy.* Washington, DC: AEI Press, 1994.

Magleby, David, and Kelly Patterson. "Consultants and Direct Democracy." *PS: Political Science and Politics* 31 (1998): 160–69.

Mahtesian, Charles. "Grassroots Charade." *Governing,* November 1998, 38–42.

Mansbridge, Jane. *Beyond Adversary Democracy.* Chicago: University of Chicago Press, 1983.

March, James, and Johan Olsen. "The New Institutionalism: Organizational Factors in Political Life." *American Political Science Review* 78 (1984): 734–49.

March, James, and Johan Olsen. *Rediscovering Institutions: The Organizational Basis of Politics.* New York: Free Press, 1989.

Matsusaka, John. "Fiscal Effects of the Voter Initiative: Evidence from the Last 30 Years." *Journal of Political Economy* 103 (1995): 587–623.

Matsusaka, John. "Problems with a Methodology Used to Evaluate the Voter Initiative." *Journal of Politics* 63 (2001): 1250–56.

Mattson, Kevin. *Creating a Democratic Public: The Struggle for Urban Participatory Democracy during the Progressive Era.* University Park: Pennsylvania State University Press, 1998.

McCall, Samuel. "Representative as against Direct Legislation." In William B. Munro, ed., *The Initiative, Referendum, and Recall.* New York: Appleton, 1912.

McChesney, Robert. *Rich Media, Poor Democracy: Communication Politics in Dubious Times.* Urbana: University of Illinois Press, 1999.

McCombs, M. E., and D. L. Shaw. "The Agenda-Setting Function of Mass Media." *Public Opinion Quarterly* 36 (1972): 176–87.

McCuan, David, Shaun Bowler, Todd Donovan, and Ken Fernandez. "California's Political Warriors: Campaign Professionals and the Initiative Process." In Shaun Bowler, Todd Donovan, and Caroline J. Tolbert, eds., *Citizens as Legislators: Direct Democracy in the United States.* Columbus: Ohio State University Press, 1998.

McLeod, J., and D. McDonald. "Beyond Simple Exposure: Media Orientations and Their Impact on the Political Process." *Communication Research* 12 (1985): 3–34.

McSeveney, Samuel. "The Fourth Party System and Progressive Politics." In L.

Sandy Maisel and William Shade, eds., *Parties and Politics in American History.* New York: Garland, 1994.

Mendelsohn, Matthew, and Fred Cutler. "The Effect of Referenda on Democratic Citizens: Information, Politicization, Efficacy, and Tolerance." *British Journal of Political* Science 30 (2000): 669–98.

Mendelsohn, Matthew, and Andrew Parkin, eds. *Referendum Democracy: Citizens, Elites, and Deliberation in Referendum Campaigns.* New York: Palgrave, 2001.

Meyer, H. H. B. *Select List of References on Initiative, Referendum, and Recall.* Washington, DC: Library of Congress, 1911.

Milkis, Sidney. *Political Parties and Constitutional Development: Remaking American Democracy.* Baltimore: Johns Hopkins University Press, 1999.

Miller, Kenneth. "Constraining Populism: The Real Challenge of Initiative Reform." *Santa Clara Law Review* 41 (2001): 1037–84.

Mills, Katherine. "Direct Legislation." *Twentieth Century Magazine* 18 (1911): 556–58.

Mitchell, William, and Michael Munger. "Economic Models of Interest Groups: An Introductory Survey." *American Journal of Political Science* 35 (1991): 512–46.

Morell, M. "Citizens' Evaluations of Participatory Democratic Procedures: Normative Theory Meets Empirical Science." *Political Research Quarterly* 52 (1999): 293–322.

Mossberger, Karen, Caroline J. Tolbert, and Mary Stansbury. *Virtual Inequality: Beyond the Digital Divide.* Washington, DC: Georgetown University Press, 2003.

Mueller, Dennis. *The Political Economy of Growth.* New Haven: Yale University Press, 1983.

Munro, William B. *The Government of the United States: National, State, and Local.* 3d ed. New York: Macmillan, 1931.

Munro, William B., ed. *The Initiative, Referendum, and Recall.* New York: Appleton, 1912.

National Conference of State Legislatures. *Initiative and Referendum in the Twenty-first Century: Final Report and Recommendations of the NCSL I&R Task Force.* Denver: National Conference of State Legislatures, 2002.

Nelson, Galen. "A Bullet through the Ballot: On Killing Election Reform." At www.tompaine.com/feature.cfm/ID/7162, February 4, 2003.

Nelson, Galen. "Fighting Regressive Tax Measures." At www.ballot.org/resources/galentaxes.html, September 10, 2002.

Nie, Norman, and Kristi Andersen. "Mass Belief System Revisited: Political Change and Attitude Structure." *Journal of Politics* 36 (1974): 541–91.

Nie, Norman, Sidney Verba, and John Petrocik. *The Changing American Voter.* Cambridge: Harvard University Press, 1979.

Niemi, Richard, Stephen Craig, and F. Mattei. "Measuring Internal Political Efficacy in the 1988 National Election Study." *American Political Science Review* 85 (1991): 1407–13.

Norquist, Grover. "Prelude to a Landslide: How Grass-Roots Populism Could Help Republicans in 1996." *Policy Review* 66 (1993): 30–35.

Norris, Frank. *The Octopus: A Story of California.* New York: Doubleday, Page, 1901.

Norris, Pippa. *Critical Citizens: Global Support for Democratic Governance.* Oxford: Oxford University Press, 1999.

Norris, Pippa. *Digital Divide: Civic Engagement, Information Poverty, and the Internet Worldwide.* New York: Cambridge University Press, 2001.

Nye, Joseph, Philip Zelikow, and David King, eds. *Why People Don't Trust Government.* Cambridge: Harvard University Press, 1997.

Oberholtzer, Ellis P. *The Referendum in America (Together with Some Chapters on the Initiative and the Recall).* Rev. ed. New York: Scribner's, 1911.

Osborne, David, and Ted Gaebler. *Reinventing Government: How the Entrepreneurial Spirit Is Transforming the Public Sector.* Reading, MA: Addison-Wesley, 1992.

Owens, John R., and Larry L. Wade. "Campaign Spending on California Ballot Propositions, 1924–1984: Trends and Voting Effects." *Western Political Quarterly* 39 (1986): 675–89.

Parsons, Frank. *Direct Legislation; or, The Veto Power in the Hands of the People.* Philadelphia: Taylor, 1900.

Pateman, Carole. *Participation and Democratic Theory.* New York: Cambridge University Press, 1970.

Patterson, Thomas. *The Vanishing Voter: Public Involvement in an Age of Uncertainty.* New York: Knopf, 2002.

Peltier, Michael. "Bush's Biggest Foe May Be Education Initiative." *Naples Florida News,* June 17, 2002, p. B1.

Peters, B. Guy. *The Future of Governing: Four Emerging Models.* Lawrence: University Press of Kansas, 1996.

Peters, B. Guy. *Institutional Theory in Political Science: The New Institutionalism.* London: Pinter, 1999.

Piott, Steven. "The Origins of the Initiative and Referendum in America." *Hayes Historical Journal* 11 (1992): 5–17.

Piott, Steven. *Giving Voters a Voice: The Origins of the Initiative and Referendum in America.* Columbia: University of Missouri Press, 2003.

Piven, Frances Fox, and Richard Cloward. *Why Americans Don't Vote.* New York: Pantheon, 1988.

Piven, Frances Fox, and Richard Cloward. *Why Americans Still Don't Vote: And Why Politicians Want It That Way.* Boston: Beacon, 2000.

Powell, G. B. "American Voter Turnout in Comparative Perspective." *American Political Science Review* 80 (1986): 17–43.

"Power to the People: A Pervasive Web Will Increase Demands for Direct Democracy." *The Economist,* January 25, 2003, 17–23.

Price, Charles. "The Initiative: A Comparative State Analysis and Reassessment of a Western Phenomenon." *Western Political Quarterly* 28 (1975): 243–62.

Pritchell, Robert. "The Influence of Professional Campaign Management Firms in Partisan Elections in California." *Western Political Quarterly* 11 (1958): 278–300.

Putnam, Robert. *Bowling Alone: The Collapse and Revival of American Community.* New York: Simon and Schuster, 2000.

Qvortrup, Mads. *A Comparative Study of Referendums: Government by the People.* Manchester: Manchester University Press, 2002.

Raine, William MacLeod. "The Rebellion against Privilege in Colorado." *Twentieth Century Magazine* 14 (1910): 100–107.

Reinsch, Paul. "The Initiative and Referendum." *Proceedings of the Academy of Political Science in the City of New York* 3 (1912): 155–61.

Roosevelt, Theodore. "Nationalism and Popular Rule." *The Outlook,* January 21, 1911.

Rosenstone, Steven, and John Mark Hansen. *Mobilization, Participation, and Democracy in America.* New York: Macmillan, 1993.

Rosenthal, Alan. *The Decline of Representative Democracy: Process, Participation, and Power in State Legislatures.* Washington, DC: CQ Press, 1998.

Rossiter, Clinton, and James Lare, eds. *The Essential Lippmann: A Political Philosophy for Liberal Democracy.* New York: Random House, 1963.

Schattschneider, E. E. *The Semisovereign People.* New York: Holt, Rinehart, and Winston, 1960.

Scheiber, Harry. "Foreword: The Direct Ballot and State Constitutionalism." *Rutgers Law Journal* 28 (1997): 787–823.

Schlozman, Kay. "What Accent the Heavenly Chorus? Political Equality and the American Pressure System." *Journal of Politics* 46 (1984): 1006–32.

Schlozman, Kay, and John Tierney. *Organized Interests and American Democracy.* New York: Harper and Row, 1986.

Schlup, Leonard. "Republican Insurgent: Jonathan Bourne and the Politics of Progressivism, 1908–1912." *Oregon Historical Quarterly* 87 (1986): 229–44.

Schmidt, David. *Citizen Lawmakers: The Ballot Initiative Revolution.* Philadelphia: Temple University Press, 1989.

Schnader, W. A. "Proper Safeguards for the Initiative and Referendum Petition." *American Political Science Review* 10 (1916): 515–31.

Schrag, Peter. "Take the Initiative, Please." *American Prospect,* October 1, 1996, pp. 1–3.

Schrag, Peter. *Paradise Lost: California's Experience, America's Future.* New York: New Press, 1998.

Schuman, David. "The Origins of State Constitutional Direct Democracy: William Simon U'Ren and the Oregon System." *Temple Law Review* 67 (1994): 947–63.

Shafroth, John. "Imperative Need of Direct Legislation." *Twentieth Century Magazine* 24 (1911): 516–19.

Shefter, Martin. *Political Parties and the State: The American Historical Experience.* Princeton: Princeton University Press, 1994.

Shockley, John. "Direct Democracy, Campaign Finance, and the Courts: Can Corruption, Undue Influence, and Declining Voter Confidence Be Found?" *University of Miami Law Review* 39 (1985): 377–428.

Shockley, John. "Money in Politics: Judicial Roadblocks to Campaign Finance Reform." *Hastings Constitutional Law Quarterly* 10 (1983): 679–92.

Silbey, Joel. *The American Political Nation, 1838–1893.* Stanford, CA: Stanford University Press, 1991.

Simon, Herbert. "A Behavioral Model of Rational Choice." *Quarterly Journal of Economics* 69 (1955): 99–118.

Skocpol, Theda, and Morris Fiorina, eds. *Civic Engagement in American Democracy*. Washington, DC: Brookings Institution Press, 1999.

Smith, Bradley. *Unfree Speech: The Folly of Campaign Finance Reform*. Princeton: Princeton University Press, 2001.

Smith, Daniel A. "Campaign Financing of Ballot Initiatives in the American States." In Larry Sabato, Bruce Larson, and Howard Ernst, eds., *Dangerous Democracy? The Battle over Ballot Initiatives in America*. Lanham, MD: Rowman and Littlefield, 2001.

Smith, Daniel A. "Homeward *Bound?* Micro-Level Legislative Responsiveness to Ballot Initiatives." *State Politics and Policy Quarterly* 1 (2001): 50–61.

Smith, Daniel A. "Howard Jarvis' Legacy? An Assessment of Antitax Initiatives in the American States." *State Tax Notes* 22 (2001): 753–64.

Smith, Daniel A. "Overturning Term Limits: The Legislature's Own Private Idaho?" *PS: Political Science and Politics* 36 (2003): 215–20.

Smith, Daniel A. "Representation and the Spatial Dimension of Direct Democracy." Paper presented at American Political Science Association Conference, Boston, August 29–September 1, 2002.

Smith, Daniel A. "Representation and the Urban Bias of Direct Democracy." Paper presented at the Western Political Science Association Conference, Long Beach, CA, March 21–24, 2002.

Smith, Daniel A. "Special Interests and Direct Democracy: An Historical Glance." In M. Dane Waters, ed., *The Battle over Citizen Lawmaking*. Durham, NC: Carolina Academic Press, 2001.

Smith, Daniel A. "Strings Attached: Outside Money in Colorado's Seventh Congressional District." In David Magleby and Quin Monson, eds., *The Last Hurrah? Soft Money and Issue Advocacy in the 2002 Congressional Elections*. Washington, DC: Brookings Institution, 2004.

Smith, Daniel A. *Tax Crusaders and the Politics of Direct Democracy*. New York: Routledge, 1998.

Smith, Daniel A. "Unmasking the Tax Crusaders." *State Government News* 41 (March 1998): 18–21.

Smith, Daniel A., and Robert J. Herrington. "The Process of Direct Democracy: Colorado's 1996 Parental Rights Amendment." *Social Science Journal* 37 (2000): 179–94.

Smith, Daniel A., and Joseph Lubinski. "Direct Democracy during the Progressive Era: A Crack in the Populist Veneer?" *Journal of Policy History* 14 (2002): 349–83.

Smith, Daniel A., and Caroline J. Tolbert. "The Initiative to Party: Partisanship and Ballot Initiatives in California." *Party Politics* 7 (2001): 739–57.

Smith, Mark. "Ballot Initiatives and the Democratic Citizen." *Journal of Politics* 64 (2002): 892–903.

Smith, Mark. "The Contingent Effects of Ballot Initiatives and Candidate Races on Turnout." *American Journal of Political Science* 45 (2001): 700–706.

"Statewide Initiative and Referendum." In *The Book of the States,* vol. 33. Lexington, KY: Council of State Governments, 2001.

Steinmo, Sven. "Political Institutions and Tax Policy in the United States, Sweden, and Britain." *World Politics* 41 (1989): 500–534.

Steinmo, Sven, Kathleen Thelen, and Frank Longstreth, eds. *Structuring Politics: Historical Institutionalism in Comparative Analysis.* New York: Cambridge University Press, 1992.

Stimson, Frederick. "Certain Retrogressive Policies of the Progressive Party." *Proceedings of the American Political Science Association* 9 (1912): 149–61.

Stitton, Tom. *John Randolph Haynes: California Progressive.* Stanford, CA: Stanford University Press, 1992.

Sullivan, James W. *Direct Legislation by the Citizenship through the Initiative and Referendum.* New York: True Nationalist, 1893.

Taft, William Howard. *Popular Government: Its Essence, Its Permanence, and Its Perils.* New Haven: Yale University Press, 1913.

Tolbert, Caroline J. "Changing Rules for State Legislatures: Direct Democracy and Governance Policies." In Shaun Bowler, Todd Donovan, and Caroline J. Tolbert, eds., *Citizens as Legislators.* Columbus: Ohio State University Press, 1998.

Tolbert, Caroline J. "Rethinking Lowi's Constituent Policy: Governance Policy and Direct Democracy." *Environment and Planning C:* Government and Policy 20 (2002): 75–93.

Tolbert, Caroline J. "Direct Democracy and Institutional Realignment in the American States." *Political Science Quarterly* 118 (2003): 467–89.

Tolbert, Caroline J. "Public Policy and Direct Democracy in the Twentieth Century: The More Things Change, the More They Stay the Same." In M. Dane Waters, ed., *The Battle over Citizen Lawmaking.* Durham, NC: Carolina Academic Press, 2001.

Tolbert, Caroline J., and John Grummel. "White Voter Support for California's Proposition 209: Revisiting the Racial Threat Hypothesis." *State Politics and Policy Quarterly* 3 (2003): 183–202.

Tolbert, Caroline J., John Grummel, and Daniel A. Smith. "The Effect of Ballot Initiatives on Voter Turnout in the American States." *American Politics Research* 29 (2001): 625–48.

Tolbert, Caroline J., and Rodney Hero. "Dealing with Diversity: Racial/Ethnic Context and Social Policy Change." *Political Research Quarterly* 54 (2001): 571–604.

Tolbert, Caroline J., and Rodney Hero. "Race/Ethnicity and Direct Democracy: An Analysis of California's Illegal Immigration Initiative." *Journal of Politics* 58 (1996): 806–18.

Tolbert, Caroline J., Daniel Lowenstein, and Todd Donovan. "Election Law and Rules for Using Initiatives." In Shaun Bowler, Todd Donovan, and Caroline J. Tolbert, eds., *Citizens as Legislators: Direct Democracy in the United States.* Columbus: Ohio State University Press, 1998.

Tolbert, Caroline J., and Ramona S. McNeal. "Unraveling the Effects of the Internet on Political Participation." *Political Research Quarterly* 56 (2003): 175–85.

Tolbert, Caroline J., Ramona S. McNeal, and Daniel A. Smith. "Enhancing Civic

Engagement: The Effect of Direct Democracy on Political Participation and Knowledge." *State Politics and Policy Quarterly* 3 (2003): 23–41.

Truman, David. *The Governmental Process: Political Interests and Public Opinion.* New York: Knopf, 1951.

U'Ren, William S. "Remarks on Mr. Herbert Croly's Paper on 'State Political Reorganization.'" *Proceedings of the American Political Science Association* 8 (1911): 136–39.

Verba, Sidney, Kay Schlozman, and Henry Brady. *Voice and Equality: Civic Voluntarism in American Politics.* Cambridge: Harvard University Press, 1995.

Washington Public Disclosure Commission. "1998 Ballot Measures—Contribution and Expenditure Totals." 1999. At <www.pdc.wa.gov/>, November 30, 2002.

Waters, M. Dane, ed. *The Battle over Citizen Lawmaking.* Durham, NC: Carolina Academic Press, 2001.

Waters, M. Dane. "Initiative and Referendum Institute's November 2002 General Election Pre-Election Report." At <www.iandrinstitute.org>, August 10, 2002.

Waters, M. Dane. "Trends in State Initiatives and Referenda." In *The Book of the States,* vol. 34. Lexington, KY: Council of State Governments, 2002.

Weatherford, M. Stephen. "Measuring Political Legitimacy." *American Political Science Review* 86 (1992): 149–66.

Weaver, D. H. "What Voters Learn from Media." *Annual of the AAPSS* 546 (1996): 34–47.

Weaver, D. H., and D. Drew. "Voter Learning in the 1990 Off-Year Election: Did the Media Matter?" *Journalism Quarterly* 70 (1993): 356–68.

Weaver, D. H., D. A. Graber, M. E. McCombs, and C. H. Eyal. *Media Agenda-Setting in a Presidential Election: Issues, Images, and Interest.* New York: Praeger, 1981.

Wenzel, James, Todd Donovan, and Shaun Bowler. "Direct Democracy and Minorities: Changing Attitudes about Minorities Targeted by Initiatives." In Shaun Bowler, Todd Donovan, and Caroline J. Tolbert, eds., *Citizens as Legislators: Direct Democracy in the United States.* Columbus: Ohio State University Press, 1998.

Weyl, Walter. *The New Democracy.* New York: Macmillan, 1912.

White, William Allen. *The Old Order Changeth: A View of American Democracy.* New York: Macmillan, 1910.

Wilcox, Delos F. *Government by All the People; or, The Initiative, the Referendum, and the Recall as Instruments of Democracy.* New York: Macmillan, 1912.

Wilson, Woodrow. *Constitutional Government in the United States.* New York: Columbia University Press, 1908.

Wilson, Woodrow. "The Issues of Reform." In William B. Munro, ed., *The Initiative, Referendum, and Recall.* New York: Appleton, 1912.

Wilson, Woodrow. *The Papers of Woodrow Wilson.* Ed. Arthur Link. Princeton: Princeton University Press, 1977.

Wilson, Woodrow. *The State: Elements of Historical and Practical Politics.* Rev. ed. Boston: Heath, 1898.

Wolak, Jennifer, Adam Newmark, Todd McNoldy, David Lowery, and Virginia Gray. "Much of Politics Is Still Local: Multi-State Lobbying in State Interest Communities." *Legislative Studies Quarterly* 27 (2002): 527–55.

Wolfensberger, Donald. *Congress and the People: Deliberative Democracy on Trial.* Washington, DC: Woodrow Wilson Center Press, 2000.

Wolfinger, Raymond, and Steven Rosenstone. *Who Votes?* New Haven: Yale University Press, 1980.

Works, John. "The Political Regeneration of California." *Twentieth Century Magazine* 23 (1911): 387–94.

Zaller, John. *The Nature and Origins of Mass Opinion.* Cambridge: Cambridge University Press, 1992.

Zisk, Betty. *Money, Media, and the Grass Roots: State Ballot Issues and the Electoral Process.* Newbury Park, CA: Sage, 1987.

Zueblin, Charles. "The Training of the Citizen." *Chautauquan* (October 1903): 161–68.

Index